The COALITION YEARS
1996–2012

Other books by the author

Beyond Survival: Emerging Dimensions of Indian Economy (1984)
Off the Track (1987)
Saga of Struggle and Sacrifice (1992)
Challenges Before the Nation (1992)
Thoughts and Reflections (2014)
The Dramatic Decade: The Indira Gandhi Years (2014)
The Turbulent Years (2016)

The COALITION YEARS
1996–2012

PRANAB MUKHERJEE

RUPA

First published by
Rupa Publications India Pvt. Ltd 2017
7/16, Ansari Road, Daryaganj
New Delhi 110002

Sales Centres:

Allahabad Bengaluru Chennai
Hyderabad Jaipur Kathmandu
Kolkata Mumbai

Copyright © Pranab Mukherjee 2017
Photos courtesy:
Anandabazar Patrika Archive: 1, 2, 3, 4, 6, 7, 8, 14, 19, 21, 24, 27, 30, 31, 34, 36, 37
Hindustan Times: 5, 9, 10, 11, 12, 13, 15, 16, 25, 26
Photo Division: 22, 29, 32, 33, 35
Author Archives: 17, 18, 20, 23, 28

The views and opinions expressed in this book are the author's own
and the facts are as reported by him which have been verified to the
extent possible, and the publishers are not in any way liable for the same.

All rights reserved.

No part of this publication may be reproduced, transmitted,
or stored in a retrieval system, in any form or by any means,
electronic, mechanical, photocopying, recording or otherwise,
without the prior permission of the publisher.

ISBN: 978-81-291-4905-3

Ninth impression 2022

15 14 13 12 11 10 9

The moral right of the author has been asserted.

Printed at Saurabh Printers Pvt. Ltd, Noida

This book is sold subject to the condition that it shall not,
by way of trade or otherwise, be lent, resold, hired out,
or otherwise circulated, without the publisher's prior consent, in any
form of binding or cover other than that in which it is published.

*Dedicated to
the Indian Voter*

CONTENTS

Preface	ix
1. In Parliament	1
2. The Congress After Rajiv	12
3. Sonia Gandhi Takes Charge	38
4. NDA, 1998–99	45
5. 2004	61
6. In Defence	79
7. Managing the External Environment	100
8. India–US Civil Nuclear Cooperation Agreement	127
9. Returning to Finance	160
10. To Rashtrapati Bhavan	204
Epilogue	231
Appendices	235
Acknowledgements	267
Index	269

PREFACE

My journey of 37 years as a parliamentarian came to an end in July 2012 when I was elected the President of India. However, I continued to have a tenacious link with this revered institution; in fact, I became an integral part of it as the President of the Republic.

Five years later, on 25 July 2017, my association with the Parliament came to an end when I demitted the highest office of the country. After 48 action-packed years, I left this hallowed institution with a tinge of sadness and a rainbow of memories. I left with a sense of fulfilment and happiness at having served the people of this great country through this institution. How successful I was in discharging my responsibilities will be judged, over time, by the critical lens of history.

Today, I am no longer the president but a citizen, a pilgrim just like you in India's march towards glory. As I reflect on my political journey, I feel privileged to have witnessed and participated in the emergence of a great nation. I learnt from my travels across the length and breadth of the country and my conversations with people across the social spectrum—students, scientists, innovators, scholars, jurists, authors, artistes and leaders from all over the world. I intend to continue this journey of learning in the years to come.

The Coalition Years is third in the trilogy titled *Dramatic Decades*, beginning with *The Indira Gandhi Years 1969–1980* and followed by *The Turbulent Years 1980–1996*, which chronicle my life as a parliamentarian from 1969 to 1996. This volume is a recollection of my experiences from 1996–2012—the triumphs and tribulations that characterized post-Congress polity and the fascinating encounters with leaders across the political divide. Whether it was the creation of a streamlined defence procurement procedure, the successful conclusion of the Indo–US nuclear deal, or the establishment of a social security net through landmark legislations like MGNREGA, and the introduction of Aadhaar, as Cabinet Minister heading the ministries of Defence, External Affairs and Finance, I had the opportunity to preside over agendas that formed the cornerstone of Congress policies for the making of an inclusive India.

The process of writing this book has been stimulating as well as illuminating. I offer *The Coalition Years* to you, dear reader, in the hope that you will gain new insight into the behind-the-scenes action in the areas of decision-making, policy formulation and its implementation in the government.

I hope you will enjoy reading the book as much as I have enjoyed writing it.

Pranab Mukherjee
New Delhi, October 2017

CHAPTER 1

IN PARLIAMENT

My journey as a parliamentarian began decades ago when I became a member of the Congress Parliamentary Party (CPP), when the Bangla Congress merged with the Indian National Congress (INC) towards the end of 1971. Before that I was an independent Member representing Bangla Congress—a regional party—from 1969 to 1971. I was a member of the Rajya Sabha for five terms till 2004 when I was elected to the Lok Sabha. There was, however, a short period—1987 to 1993—when I was out of the Parliament. And from 1987 to 1988, I was out of the Congress too, virtually on a sabbatical from politics.

That break notwithstanding, my long career has been enriching and has shaped my political outlook and persona. I entered the Parliament at a time when the Rajya Sabha was full of experienced parliamentarians and leaders of the freedom movement, many of whom were brilliant speakers such as M.C. Chagla, Ajit Prasad Jain, Jairamdas Daulatram, Bhupesh Gupta, Joachim Alva, Mahavir Tyagi, Raj Narain, Bhai Mahavir, Dahyabhai Patel and Maniben Patel (Sardar Vallabhbhai Patel's son and daughter respectively) and Loknath Misra.

Bhupesh Gupta, a leader of the Communist Party of India

(CPI), was truly a legend in the Rajya Sabha and left an indelible impression on me. He was in a way my mentor in the Parliament. It is not as if I did not have any differences with him. I would like to recount one particular incident that highlights his graciousness and civility in the Parliament.

In 1980, when I was the minister in charge of Commerce, Textiles, Steel and Mines and Civil Supplies, the President, in 1979, had issued an ordinance sanctioning preventive detention to maintain essential supplies. This was opposed by the Opposition parties including the Left under Bhupesh Gupta's leadership. A debate on this issue continued in the Rajya Sabha till late at night. As the minister in charge, and in accordance with the custom, I enquired of the members about the time they would like to be served dinner. No sooner had I asked, than Gupta rose and said aggressively, 'We will have a sumptuous meal at your expense and inflict on you a crushing defeat.' I was taken aback and retorted, 'Neither you nor I am the master of the House. Do not arrogate to yourself the position of the spokesperson of the House.'

Ms Indira Gandhi, who was seated beside me, thought that I had exceeded my brief and said, 'You have been unnecessarily rude to Gupta.' I also realized my mistake and immediately sent a note to Gupta expressing regret. He nodded with a gracious smile and the matter was put to rest.

Gupta began his career in the Parliament in 1952 when the House was constituted and continued to be its member till 1981, when he passed away while undergoing treatment in Moscow. I still remember the glowing tributes paid to him across the political spectrum.[1] Prime Minister Indira Gandhi had said that the Rajya Sabha would not be the same without him.

---

[1] 'Bhupesh: Some Reminiscences', *Mainstream Weekly*, Vol. LII, 18 October 2014, http://www.mainstreamweekly.net/article5257.html

My career as a parliamentarian was mentored by Ms Indira Gandhi. Her steely determination, clarity of thought and decisive actions made her a towering personality. She never hesitated to call a spade a spade. I remember we had gone to London in November 1978, after the defeat of the Congress in the post-Emergency elections in 1977. A large number of media persons in a fairly aggressive mood were waiting for Ms Gandhi at the Heathrow Airport lounge. The first question that was flung at her was, 'What have been your gains from the Emergency?' Looking the journalist squarely in the eye, she replied in a level voice, 'In those 21 months, we comprehensively managed to alienate all sections of the Indian people.' A moment of silence followed by loud laughter! Not one question was asked after that and the media persons just melted away. I also learnt an early lesson of acknowledging mistakes and rectifying them. Self-correction in such situations is always a better option than self-justification.

THE EVOLVING COMPOSITION: RAJYA SABHA AND LOK SABHA

Till 1969, the composition of the Rajya Sabha and the Lok Sabha followed a similar pattern, wherein both had a majority of the ruling party—the Congress. However, with the split in the Congress in 1969, aimed at marginalizing Indira Gandhi by the syndicate Congress, and the subsequent elections in 1971 when her Congress—Congress (I)—was elected with a thumping majority, this equation changed.[2] The Congress had majority in the Lok Sabha, but because of the split, it was reduced to a strength of 90 members in a House of 245.

---

[2]Statistical Report on General Elections, 1971 To The Fifth Lok Sabha, Vol. I, Election Commission of India, New Delhi, http://eci.nic.in/eci_main/StatisticalReports/LS_1971/Vol_I_LS71.pdf

As a consequence, the Upper House started asserting itself against the government, and rejected many important legislations and constitutional amendments in spite of the fact that they were supported in the Lok Sabha. For example, the constitution amendment bill of 1970 which sought to abolish privy purses, failed to get two-thirds majority in the Rajya Sabha by a fraction of votes.[3]

This was the first time that a ruling party—with a mandate from the people in the Lok Sabha—found it difficult to get even a working majority in the Rajya Sabha. This situation continues even today, with many such occurrences over the years.

So, what does one do when a party or coalition secures a decisive mandate in Lok Sabha election but finds that some of its plans are stymied in the Rajya Sabha where it is in minority? Going by the debates in the Constituent Assembly, it is clear that the makers of the Indian Constitution did not anticipate that the Upper House could become an impediment to lawmaking and governance. They also did not visualize a situation where the country's polity would become so fractured as to squeeze and marginalize national parties while nurturing dozens of regional, denominational and caste-based parties in the states, leading to representation of a plethora of parties in the Upper House. In 1952, there were just six recognized political parties in the Rajya Sabha, whereas today there are 30.[4]

However, while such a situation lends complexity to the smooth functioning of the Parliament, the fact remains that a simple majority or even a two-thirds majority in the Lok Sabha does not impact the composition of the Rajya Sabha. The latter's

---

[3]Point of privilege (Rajya Sabha, 1971), New Delhi, http://rajyasabhahindi.nic.in/rshindi/privileges_digest/priv-95.pdf
[4]Party Position in the Rajya Sabha as on 07/07/2017, Rajya Sabha website, http://164.100.47.5/Newmembers/partypositionsummary.aspx

composition is such, that the six states with the highest population and *their* ruling parties (rather than the ruling party at the Centre) determine the majority in the Rajya Sabha.

A look at the history of creation of the Rajya Sabha is in order.

In its report presented to the Constituent Assembly on 21 July 1947, the Union Constitution Committee, set up by the Constituent Assembly under Jawaharlal Nehru, made the following proposals for Rajya Sabha:[5,6]

- The two chambers should be named as the (1) Council of States and (2) House of People. These names are indicative of the manner in which each chamber would be constituted. The Parliament of the Union would be designated 'National Assembly'.
- The Council of States shall have 250 members.
- The units should have representation in the Council of States on the basis of one member for every whole million population up to five million, plus one member for every two additional million—subject to a maximum of twenty for a unit.

However, the Constituent Assembly made some changes which are reflected in the Constitution. As a result, unless the ruling party or the ruling combination had a majority in the assemblies of these six states—undivided Uttar Pradesh (34 seats), undivided Bihar (22 seats), undivided Bombay (27 seats), Madras (17 seats),

---

[5]Constituent Assembly of India Debates (Proceedings)-Vol. IV, 21 July 1947, http://164.100.47.132/lssnew/constituent/vol4p6.pdf
[6]'Rajya Sabha: Evolution, Powers and Position', Chapter 1, Rajya Sabha website, http://rajyasabha.nic.in/rsnew/rsat_work/chapter-1.pdf. This formula was recommended by a sub-committee consisting of Dr B. R. Ambedkar, Gopalaswamy Ayyangar, K.M. Munshi and Sardar K.M. Panikkar.

undivided Andhra Pradesh (18 seats) and West Bengal (16 seats)—no ruling party or combination could get a simple majority in the Rajya Sabha. These numbers are set out in the Fourth Schedule and can be altered only by constitutional amendments. As such, it is impossible to have a two-thirds majority, or even a simple majority, unless the ruling party wins all of these six large State Assemblies, or all others, through a process of simultaneous election (which in turn is impossible because that too would require a constitutional amendment).

Since the 1990s neither the BJP nor the Congress, the two national parties that have led coalition governments at the Centre, have enjoyed the majority to rule these states. Both these parties may have formed governments (in Uttar Pradesh [UP] and Andhra Pradesh) but not continuously. The BJP had to enter into alliances with regional parties in UP to form the government in 1991–92, 1997–99, 1999–2000 and 2000–02.[7] In other words, till 2017, only regional parties have ruled UP, Bihar, Tamil Nadu, Andhra Pradesh and West Bengal. Since 1967, Tamil Nadu has been governed by either the DMK or the AIADMK. From 1977 to 2011, West Bengal was ruled by the Left Front led by the CPI (M), after which another regional party, the Trinamool Congress (TMC), took over. This clearly highlights the fact that having a majority in the Lok Sabha does not guarantee a majority for the mainstream ruling party in the Rajya Sabha.

While the ruling party's lack of numerical strength in the Rajya Sabha has been exploited by various opposition groups since the 1990s, the more recent practice of disruption of the House was not in vogue during my early days in the Parliament. Or, if at all, such aberrations were infrequent. At times, members

---

[7]Ex. CHIEF MINISTERS OF UTTAR PRADESH, Government of Uttar Pradesh Official website, http://up.gov.in/upexcms.aspx

hotly debated issues pertaining to the states, of course with the permission of the Chair at Zero Hour, but without causing any disruptions.

PARLIAMENT: THE FOUNTAINHEAD OF INDIAN DEMOCRACY

Parliament is the 'Gangotri' of Indian democracy. It represents the will and the aspirations of one billion-plus people and is also the link between the people and the government. If Gangotri gets polluted, neither the Ganga nor any of its tributaries can stay unpolluted. Therefore, it is incumbent upon all parliamentarians that they maintain the highest standards of democracy and parliamentary functioning.

THE 3Ds

Effective parliamentary democracy relies on the 3Ds—Debate, Dissent and Decision. However, over a period of time, a fourth D—'Disruption'—has been injected into the system. This puts serious pressure on the government and its ability to govern, thus negating the very purpose of a parliament. Disruption hurts the Opposition more than the government since it denies them the opportunity to raise the concerns of the people. We need to correct this situation by practising tolerance and accommodation. It is the job of the leader of the House and the leader of the Opposition to work together to carry forward the agenda of the House. As the leader of the House, I had frequent discussions with the Leader of the Opposition and other leaders on ways to ensure smooth functioning of the Parliament.

The evolutionary principle of effective functioning of the parliamentary system is that the majority will rule and the minority will oppose, expose and, if possible, depose. However, the minority must accept the decisions of the majority, just as the majority must respect the views of the minority. And all the while, discipline and decorum must be maintained and rules, conventions and etiquette observed. Dissent should be expressed with decency and within the framework of parliamentary devices. The recent passage of Goods and Services Tax (GST) and its launch on 1 July 2017 is a good example of cooperative federalism and speaks volumes about the maturity of the Indian Parliament.

EFFECTIVE USE OF TIME

During the 1950s, '60s and '70s, our Parliament witnessed illuminating and exhaustive discussions on budget and financial legislations even though these financial transactions were miniscule compared to present-day allocations. In fact, though the total budgetary transactions, receipts and expenditure in Independent India's first budget totalled a mere ₹197 crore, the Parliament devoted a good deal of time in discussing and debating it. Not only that, though the size of the First Five-Year Plan was approximately ₹2,000 crore, the Approach Paper was debated for almost four days. Such discussions are necessary as they determine the direction of the development of the nation towards the objectives as enshrined in our Constitution.

Today, our budgetary transactions have increased manifold but the absence of parliamentary debates and informed discussions prevent us from appreciating their true significance. Even vital documents like the Five-Year Plans have gone undebated in the recent past. It is imperative that we go back to the essentials of engaging, discussing and debating before taking decisions regarding matters of national importance.

An example of this lack of interest in engagement and

discussion was evident when I was Deputy Chairman of the Planning Commission. P.V. Narasimha Rao, as the Chairman of the Planning Commission (in his capacity as the prime minister), decided to call for a meeting of the Consultative Committee attached to the Ministry of Planning and Programme Implementation. He arrived for the meeting with a battery of senior officials along with Minister of State (MoS) Hans Raj Bhardwaj. However, not one member of the Consultative Committee turned up! If this does not show the total lack of interest in discussion and debate, I don't know what does.

It is unfortunate that the parliamentary time devoted to legislation has been gradually declining. With the heightened complexity of administration, legislation must be preceded by adequate discussion and scrutiny. If not, it will fail to deliver the desired results or meet its objectives. It must be kept in mind that no expenditure can be incurred by the Executive, no tax levied and no money withdrawn from the Consolidated Fund of the Centre and States without the approval of the elected legislature.

ORDINANCES

Ordinances are yet another aspect of the distortion in our parliamentary functioning. The instrument of ordinances gives the Executive extraordinary powers to make laws to meet exigencies during a time when the Parliament (or State Assembly) is not in session. However, while the Executive can take this route to tackle an emergent situation, it has to be borne in mind that any such ordinance needs to be approved by the Parliament (or the State Assembly concerned) within six weeks of the next session of the legislature.

However, it has been seen that often the ordinance route

is used by governments to pass legislation on subjects that are currently pending in the Parliament, as was the case with the Food Security Ordinance in 2013. There have also been instances when an ordinance has been promulgated multiple times. This can lead to the weakening of the Parliament, and violates the spirit of the Constitution.

> According to the data published in reports of 2013, there are two distinct periods when the central government resorted to ordinances quite frequently: the period coinciding with Indira Gandhi's tenure, and the early to mid-1990s. Both these periods, for various reasons, can be characterized as those of a muscular Executive and a comparatively weak and/or unstable Parliament. The mid-1990s were especially marked by the beginning of coalition politics and short-lived governments. Though by no means conclusive, the linkage between weak Parliament and proactive ordinance-making is disturbing. If nothing else, it indicates a casual disregard of legislatures whenever the Executive is in a position to do so.[8]

Within three years of the current Lok Sabha, 28 ordinances have been promulgated. In contrast, 25 ordinances were promulgated in the 15th Lok Sabha and 36 in the 14th Lok Sabha. When the Parliament fails in discharging its lawmaking role or enacts law without discussion, it breaches the trust reposed in it by the people. I am of the firm belief that the ordinance route should be used only in compelling circumstances and that there should be absolutely no recourse to ordinances on monetary matters, which has been the practice so far with all Union governments.

---

[8]Anirudh Burman, 'Ordinance route', *Frontline*, 9 August 2013, http://www.frontline.in/the-nation/ordinance-route/article4944717.ece

No government should resort to the ordinance route on matters which are being considered, or have been introduced in the House, or a committee of the House. If a matter is deemed urgent, the committee concerned should be made aware of the situation, and should be mandated to present its report of findings strictly within the set time frame. That is, no extension should be allowed to a committee deliberating on an urgent matter.

During my days in the Rashtrapati Bhavan, on several occasions my observations on ordinances were communicated to the minister concerned or to the prime minister. But I never allowed these differences to be brought to the media glare. We need to use this instrument in the spirit in which it was meant by the makers of the Indian Constitution.

CHAPTER 2

THE CONGRESS AFTER RAJIV

P.V. Narasimha Rao provided stellar leadership to India at a critical juncture. Not only did he stabilize and turn around the nose-diving economy, he also revitalized India's foreign policy. The fact that he led a minority government did not stop him from putting in place the necessary correctives.

P.V. LEADS CONGRESS TO DEFEAT IN 1996

In the 1996 general election, the Congress party under the leadership of P.V. Narasimha Rao faced a major defeat, reducing its strength from 232 to 140 in the Lok Sabha.[9,10] The Congress lost over 42.6 per cent of its seats in the Lower House. The BJP got 161 seats.[11] There was a massive 8.4 per cent swing away

---

[9]Statistical Report on General Elections, 1991, to the Tenth Lok Sabha, Vol. I, Election Commission of India, http://eci.nic.in/eci_main/StatisticalReports/LS_1991/VOL_I_91.pdf

[10]Statistical Report on General Elections, 1996 To The Eleventh Lok Sabha, Vol. I, Election Commission of India; http://eci.nic.in/eci_main/StatisticalReports/LS_1996/Vol_II_LS96.pdf

[11]Statistical Report on General Elections, 1996 To The Eleventh Lok Sabha, Vol. I, Election Commission of India, http://eci.nic.in/eci_main/StatisticalReports/LS_1996/Vol_II_LS96.pdf

from the Congress, and its electoral support dropped from 36.5 per cent in 1991 to 28.1 per cent in 1996.[12]

This electoral loss was inexplicable, given that it came after P.V.'s exemplary steering of the economy through the balance of payments crisis and the introduction of major economic reforms. P.V. was, however, not surprised. In fact, he had shared with me his fears of Congress defeat ahead of the elections.

The fact was that in the initial phase, economic reforms largely affected the elite, and the potential benefits were yet to percolate to the masses. Elections are essentially a function of the politics of the masses and the performance of the Rao government had little to show in terms of its populist appeal.

> In the largest ever survey of mass political attitudes in India conducted between April–July 1996, only 19 per cent of the electorate reported any knowledge of economic reforms, even though reforms had been in existence since 1991.[13]
>
> Of the rural electorate, only about 14 per cent had heard of reforms, whereas the comparable proportion in the cities was 32 per cent... These statistics highlight that the raging debate over economic reforms in India was, for all practical purposes, confined to the English language newspapers, the country's graduates, the discourse on the internet, the Bombay stock market, and Delhi's India International Centre and its economic ministries. That was the circle of India's elite politics. Economic reforms were simply a non-issue in the 1996 and 1998 elections.[14]

---

[12]Stanley A. Kochanek and Robert Hardgrave, *India: Government and Politics in a Developing Nation*, 2008.
[13]Ashutosh Varshney, 'India's Democratic Challenge', *Foreign Affairs*, March–April 2007, https://www.foreignaffairs.com/articles/india/2007-03-01/indias-democratic-challenge
[14]Ashutosh Varshney, 'Mass Politics or Elite Politics? India's Economic Reforms in Comparative Perspective', *The Journal Of Policy Reform*, Vol. 2, Issue. 4, 1998 p 225.

Clearly, the wide-ranging economic reforms could not win Congress the election. What were the other issues that went wrong?

One, the alienation of the Muslims as a consequence of the Babri Masjid issue. As I have said in the earlier volume,[15] P.V.'s inability to prevent the demolition of the Masjid was one of his biggest failures—and that had a catastrophic impact on the fortunes of the party.

Two, it was the inability to structure effective alliances. The prime example of this was Tamil Nadu, and Congress's electoral alliance with Jayalalithaa's AIADMK. As a result of this alliance, G.K. Moopanar and P. Chidambaram formed the Tamil Maanila Congress and aligned with Karunanidhi's DMK. The results were disastrous for the Congress in Tamil Nadu.

> If the decline in the party's Hindi hinterland had been apparent for some time, what came as a rude shock was its performance in Maharashtra and Tamil Nadu. These two states had always elected an overwhelming majority of MPs from the Congress and its allies, not breaking the pattern even in the most disastrous elections for the Congress till that stage, the 1977 elections. In 1996, the Congress drew a complete blank in Tamil Nadu and won just 15 of the 48 seats in Maharashtra.[16]

I still remember 9 May 1996. The Congress Parliamentary Party met at P.V. Narasimha Rao's residence to work out the future strategy. It was clear that a coalition would have to be structured to stake a claim—and the party was of the view that in this

---

[15]Pranab Mukherjee, *The Turbulent Years*, Rupa Publications, 2016.
[16]Statistical Report on General Elections, 1996 To The Eleventh Lok Sabha, Vol. I, Election Commission of India, http://eci.nic.in/eci_main/StatisticalReports/LS_1996/Vol_II_LS96.pdf

state of limbo, we could encourage the formation of a coalition and support it from the outside. While these discussions were in progress, we heard that President Shankar Dayal Sharma had invited Atal Bihari Vajpayee to form the government on the principle of being the leader of the single largest party in the Lok Sabha. This was in spite of the fact that its seat strength in the Lok Sabha was barely 30 per cent. This, in my view, was a simplistic approach. Perhaps President Sharma thought that as the leader of the single largest group it would be easier for him to manage the support of others. But the result was instability in the governance. The Vajpayee government lasted only 13 days. The mandate of the President is to judiciously, and within the provisions of the Constitution, provide for a stable government.

Inviting the leader of the single largest (but still a minority) party in a divided House without ascertaining his support in the Parliament was highly risky. In two earlier cases, of 1989 and 1991, it was reasonably clear that the other parties would not, at least immediately, outvote the minority government. President Venkataraman had therefore been on fairly safe ground in taking the decisions he did.

But this was not the case in 1996. In a scenario where other parties/coalitions had declared their opposition to the largest party, it seemed futile to invite him to form the government.

In a 535-member House, the BJP and its allies numbered 186 against the United Front's 215 and the Congress's 139. There was no prospect of either the United Front or the Congress lending support to the BJP. Within 13 days of forming the government, Vajpayee was staring at defeat when he lost the Motion of Confidence in the Parliament.[17]

---

[17]'President and precedent', *Indian Express*, http://indianexpress.com/article/opinion/columns/president-and-precedent/

The Congress went back to its original plan of supporting a non-BJP coalition from the outside. V.P. Singh was expectedly the first choice, but he refused. Further discussions led to the choice of H.D. Deve Gowda to head the government.

UNITED FRONT GOVERNMENT

In the first week of June, the United Front government was formed with Deve Gowda as prime minister. The Congress decided to extend support to this government from the outside. That was the objective of the Left parties too. Deve Gowda's government was not only backed by the Left parties (CPI, CPI [M], RSP and Forward Bloc), but CPI went ahead to join the government, and two veteran leaders—Indrajit Gupta and Chaturanan Mishra—became Cabinet ministers holding important portfolios of Home and Agriculture, respectively.

The United Front government had many talented ministers like veteran former Congress leader I.K. Gujral, who was a minister in Indira Gandhi's Cabinet from 1967 to 1976 and India's Ambassador to the erstwhile USSR thereafter.[18] I.K. Gujral was entrusted with the Ministry of External Affairs. Jaipal Reddy, though not in the Cabinet, was a good resource in the Parliament.

The Tamil Maanila Congress, which had 20 seats in the Lok Sabha from Tamil Nadu, was an important constituent of the United Front government.[19] P. Chidambaram, who had left the Congress a few months earlier to co-found the Tamil Maanila Congress in 1996, was now appointed the finance minister.

---

[18]Biographical Sketch Member of Parliament 12th Lok Sabha - GUJRAL, SHRI INDER KUMAR, http://www.indiapress.org/election/archives/lok12/biodata/12pn04.php

[19]Statistical Report on General Elections, 1996 To The Eleventh Lok Sabha, Vol. I, Election Commission of India, http://eci.nic.in/eci_main/StatisticalReports/LS_1996/Vol_II_LS96.pdf

P. CHIDAMBARAM

Chidambaram entered politics much later than I did, but I had worked with him between 1991 and 1995 when he was the commerce minister in P.V. Narasimha Rao's Cabinet. However, he did not complete the full five-year term in that government as he had to resign due to some allegations of financial irregularity, which were never substantiated. Thereafter, he left the party and formed the Tamil Maanila Congress in 1996.

As finance minister in the United Front government, Chidambaram presented two budgets, in 1996–97 and 1997–98. He made a directional change in the budgetary exercise and his second budget was described by industrialists, taxpayers, and others as a 'dream budget'.

Unfortunately, the dream budget did not remain so. Though it did not exactly morph into a nightmare, in the course of the year it was found that many of the projections of revenue receipts and expenditures were off the mark and did not conform to targets that were taken into account while preparing budgetary calculations. Consequently, there was a decline in the rate of growth and employment generation, coupled with rising inflation.

Be that as it may, Chidambaram set a trend and gave a new direction to the Indian taxation system by drastically reducing the rates of taxation from excessively high levels to reasonably low levels. His analysis of the economic situation within India and outside was pragmatic, professional and acted as the guide to future policymakers.

Chidambaram has presented second highest number of budgets in the country after a record 10 by former Prime Minister Morarji Desai. He is intellectually sharp and well-informed, though he sometimes appears to be arrogant because of his very strong convictions and style of presentation.

Much has been talked about differences between Chidambaram and me. I will say that any differences that there might have been, were due to our differing perspectives on the economy. While I was conservative and believed in reforms as a continuous process and favoured an inclusive and gradual transformation of the economy—a controlled regime. He is a pro-liberalization and pro-market economist—a good example of this is the retrospective tax proposal, which we shall discuss later.

FROM P.V. TO KESRI

Towards the end of September 1996, P.V. Narasimha Rao had to resign as Congress president after being accused of corruption. He declared that he would not face the charges in court while serving as the president of the Indian National Congress. Sitaram Kesri was elected as his successor.

I clearly remember the evening Sitaram Kesri was elected. A meeting of the Congress Working Committee (CWC) had been convened and members as well as special invitees were urgently summoned to P.V.'s residence at 9, Motilal Nehru Marg. P.V. explained the situation and consulted each and every member present there, on his successor. He called me almost towards the end of the meeting (I was a special invitee), and to my utter surprise mentioned that Sitaram Kesri was the near-unanimous choice as the party president. Although I also gave my support, I had expected some other outcome. Other than me, Kesri was the most senior member of the CWC at that time (as I mentioned, I was just an invitee and not a full member of CWC).

Sitaram Kesri had risen from the ranks of the Congress organization and had become a member of the All India Congress Committee (AICC). He was the president of the Bihar Pradesh Congress Committee and MoS for parliamentary affairs in

Indira Gandhi's Cabinet in 1980. It was in January 1980 that he succeeded me as the treasurer of the AICC, when I had resigned from that office to contest the Lok Sabha election from Bolpur, my home district in West Bengal.[20] Kesri became a Cabinet Minister in P.V. Narasimha Rao's government, but he continued as party treasurer till he became the president in 1996.

At the CWC meeting, P.V. announced Sitaram Kesri's appointment and symbolically offered Kesri his seat as he moved to another. Kesri expressed his gratitude to the CWC, saying that it was an honour for him to rise from being a humble Seva Dal volunteer to the post of the party president.

Kesri's tenure as treasurer was sixteen years long and he became a butt of a few jokes within the AICC, with one being about his accounting procedures: *'Na khaata, na bahi, jo Kesri ji kahen wahi sahi.'* Though the detailed annual accounts of the Congress were presented regularly at the AICC and plenary sessions, the report on the scrutiny of receipts and expenditure was given only in the form of a statement.[21]

Once appointed as president of the Congress, Sitaram Kesri could appoint his own team as office bearers, but he chose to retain almost all from P.V.'s time. He also retained Jitendra Prasada as vice president.[22] He made only one new appointment—his close confidant and member of the Rajya Sabha from Bihar, Tariq Anwar, who was made general secretary.

As president, Sitaram Kesri reorganized some departments of AICC. He made me in charge of the department of foreign

---

[20]Volume 1, *The Dramatic Decade*, carries a detailed account of my first unsuccessful attempt at getting elected to the Lok Sabha, and relates how angry Indira Gandhi was at my foolhardiness of contesting from a communist citadel.
[21]While there was little discussion at the meetings of the AICC and the plenary, the CWC did discuss the accounts in detail.
[22]The post of vice president had been created for Kamalapati Tripathi in 1980 during the presidentship of Indira Gandhi.

affairs with an office in the annexe of AICC building (24, Akbar Road). I continued to operate from that office till 1998 when Sonia Gandhi took over as the Congress president. During his long innings as treasurer and later as Congress president, I shared an excellent working relationship with Kesri.

KESRI'S ROLE IN DESTABILIZING THE UNITED FRONT

Sitaram Kesri played a crucial role in destabilizing the United Front government, first led by Deve Gowda in 1996–97[23] and then by I.K. Gujral in 1997–98.[24]

The Deve Gowda government had been deliberately targeting the Congress. Members of the Congress, including former Prime Minister Narasimha Rao, were being prosecuted by the police on charges of corruption. The Bofors issue too was once again resurrected by the Gowda government.

In fact, most of the ministers in Deve Gowda's government had been vocal against the previous Congress government and had vowed that they would carry on the Bofors case investigation with all seriousness.

Events took a dramatic turn when CBI Director Joginder Singh came back from Geneva on 22 January 1997 with a box which allegedly contained vital documents related to the payoffs in the Bofors deal.[25] The manner in which the CBI Director showed the box clearly demonstrated the intent to dramatize the entire episode.

---

[23]Tarun J. Tejpal, 'Villan no. 1: Sitaram Kesari', *Outlook*, https://www.outlookindia.com/magazine/story/villain-no-1-sitaram-kesri/204883

[24]Praveen Swami and Venkitesh Ramakrishnan, 'The politics of blackmail', *Frontline*, Vol. 14, No. 24, 29 Nov–12 Dec, 1997, http://www.frontline.in/static/html/fl1424/14240040.htm

[25]Ananth V. Krishna, *India Since Independence: Making Sense Of Indian Politics*, Pearson Education India, 2010, p 402.

However, in subsequent investigations or the follow-ups of the case, there was no reference to the 'documents on Bofors' brought from abroad by the CBI Director himself. It confirmed the suspicion of the Congress members that the Deve Gowda government wanted to discredit the Congress while enjoying its support to rule.

That the Deve Gowda government was utilizing its official position to malign the Congress led to the clamour within the party for withdrawing support to the government.

The Congress party could not support a government which was bent upon maligning and persecuting its leadership.

In March 1997, Sitaram Kesri took into confidence a group of Congress leaders including Sharad Pawar, the leader of the Congress in the Lok Sabha, Jitendra Prasada, Arjun Singh and me. He may have taken Tariq Anwar into confidence too. I drafted a letter addressed to the President informing him about the party's decision to withdraw support from the government.

Rumours were afloat that the strategy of destabilizing the United Front government was the result of Kesri's ambition. I was not aware of any such intention though. Many believed that the Congress could get a chance to form the government. This optimism rested on the fact that a few months earlier, Atal Bihari Vajpayee had made an unsuccessful bid to come to power at the Centre.

A few of us, rather than involving the entire CWC, finalized the letter at Kesri's home for taking it to the President. In a bid to maintain secrecy and not allow the reporters waiting outside his residence to get any hint of what was on the anvil, Kesri took me along in his car while mine followed. We took a circuitous route to Rashtrapati Bhavan to throw off any enterprising reporter who might have thought of following us. Close to the destination, I got off Kesri's car, got into mine and headed home, while Kesri went to Rashtrapati Bhavan.

There was strong reaction to this decision of withdrawal of support from Congress MPs in the Lok Sabha. Several MPs gathered at Sharad Pawar's residence, who called me with a request to pacify them.

I had been told that some Congress members had doubts about Sitaram Kesri having written the resolution to withdraw Congress support from the government. They thought it was my handiwork, given that I normally drafted resolutions on behalf of the Congress party. So, I rushed to Sharad Pawar's residence and faced the ire of the party MPs congregated there. They were concerned that the withdrawal would lead to the dissolution of the House. Their worry was that as MPs in the Lok Sabha, they would have to face the electorate again, with no guarantee of winning. Some members even accused me of being party to this decision since I was in the Rajya Sabha and wouldn't have to worry about losing my parliamentary seat. They pointed out that leaders belonging to the Rajya Sabha did not understand the burden of frequent elections in the Lok Sabha. (Sitaram Kesri, Jitendra Prasada, Arjun Singh and I were all members of the Rajya Sabha!)

I tried to explain the rationale of this decision to them. While I agreed with their concern that it would be harsh to face fresh elections, I asked them how, as a party, could we keep on supporting a government which had accused the Congress of being corrupt. I repeated to them the wild allegations which were being hurled against Congress leaders.

Thereafter, I came back to AICC headquarters and reported the substance of my meeting and the feelings of the agitated members to Kesri, who just listened silently.

We then started conferring with the ruling party to determine the next course of action. During my conversations, I told them that the Congress wanted to explore the possibility of having another non-Congress, non-BJP government led by somebody else. Finally, Janata Party decided on a change of leadership from Deve Gowda to I.K. Gujral (who was the External Affairs Minister in the Deve Gowda government). The Congress extended support to the new dispensation and approved the budget proposals so that there was no financial deadlock. The budget was passed and the Deve Gowda government continued.

I.K. GUJRAL

I.K. Gujral came from a family of freedom fighters, and was one himself. Having been a student politician, he later joined Indira Gandhi's government in 1967. However, he seemed to have had disagreements with Sanjay Gandhi during the Emergency. A few years later, he left the Congress to join the Janata Dal and didn't return to the fold even when the offer was made. I am convinced that had he remained with the Congress, he would have risen to greater heights.

Gujral's tenure was short, and it would be unfair to judge it from a durability point of view. Even in this short period he left his mark on foreign policy with the 'Gujral Doctrine'.

> These principles, scrupulously observed, will, I am sure, recast South Asia's regional relationship, including the tormented relationship between India and Pakistan, in a friendly, co-operative mould,' he declared. The theory might have been scoffed at by the more hard-bitten politicians, used to the rough and tumble of South Asian strategic affairs. But against the odds, the ever-diplomatic Gujral secured results. Perhaps the most significant was the signing of the Ganga Waters Accord with Bangladesh, but he also improved relations

with Pakistan and made a personal appeal to its prime minister, Nawaz Sharif.[26]

Despite the fact that he led a motley coalition precarious from the start, Gujral refused to yield to the Congress's demand of dropping DMK from the coalition after the Jain Commission's findings were released. He held his ground. A man of principle, Gujral insisted that the investigations in the case of Rajiv Gandhi's assassination would continue. He refused to play into the hands of the Congress and left the office of the PM with his head held high.

KOLKATA PLENARY

In August 1997, the 80th Plenary Session of the Congress was organized in Kolkata. Sitaram Kesri was slowly losing support. He was not popular amongst senior CWC leaders even though they had gone along with P.V.'s proposal to appoint him president. That, coupled with the disenchantment of the Congress MPs in the Lok Sabha with the actions of the party under Kesri's leadership, affected his already receding support base.

The Kolkata Plenary was significant for three reasons.

One, it was here that Sonia Gandhi formally became a primary member of the Congress. She addressed the plenary, and was received very enthusiastically by all members. This was significant since it was her first political outing after a consistent refusal to join politics, and the rest, as they say, is history.

Two, there was a split in the West Bengal Pradesh Congress Committee (WBPCC), with the emergence of Mamata Banerjee.

---

[26] Andrew Buncombe, 'IK Gujral: Politician who improved India's foreign relations', *The Independent* (UK), http://www.independent.co.uk/news/obituaries/ik-gujral-politician-who-improved-india-s-foreign-relations-8420898.html

She mocked the Congress session held at Netaji Indoor Stadium and did not participate in it. Mamata insisted that her Congress was the real Congress and organized a huge public meeting at Brigade Parade Ground in Kolkata and called it the 'Outdoor' Session. This was practically the flashpoint as after that she formally launched the Trinamool Congress during the 1998 general election. She contested Lok Sabha elections and won spectacularly with seven Lok Sabha seats in Kolkata and surrounding areas.[27]

Three, it was at this session that AICC elections took place (for the last time till date), after the Tirupati session, which was held in 1992 under P.V. Narasimha Rao.

I contested the election to the CWC, and won hands down. Standing fifth in the order of the votes received, I became a full-fledged member of CWC—I had been its member from 1978–86 and its invitee from 1991–97—and remained one till 2012 when I was elected the 13th President of India.

KESRI'S ELECTION

Before the Kolkata session, Kesri was elected as Congress president, defeating Sharad Pawar and Rajesh Pilot.

However, this election to the office of the Congress president was not smooth. Sitaram Kesri wanted to continue, as his tenure had been short. Jitendra Prasada and a couple of other members supported him. He also claimed that he had the support of 10 Janpath—meaning Sonia Gandhi, though she was not involved in party matters or in any other public policy at that time. Without being very vocal about it, Ms Gandhi did extend her support to Kesri.

---

[27]Statistical Report on General Elections, 1998 To the 12th Lok Sabha, Vol. I, Election Commission of India, http://eci.nic.in/eci_main/StatisticalReports/LS_1998/Vol_I_LS_98.pdf, p.109

However, two prominent Congress leaders, Sharad Pawar from Maharashtra and Rajesh Pilot from Rajasthan, decided to contest this election. Some of us tried to avoid a contest and get a consensus candidate, but failed. Finally, I threw my lot with Kesri. I essentially became his campaign manager. I would often hold press conferences to elaborate on organizational issues and how a consensus candidate was preferable. My residence at 13 Talkatora Road, virtually became the war room for his campaign. A.K. Antony, Jitendra Prasada, R.K. Dhawan, Tariq Anwar and others would visit and discuss various election-related issues. I even went to campaign in some of the states in the Northeast, as well as Madhya Pradesh and Rajasthan.

A.R. Antulay became Sharad Pawar's election agent. This was rather odd as Pawar and Antulay were in opposing camps. But in this election, many strange things seemed to be happening.

Needless to say, Kesri won the election with an overwhelming majority. That Kesri's high-profile opponents fared miserably was no surprise to me since they had little following among Congress workers—they were leaders in the media. Kesri, on the other hand, enjoyed tremendous support. He was backed by Pradesh Congress Committee (PCC) leaders—all major states, including Congress-ruled state governments from the Northeast to the South and the West supported Sitaram Kesri. This was one of the very few occasions when the office of the Congress president was keenly contested by rival candidates.

HISTORY OF CONTESTS FOR CONGRESS PRESIDENCY

In the long history of the Congress, a really serious contest for presidency was first fought between Subhas Chandra Bose and Pattabhi Sitaramayya in 1939. Though Sitaramayya was backed by senior leaders like Gandhiji, Bose was the more popular icon, enthusiastically supported by the youth. Subhas Chandra Bose won a massive victory. But it created an awkward situation, resulting in Gandhiji insisting that Sitaramayya's defeat was his own defeat.

The ensuing estranged relationship between Gandhiji and Bose in the late 1930s was an unfortunate chapter in the history of the Congress. But since then, senior Congress leaders have scrupulously tried to avoid such a situation, even though sometimes it became inevitable. Before Sitaram Kesri's election, another major contest for the Congress presidency took place in 1950 between J.B. Kripalani and Purushottam Das Tandon, prior to the Nasik session of the Congress. The outcome was not pleasant. J.B. Kripalani left Congress and formed his own outfit, Kisan Mazdoor Praja Party (KMPP).

However, Tandon had to quit the Congress president's office owing to his differences with the then Prime Minister, Jawaharlal Nehru. At that juncture, Nehru was requested to assume the presidentship of the Congress; thus, from 1951 to 1955 he combined the office of Congress president with the office of the prime minister. However, Nehru was against one person holding both offices simultaneously, and corrected this situation at the Congress session in Avadi in 1955. There, U.N. Dhebar succeeded Nehru as Congress president. Thereafter, the unanimous election of the Congress president continued till the split of Indian National Congress in 1969.

I mention these examples and contests only to highlight the importance given to the office of the Congress president. I personally subscribe to the theory that certain offices should not be sought; rather, they should be offered. I consider the Congress presidency to be one such office. The old practice of inviting an eminent person to preside over the annual session of Indian National Congress and that person holding office till the next annual session was truly remarkable for any political organization, including the Congress. Therefore, my efforts were always focused at having a unanimously chosen or consensus candidate for the office of the Congress President. That is what prompted me to work for a consensus in favour of Kesri, failing which I supported him.

UNITED FRONT II FALLS

A couple of months after the Kolkata Plenary, the government faced another serious crisis when the preliminary report of the Jain Commission, set up to investigate the assassination of Rajiv Gandhi at Sriperumbudur on 21 May 1991, was released on 28 August 1997.[28]

Justice M.C. Jain's interim report[29] suggested that the DMK and its leadership had been involved in encouraging Velupillai Prabhakaran, the leader of the Liberation Tigers of Tamil Eelam (LTTE), and his followers. There were also references to poor security arrangements for Rajiv Gandhi. While the report did not refer to any particular leader or involvement of any party in the conspiracy, it was a problematic situation for the United Front government. The DMK was a member of the coalition group, which the Congress supported from the outside. Also, the Cabinet had a few DMK ministers, including Murasoli Maran, who held important portfolios.[30]

The winter session of the Parliament in 1997 witnessed hectic parleys in an attempt to diffuse the crisis. Some Congress leaders—Sitaram Kesri, Jitendra Prasada, Arjun Singh, Sharad Pawar and

---

[28] Ananth V. Krishna, *India Since Independence: Making Sense of Indian Politics*, Pearson Education India, 2010, p 406.
[29] Lok Sabha debates, 25.11.91.
[30] Members Bioprofile, Maran, Shri Murasoli, Lok Sabha website, http://164.100.47.194/LOKSabha/Members/MemberBioprofile.aspx?mpsno =243&lastls=13

I—were invited by Prime Minister Gujral for dinner at his official residence.[31] We discussed the issue; the Prime Minister said that there was no direct evidence of the involvement of any particular leader of the DMK, let alone any minister. He went on to say that in such a situation, it would send a wrong message if he were to take action against the DMK. The government would be seen as succumbing to the pressure of a supporting party, and its capacity to govern would become extremely limited. Gujral was firm in his view that the credibility of the government could not be undermined. We told him that we would like to take the issue and his point of view to the CWC, which would ultimately take a decision.

A large number of Congress members, including a part of the leadership, were not favourably disposed towards what now seemed to be a frequent withdrawal of support to the government. These members were mostly those elected to the Lok Sabha, and rightly feared that fresh elections, as a result of withdrawal of support to the government, may not favour them. Also, I.K. Gujral was quite popular among the Leftists and had the support base of academicians and intellectuals.[32] He had also been a long-time colleague of Indira Gandhi. Despite all these compelling factors, the Congress took a stand, and withdrew support.

This time, the letter to the President about withdrawing support, was not drafted secretly as was done in the case of the

---

[31]Praveen Swami and Venkitesh Ramakrishnan, 'The politics of blackmail', *Frontline*, New Delhi, Vol. 14, No. 24, 29 Nov–12 Dec, 1997, http://www.frontline.in/static/html/fl1424/14240040.htm

[32]The 'old friends' who helped him become India's 12th Prime Minister (pipping Moopanar and Mulayam Singh Yadav to the post) included the CPI (M)'s Jyoti Basu, former Vice President Krishan Kant (who was Andhra Pradesh Governor at the time) as mentioned in 'Politician who was gentleman first', *The Hindu*, 1 December 2012, http://www.thehindu.com/todays-paper/tp-opinion/politician-who-was-gentleman-first/article4152541.ece

Deve Gowda government. After open discussions at the CWC, a resolution was passed that the Congress would withdraw support if the Prime Minister refused to drop the DMK ministers from his Cabinet.

In doing so, the Congress chose to forget, or simply overlook, the compulsions of politicians in Tamil Nadu who were not in a position to vocally oppose the leaders of Sri Lankan Tamils. Apart from ethnic and linguistic congruity between the people of Tamil Nadu and Sri Lankan Tamils, there were living ties between them too—many had community connections across generations, separated by the ocean.

However, there were occasions when matters of principle would outweigh even the strongest of connections. In early 1995, on the eve of the visit of Sri Lankan President Chandrika Kumaratunga, I was asked by a section of the media if I, in my capacity as the country's Minister for External Affairs, would press for the extradition of LTTE leader, V. Prabhakaran. My response was an emphatic yes, much to the consternation of the visiting leader. When P.V. apprised me of the sense of disquiet that my statement had generated, I informed him that I would be failing in my duties as the External Affairs Minister if I didn't raise the issue of the extradition of those responsible for the assassination of one of India's former prime ministers.

So why did the Congress withdraw support? What did Kesri mean by his oft-repeated comment, *'Mera paas waqt nahin hai'* (I have no time)? Many Congress leaders interpreted it as his ambition to become prime minister. He tried to exploit the overarching anti-BJP sentiment while simultaneously undermining the United Front government with the aim of thrusting himself as the head of a non-BJP government.

Whatever the reason, I.K. Gujral stood firm in his resolve not to drop the DMK ministers.

Eventually, the Congress withdrew support to the government. Gujral resigned on 28 November 1997, and the President dissolved the Lok Sabha on 4 December 1997. Mid-term elections were announced for February 1998.

On 29 December 1997, Sonia Gandhi, who was now a primary member of Congress, announced that she would campaign for the party in the upcoming general election. At a press briefing held that day, the Congress announced that:

> A large number of Congress workers from all over the country have requested Sonia Gandhi to take active interest in the affairs of the Congress Party which is at the moment passing through a very crucial phase. On 17 December 1997, the Congress president conveyed to Mrs. Gandhi the unanimous request of the extended Congress Working Committee to campaign for the party at this difficult moment. Mrs. Gandhi has acceded to these requests. Details for putting this decision into practice are being worked out by the AICC.[33]

However, while Sonia Gandhi did campaign across the length and breadth of the country, drawing large crowds wherever she went, she was still adamant that she would not herself contest the Lok Sabha elections. The media reported laudably on her campaign and her growing popularity.

> These days, Sonia is fluent in both Hindi and English. Way back, when she first headed the Congress election campaign, she read out her Hindi speeches, written in Roman script and laced with the Italian accent, with some difficulty. Yet, wherever she went—usually accompanied by

---

[33]Manini Chatterjee, 'The last straw', *Frontline,* Vol. 15, No. 01, Jan 10–23, 1998, http://www.frontline.in/static/html/fl1501/15010220.htm

daughter Priyanka, or son Rahul, or both—huge crowds applauded her. On January 11, 1998, the latest inheritor of the Nehru-Gandhi legacy made her political debut with an election rally close to the spot in the southern town of Sriperumbudur, where Rajiv was blown up by a smiling suicide bomber of the LTTE. Thereafter, no matter where she went, the welcome to her grew warmer.[34]

Under the presidentship of Sitaram Kesri, the Congress managed to get only 141 seats in the Lok Sabha. This defeat, to my mind, was a result of the erosion in upper caste votes as well as those of Muslims. The Congress, which had till now been an umbrella organization accommodating all, irrespective of caste, creed, religion, or region, was suddenly confronted with a decline of its secular credentials.

Nehru had believed in a strong, cadre-based and inclusive organization, but after him this belief was lost. Indira Gandhi divided the political spectrum, and slowly the Congress's organizational structure as well.

MAMATA BANERJEE

Mamata Banerjee emerged as a force to reckon with after the Kolkata Plenary in 1997. Mamata has had a spectacular political career. In my second volume, I have written about how she was elected to the Lok Sabha in 1984, defeating Somnath Chatterjee from the Jadavpur constituency that was considered to be a citadel of the Marxist party. This was a splendid victory and she appeared to be truly a giant killer. Throughout her subsequent

---

[34]Inder Malhotra, 'Rear View: How Sonia took over Congress', *Indian Express*, http://indianexpress.com/article/opinion/columns/rear-view-how-sonia-took-over-congress/

political life, she has always faced tough challenges bravely and tried to convert them into opportunities. Mamata left Congress and formed TMC in 1998. She faced her first and, till date, the last defeat in the 1989 general election, when she lost to the CPI (M) candidate, Malini Bhattacharya.

Mamata Banerjee is a born rebel. Nothing illustrates this innate characteristic more than the state organizational election of 1992.

In 1991, I was the deputy chairman of the Planning Commission, and was not taking much interest in the day-to-day politics of the WBPCC. But before the organizational election, there was an interesting development. There were some media reports that important Congress leaders of West Bengal, including P.R. Dasmunsi, Ajit Panja, Somen Mitra, Subrata Mukherjee, Mamata Banerjee and Atish Sinha (then leader of Congress Legislative Party [CLP]), had approached Prime Minister and Congress President P.V. Narasimha Rao with a written request to persuade me to work out an alternative to avoid an open contest at various levels of the state Congress organization. Open contest, they reportedly said, only resulted in ugly factionalism, and sometimes also to violence, thus bringing disrepute to the party. They further stated that the signatories represented all major factions of the WBPCC and also those of four frontal organizations, namely Mahila Congress, Yuva Congress, Chhatra Parishad and Bengal Provincial National Trade Union Congress. They insisted that since I did not belong to any faction or group, I would inspire confidence in the minds of ordinary Congressmen and any compromise formula put forward by me would be accepted by all.

It may be in order to understand the structure of the Congress party at the block and district levels. At the block level, four delegates are sent to the District Congress Committee (DCC) while one member, called the delegate, is sent to the PCC. The delegate attends the AICC plenary and also participates in the election of the Congress president. The delegates became the members of the general body of various PCCs.

P.V. called me and told me to work out a mechanism in consultation with the leaders. Initially, Mamata Banerjee did not have any objection; in fact, she had signed the proposal. Siddhartha Shankar Ray, who was then president of WBPCC, also told me personally that Mamata Banerjee would support me wholeheartedly.

G.K. Moopanar, a veteran Congress leader and a former general secretary of AICC, was appointed Provincial Returning Officer, and on his recommendation, K.T. Ramachandran[35] was appointed Assistant Returning Officer. I began my talks with the leaders of all factions at the district level.

One day, during the winter of that year, I requested Mamata Banerjee for a meeting to discuss some of the observations she had made about the process. G.K. Moopanar and K.T. Ramachandran were also to be part of the meeting. During the discussion, Mamata suddenly flared up and accused me along with other leaders of a conspiracy against her. She now demanded organizational election, and said she had always stood for elections so that grass-roots level workers could have their say in organizational matters. She went on to accuse me and others of distributing organizational positions amongst ourselves, thereby thwarting the electoral process.

I was flabbergasted by her reaction and wild allegations. I told her that it was at the request of the local leaders, including herself, that the whole compromise formula was being devised.

---

[35] K.T. Ramachandran was a government servant who resigned in 1967 to join the Congress.

She, however, said that she was totally opposed to my approach and wanted open elections. Having said that, she left the meeting in a huff. I was stunned, and felt humiliated and insulted. G.K. Moopanar, the level-headed and seasoned political leader that he was, told me he would make an attempt to pacify her by visiting her after some time.

On her way out of our meeting, Mamata addressed the media and made caustic comments about us wanting compromise and adjustment, while she wanted elections at the grass-roots level as she felt that it was the only way the Congress party could be saved. The media sought my comments after some time. I declined to make any comment other than what I had communicated to the Congress President and the Prime Minister: that I would not like to continue with the responsibility he had entrusted me with. Naturally, it made headlines in the next day's newspapers. In spite of requests by state Congress leaders to take my decision back, I stood firm. 'Thank you very much. But I have already decided that I will have no role in the organizational election of WBPCC.'

I returned to Delhi the next day and met P.V. with the details. I also told him that Moopanar was trying to persuade Mamata and that he could directly check with Moopanar about the outcome.

Given that organizational election in other states were advancing as per schedule, Mohsina Kidwai was sent as observer to West Bengal with the aim of resolving the issue. I was told later that a list of around 450 delegates was agreed upon and adopted.

The date for the election of WBPCC was fixed. Thirty members of PCC, including the PCC president, three vice presidents, one treasurer and 56 members of the AICC were to be elected at the meeting. Except for the state president, all other members, including me, were elected to various bodies through the unanimous approval of a resolution. Voting through secret ballot was conducted for the election of the president of WBPCC and at the end of the elections, at about two o'clock in the morning, Somen Mitra was declared elected, having defeated Mamata Banerjee by a very narrow margin.

I was present when that result was announced. An angry Mamata came up to me and asked, 'Are you happy? Has your desire to defeat me been fulfilled?' I told her that she was totally mistaken. I added that ever since she had left the meeting at Hindustan Copper Guest House, I had no role in the organizational elections except attending the meeting of the General Body that day and watching the proceedings.

Looking back, I think I should have handled the situation differently. As in my relationship with Rajiv Gandhi (which I have written about in my volume 2), I allowed my emotions and sentiments to govern my rationality. Mamata Banerjee was almost half my age, and did not have the experience comparable to mine in public life. Therefore, I should have been more understanding, sympathetic, appreciative and patient with her.

She has a unique quality which I have myself commented upon on several occasions. She has built her own career—fearlessly and aggressively—and what she is today is the outcome of her own struggle, labour and hard work. She has an aura about her which is difficult to explain but impossible to ignore.

Since 1998, the performance of the West Bengal Congress in general elections has been dismal. Even the efforts made by Sonia Gandhi to forge a coalition with the Trinamool Congress in the 2001 general election did not succeed. However, Mamata in alliance with the Congress in the 2009 Lok Sabha elections and the 2011 Assembly elections achieved spectacular success in both. After the 2009 Lok Sabha elections, she joined the UPA-II government as Cabinet Minister of Railways along with six MoS. After winning the 2011 State Assembly elections of West Bengal, she preferred to resign from Central Cabinet and donned the mantle of the Chief Minister of West Bengal. In October 2012, she left UPA-II and became totally independent. Her success in 2014 Lok Sabha elections brought down Left parties from 15 to 2 and reduced Congress from 6 to 4. The evolution of Mamata Banerjee as a political leader of substance is an important episode in contemporary politics of West Bengal.

CHAPTER 3

SONIA GANDHI TAKES CHARGE

In the Congress Constitution, there is an elaborate provision for the election of the Congress president but no provision for their removal. Perhaps the makers of the Congress Constitution assumed that this could not happen in the future as it had never happened in the past. In the long history of the Congress, there had never been an occasion where the Congress president had to be removed from the position. Whenever there was a difference between the Congress president and the High Command, the views of the High Command (Gandhiji and Nehru) prevailed and the Congress president resigned rather than having to be sacked. In fact, the Congress president had been the virtual nominee of the Congress prime minister from 1947 to 1964 and from 1971 to 1977.

In 1998, however, the CWC faced a peculiar situation with Sitaram Kesri.

After the party's dismal performance in the general election that year, a large number of Congress leaders and workers wanted a change of guard. They demanded that Sonia Gandhi be persuaded to take over the leadership of the party as president. One day, Jitendra Prasada came to me and said that Sitaram Kesri was rapidly losing popularity among the party rank and file. I asked how we could be so sure of that when just a few months ago, at the Kolkata session, he had been overwhelmingly elected as the president, defeating Sharad Pawar and Rajesh Pilot.

Prasada pointed out that as Sonia Gandhi had campaigned vigorously during the elections, she had established a rapport with the Congress masses and there was a growing sentiment that she should lead the Congress. In fact, Sharad Pawar was most vociferous in the demand for a change in leadership, motivated, in all probability, by his desire to be appointed as the party president, in case Sonia Gandhi stubbornly refused to accept the office. None of the members were in favour of bringing back P.V.

Given that the party Constitution was silent on the removal of the party president, Prasada asked me to find a solution as according to him, I possessed in-depth knowledge of the Congress Constitution and its rules.

I studied the matter, and finally did find a solution. The CWC had the power to meet such a situation. The Congress Constitution has a provision, Article XIX-J, which says that, in the event of an extraordinary situation, the CWC can resort to appropriate solutions not mentioned in the Constitution, but subject to the ratification of such a decision by the AICC within six months. After careful consideration, I told Prasada and Pawar about this provision and we decided to discuss this possibility further. A few more CWC members came to my residence for discussions and we worked out the details of the plan. The plan was:

- A CWC meeting would be called at short notice.
- If the Congress President refused to summon the Working Committee on the basis of the requisition, then the requisitioning members themselves would convene the meeting and thereafter would take an appropriate decision.

Since I knew the intricacies of the Congress Constitution, I was asked to prepare and operationalize the plan. My involvement in this particular situation was essentially academic.

In order to maintain secrecy, it was also agreed that the matter would not be discussed further.

On 5 March 1998, Congress President Sitaram Kesri convened the meeting of the CWC at the party office at 24 Akbar Road. On the day of the meeting, Jitendra Prasada, Sharad Pawar and Ghulam Nabi Azad explained the current situation and urged Kesri to respond to their suggestion by taking the initiative to invite Sonia Gandhi to take charge of the party. Sitaram Kesri refused to accept the suggestion and accused me and some others present of hatching a conspiracy against him. He then declared the CWC meeting closed and left the venue followed by his confidant, General Secretary Tariq Anwar.

All other members of the CWC, including me, were still present at the venue. I was by then an elected member of the CWC, and since I was the most senior member, I was requested to preside over the meeting. I did, and at the meeting adopted a resolution that was approved unanimously by the members of the Working Committee. In that resolution, the CWC expressed its gratitude and thanked Congress President Sitaram Kesri for his offer, reported earlier in the media, to relinquish his office if Sonia Gandhi expressed her willingness to accept the Congress presidency.[36]

The resolution further thanked Kesri for providing leadership and guidance to the Congress organization during his tenure. The resolution was carried unanimously and some of the CWC members took the typed copy to the residence of Sonia Gandhi and requested her to take up Congress presidency. Sonia Gandhi

---

[36]Rasheed Kidwai, *Sonia: A Biography*, Penguin, 2011, p 98.

accepted the request. Thereafter, she was formally elected as the president of the party by the AICC on 6 April 1998, and the decision was ratified by the plenary session of Congress in Bangalore.[37,38]

Though she was entitled as per the provisions of the Congress Constitution to have her own new team, Sonia Gandhi opted for continuity. She decided to leave the elected component of the Working Committee intact and made additions and alterations only in the nominated category. All office bearers were retained. P.A. Sangma was inducted into the Working Committee, Ambika Soni was appointed her political adviser and, later, Ahmed Patel, who continues to be her political adviser till date.

I was not in Sonia Gandhi's inner circle in her initial years as Congress president. Her close advisers comprised Natwar Singh, Arjun Singh, K. Karunakaran, Ahmed Patel and Ambika Soni. It was the Pachmarhi Conclave of the Congress which brought me close to her.

PACHMARHI CONCLAVE

After assuming office as Congress president, Sonia decided to hold a brainstorming session of senior Congressmen on 4–6 September 1998. Around 300 delegates—members of the Working Committee, invitees, AICC office bearers, PCC presidents, CLP leaders, prominent members of Parliament and other senior state Congress and national leaders—participated.

Nawal Kishore Sharma, senior Congress leader and former general secretary of the AICC, was in charge of the conclave. The delegates were divided into five focus groups to discuss

---

[37]Ed. Pranab Mukherjee, *Congress and the Making of the Indian Nation*, Academic Foundation, Vol. I, p 148, 2011.
[38]Appendix 1: Election of Smt. Sonia Gandhi as Congress President.

(1) political issues (2) economic issues (3) international issues (4) agriculture (5) organizational matters. I, along with Natwar Singh, was asked to lead the group focusing on international issues. Sonia Gandhi addressed the inaugural session and laid down the broad objectives of the conclave. Thereafter, the various groups went into their sessions. Sonia attended the deliberations of each group for around an hour. The following day, all group leaders submitted their recommendations to Sharma. On Sharma's advice, Sonia Gandhi asked me to compile them and put them together in the form of a Declaration.

With the assistance of Mani Shankar Aiyar and a couple of others, I compiled the conclusions into a Declaration for the approval of the general session on the concluding day. On that day, I was not only asked to explain the salient features of the Declaration to the delegates but also to interact with the media on the subject.[39]

This conclave was significant for the political stand it took. In her concluding remarks, Sonia Gandhi said:

> The fact that we are going through a coalitional phase at national politics reflects in many ways the decline of the Congress. This is a passing phase and we will come back again with full force and on our own steam. But in the interim, coalitions may well be needed.[40]

Thus, she asserted that in the long run, the Congress would be able to govern on its own, but at the same time anticipated what was to happen in 2004.

Following my active participation in the conclave, Sonia Gandhi started consulting me more frequently. A certain

---

[39] Appendix 2: The Pachmarhi Declaration 6th September, 1998.
[40] Edited by Pranab Mukherjee, *Congress and the Making of the Indian Nation*, Academic Foundation, Vol. I, p 150, 2011.

detachment which had earlier existed in our relationship gradually transformed into warmth and mutual respect.

I believe that this detachment and her decision of not being aligned with anybody in particular is her greatest strength. It reflects another important dimension in India's political history. Like other illustrious members of her family, Sonia has adopted a truly pan-India approach. Her ability to reach out to the masses and their acceptance of her as their leader was the single most important qualifying factor for her to become India's prime minister. She could have acquired other essential qualities for this office after assuming power.

Looking back, I can say that as the longest serving Congress president, Sonia's positive contribution to strengthen the Congress party has not received due attention in the analysis of contemporary political observers. The mere fact that the Congress party led the coalition of UPA-I and II from 2004–14, despite the lack of adequate numbers, speaks of her ability to forge an alliance with various parties including smaller entities like the Telangana Rashtra Samithi (TRS) and the Jharkhand Mukti Morcha (JMM), apart from the Rashtriya Janata Dal (RJD), DMK and CPI (M). As an astute and pragmatic political leader, she realized that ruling with an absolute majority in the Parliament may be a distant goal, but not an immediately achievable one.

THE BEGINNING OF POST-CONGRESS POLITY

This period can probably be categorized as a marker for the beginning of the post-Congress polity. Until now, the Nehruvian 'catch-all' and inclusive nature of the party, albeit diminishing over time, had ensured the party's standing and electoral success. Now one could see a discernible trend towards:

- A loss in the Congress's vote share from 39.5 per cent in 1989 to 25.9 per cent in 1998.
- An increase in the number of regional or state-level political actors.

The rise of the BJP in the 1990s as an alternate to the Congress coincided with another significant development across the nation's political landscape—the formation of alliances by smaller parties to constitute a bulwark against the Congress.

For the first time in Indian politics, a post-electoral coalition of minor state-based parties constituted the government at the Centre. The United Front government of 1996 was formed primarily by parties which were based in, and limited to, particular states. This formidable political grouping included Telugu Desam Party ([TDP] Andhra Pradesh), DMK and All India Anna Dravida Munnetra Kazhagam ([AIADMK] Tamil Nadu), Tamil Maanila Congress (Tamil Nadu) and Asom Gana Parishad (Assam). The BJP government formed in 1998 also depended upon an electoral alliance with state-based parties such as the Akali Dal, TDP and the AIADMK.

These developments stood in sharp contrast to much of the period after independence, when the Congress was either the dominant party, or one of two major parties in all of the states.[41]

---

[41]Pradeep Chhibber and Irfan Nooruddin, 1991, 'Party Competition and Fragmentation in Indian National Elections: 1957–1998', in Ramashray Roy and Paul Wallace's, *Indian Politics and the 1998 Election: Regionalism, Hindutva and State Politics*, Sage Publications, 1999.

CHAPTER 4

NDA, 1998–99

The 12th general election began in February 1998. The election results gave the Congress little reason to cheer but a lot to introspect. It was the second consecutive election in two years that the party had lost. Though the BJP won more seats than it did in the 1996 elections, no single party secured a majority in the Lok Sabha. BJP had won 182 seats, while Congress was far behind with only 141 seats.[42]

President K.R. Narayanan then decided to hold discussions, unlike President Shankar Dayal Sharma two years ago, to choose a leader who could command a majority in the Lok Sabha. While the President was engaged in the task of deciding the party that could provide a stable coalition government, veteran communist leader Harkishan Singh Surjeet, General Secretary of the CPI (M), was working hard to bring together all non-BJP parties. The Congress was also roped into this combination. However, as the single largest party in Parliament, Narayanan asked the BJP under Atal Bihari Vajpayee to provide letters of support from the

---

[42]Statistical Report on General Elections, 1998 To The 12th Lok Sabha, Vol. I, Election Commission of India, New Delhi, http://eci.nic.in/eci_main/StatisticalReports/LS_1998/Vol_I_LS_98.pdf

coalition partners. Having thus satisfied himself, he then issued a statement on 15 March 1998:

> The number of MPs supporting the formation of a government by the BJP now comes to 264. The number—264—remains short of the halfway mark in the total House of 539. However, when seen in the context of the TDP's [Telugu Desam Party] decision, as conveyed to the President by Chandrababu Naidu to remain neutral, the number of 264 does cross the mark… The President has also advised Shri Vajpayee to secure a vote of confidence on the floor of the House within ten days of his being sworn in.[43]

Vajpayee thus formed the NDA coalition government in 1998.[44]

VAJPAYEE'S 13-MONTH GOVERNMENT

Though this was a short 13-month tenure, Vajpayee took some significant decisions, and also had to face some tough choices.

Perhaps the most important decision was to conduct the second round of nuclear tests in Pokhran on 11 May 1998. Making the announcement, Vajpayee said:

> Today, at 15:45 hours, India conducted three underground nuclear tests in the Pokhran range. These tests conducted today were with a fission device, a low-yield device and a thermonuclear device. The measured yields are in line with expected values. Measurements have also confirmed that there was no release of radioactivity into the atmosphere. These were contained explosions like the

---

[43]Press Communique Rashtrapati Bhavan, 15 March 1998, New Delhi.
[44]Ibid.

experiment conducted in May 1974. I warmly congratulate the scientists and engineers who have carried out these successful tests.[45]

The tests evoked considerable pride across the nation and the political divide. Hailing the tests, Sonia Gandhi said:

> I would like to place on record in this formal meeting of the Congress Working Committee the pride we feel in the achievement of our nuclear scientists and engineers for putting India's nuclear capability in the front rank... The nuclear question is a national matter; not a partisan one. On this, every Indian stands united.[46]

However, the international response was very negative. The outcry against India was almost universal.

The tests drew immediate condemnation from the Clinton Administration, which said the United States (US) was 'deeply disappointed' and was reviewing trade and financial sanctions against India under American non-proliferation laws. Britain voiced its 'dismay' and Germany called the tests 'a slap in the face' of 149 countries that have signed the nuclear non-proliferation treaty (NPT). Kofi Annan, the UN Secretary General, also issued a statement expressing his 'deep regret'.[47]

On the back of sanctions being imposed, the Vajpayee government went into long negotiations with the West, with Jaswant Singh appointed as the primary interlocutor. The general

---

[45] Announcement by the Prime Minister, 11 May 1998, PMO New Delhi.
[46] Ed. Pranab Mukherjee, *Congress and the Making of the Indian Nation*, Vol. I, p 151, 2011.
[47] John F. Burns, 'India Sets 3 Nuclear Blasts, Defying A Worldwide Ban; Tests Bring A Sharp Outcry', *The New York Times*, 12 May 1998, http://www.nytimes.com/1998/05/12/world/india-sets-3-nuclear-blasts-defying-a-worldwide-ban-tests-bring-a-sharp-outcry.html?_r=0

consensus within the Congress party was that the tests and the resultant sanctions would have an adverse impact on the growing economy.

Although bringing India on the nuclear stage did clearly create misgivings in Pakistan too, Vajpayee remained keen to forge a harmonious relationship with Pakistan. He made his now historical bus yatra to Lahore in February 1999, after which India and Pakistan signed the Lahore Declaration to usher in peace and stability in South Asia.[48]

Within three months of the signing of this Declaration, India and Pakistan went to war at Kargil, which not only put that diplomatic initiative in jeopardy, but also threatened peace in the subcontinent. The Vajpayee government managed the situation admirably while keeping all the Opposition parties informed of the developments throughout that time.

JAYALALITHAA PULLS THE RUG

Though Vajpayee was the consummate consensus-builder, the coalition was fraught with internal friction. This came to a head when J. Jayalalithaa, General Secretary of AIADMK, who had 17 members in the Lok Sabha, withdrew support from the NDA government in writing on 14 April 1999.[49] A Motion of Confidence was brought in the Lok Sabha on 17 April by Prime Minister Vajpayee before the end of the budget session. It was defeated in the House by one vote in a controversial decision.

Congress MP Giridhar Gamang had replaced Janaki Ballabh Patnaik as chief minister of Odisha. Gamang had to get himself

---

[48]Lahore Declaration, 2 February 1999, http://mea.gov.in/in-focus-article.htm?18997/Lahore+Declaration+February+1999

[49]Suhasini Haidar, 'Jaya meets President, withdraws support', 14 April 1999, http://www.rediff.com/news/1999/apr/14jaya.htm

elected to the Orissa legislative assembly within six months of his assumption of office as chief minister. At the time of the Confidence Motion, Gamang was still a sitting member of the Lok Sabha. His services were requisitioned by the party, and he participated in the proceedings but did not speak. When the Motion was put to vote, he voted against it and made the crucial difference.

Members of the ruling party questioned Gamang's participation in any proceedings of the Lok Sabha since he was the chief minister of a state. However, Lok Sabha Speaker G.M.C. Balayogi ruled that as he had not resigned from his Lok Sabha seat and had not yet been elected to the State Assembly, he was entitled to cast his vote. Once the government lost the confidence of the House, Vajpayee accepted the verdict and resigned immediately. He advised the President to dissolve the Lok Sabha and hold a general election once again. President K.R. Narayanan accepted the recommendation and ordered fresh elections and asked Vajpayee and his Cabinet to continue till alternative arrangements were made after the elections. Fresh elections were thus scheduled for September–October 1999.[50]

After the defeat of the Vajpayee government, the CWC met on 17 April in the AICC office at 8 p.m. The following resolution was adopted:

> The CWC places on record its deep appreciation of the role played by the Congress President in helping to marshal all the secular forces with the active assistance of secular parties in the country and in defeating the Vote of Confidence tabled in Lok Sabha by Shri Atal Bihari Vajpayee. The CWC

---

[50]Statistical Report on General Elections, 1999 To The 13th Lok Sabha, Vol. I, Election Commission of India, New Delhi, http://eci.nic.in/eci_main/StatisticalReports/LS_1999/Vol_I_LS_99.pdf

authorizes the Congress President to take all further action in this regard.

It was also decided at that meeting that the situation should not lead to any financial crisis in the country, especially since it happened during the Budget Session. The Congress President appointed a sub-committee consisting of Sharad Pawar, Dr Manmohan Singh and me to look into budget-related issues and to ensure that no financial crisis occurred as a result of this defeat.

SONIA GANDHI STAKES CLAIM

As the second largest party after the BJP, the Congress, with Sonia Gandhi as its president, immediately staked claim to form the government.[51] But the support which had been mustered to vote out the BJP dissipated. Some political parties like the Samajwadi Party expressed reservations in supporting a government led by the Congress. Sonia, when staking her claim, told media persons that she had the support of 276 members of the Lok Sabha. She calculated the numbers on the basis of votes against the Motion of Confidence, believing that the 276 members not in support of the government would rally behind the Congress. However, all these parties did not confirm their support in writing for Sonia to form the government. The President had no option but to accept the recommendation of the outgoing Prime Minister.

The CWC met on 25 April at Sonia Gandhi's residence where she briefed the members on the situation. She said that she had told the President that the Congress did not have the requisite numbers and, therefore, she would be unable to form the government.

---

[51]'Making of a leader', *India Today*, 17 January 2005, http://indiatoday.intoday.in/story/a-quick-look-at-the-life-and-times-of-sonia-gandhi/1/194439.html

Another attempt was made to form a government with the support of the Congress from outside.

The Congress president sought the opinion of the CWC on extending support to the proposed Third Front government. She asked me to initiate the discussion for it. I strongly opposed this move, pointing out that while the Third Front would survive with the support of the party, the Congress would be held accountable for the coalition's misdeeds. The Congress would be entrusted with responsibility without any authority, which to my mind, was unacceptable, especially in the context of the experience during the United Front regime from 1996–98. I argued that it would be preferable to go to polls than fall into that trap. Senior CWC leaders like Sharad Pawar, K. Karunakaran and many others took part in the discussion that followed. Finally, the following resolution was passed:

> This meeting of the CWC, after reviewing the prevailing political situation arising out of the defeat of the BJP coalition government on 17th April 1999 in the Vote of Confidence, resolved unanimously that the Congress Party should not extend support to any party or coalition of parties to form the government at the Centre. The Congress Party feels that some of the non-BJP secular parties who declined to extend support to the Congress party to form government at the Centre, betrayed the process of consolidation of secular forces and the Congress urges upon all other secular forces to prevail upon recalcitrant parties to fall in line with other parties who have extended their support to the Congress to form the government.

The CWC meeting strongly criticized the recalcitrant attitude of some non-BJP parties in not supporting the Congress in its bid to form an alternative government. It also spoke against the vicious campaign launched against the Congress party by the BJP, especially over Giridhar Gamang's vote. The CWC asked the party and its supporters to rise to the occasion and give a befitting reply to the BJP in the forthcoming Lok Sabha elections.

THE CONSTITUTIONAL PROPRIETY OF DEFEATED PM ADVISING DISSOLUTION

At this juncture, some constitutional experts wondered if a defeated prime minister could indeed recommend dissolution of the House. But President Narayanan considered all aspects and kept in mind the precedents of 1979 and 1991.

In 1979, Chaudhary Charan Singh was sworn in as prime minister by President Neelam Sanjiva Reddy on the basis of letters of support from various political parties who had members in the Lok Sabha. Singh was asked to prove his majority on the floor of the House. However, on the date fixed for seeking the Vote of Confidence, Charan Singh did not even come to the Lok Sabha to move the Motion of Confidence. He had already lost majority, as the Congress (I) had withdrawn support to his government. The party had informed the President of this decision a day earlier. Charan Singh visited the President and resigned, recommending the dissolution of the Lok Sabha. He had not faced the Lok Sabha for even a single day as prime minister. Though the President accepted Singh's resignation, he did not immediately accept his recommendation for dissolving the House. He waited for two days to study the constitutional implications and consulted legal experts. The House was in the meantime adjourned sine die, but not dissolved. After two days, the House was dissolved through a notification and fresh elections were declared.

There was a similar situation in 1991 when Chandra Shekhar

became prime minister after V.P. Singh, with the outside support of the Congress. Like Charan Singh, when he lost the support of the House due to withdrawal of the Congress support, Chandra Shekhar too tendered his resignation and recommended fresh elections to the President R. Venkataraman.

It needs to be mentioned that there is a British practice established from 1905 in this regard. Queen Victoria, on the basis of advice of Lord Salisbury, concluded that the recommendation of the prime minister for the dissolution of the House is almost mandatory to the Sovereign.

The amendment introduced in Article 74 of the Indian Constitution through the 42nd Amendment has settled the matter. The provision makes it clear that the president, in exercising his powers and discharging his responsibilities, is bound by the advice given to him by the council of ministers headed by the prime minister.

The fractured mandate given by the electorate created a situation that led to four general elections between 1991 and 1999. Forming the government with the support of coalition parties was always fraught with risks. The inability of the government to meet the expectations of the supporting parties only reinforced the fragility of the coalition.

SONIA GANDHI'S FOREIGN ORIGIN

It was during this time that a controversy erupted around Sonia Gandhi's Italian origin. Three members of the CWC—Sharad Pawar, P.A. Sangma (nominated as a CWC member by Sonia Gandhi) and Tariq Anwar—made a statement that no person of foreign origin should be chosen as the president, the vice president or the prime minister of India. Ahead of the 1999 elections, there seemed to be an all-out rebellion against the possibility that Sonia Gandhi might be the Congress's prime ministerial candidate.

Rasheed Kidwai, in his book on Sonia Gandhi, relates this controversy:

> As recounted by those present at the meeting, Sangma slowly built a case for how the BJP campaign against Sonia's foreign origins was seeping deep down to even remote villages. Then came the unkindest cut. 'We know very little about you, about your parents,' Sangma told her. Those present claim that Sonia was shocked by Sangma's bluntness who was drafted into the CWC as her nominee. The third signatory, Sitaram Kesri's protégé Tariq Anwar, too, had survived in the CWC even after his mentor's departure, courtesy of Sonia.
>
> Then the man she had made leader of the Opposition (until Sonia herself became a Lok Sabha member in September 1999) picked up from where Sangma left off. With opening remarks as deceptive as the smile signal, Pawar said Sonia Gandhi had done a great job as the party chief.
>
> 'You brought unity in the party and revamped the organisation. However, the Congress has not succeeded in answering the BJP's campaign about your foreign origins. Let us take a serious note of it.'[52]

In my opinion, Sharad Pawar, as the leader of the Opposition in the Lok Sabha, expected the party to request him, instead of Sonia Gandhi, to stake claim to form the government. After Sonia's elevation as the Congress president, she consulted P. Shiv Shankar on all important issues rather than Sharad Pawar. This sense of alienation and disenchantment may have been responsible for his statements on Sonia's foreign origin, and his subsequent

---

[52]Rasheed Kidwai, *Sonia: A Biography*, Penguin, p 102, 2011.

1. May 1996: H.D. Deve Gowda, United Front Prime Miniterial candidate with Pranab Mukherjee in New Delhi.

2. January 1997: Pranab Mukherjee with Sitaram Kesri and V.N. Gadgil in New Delhi.

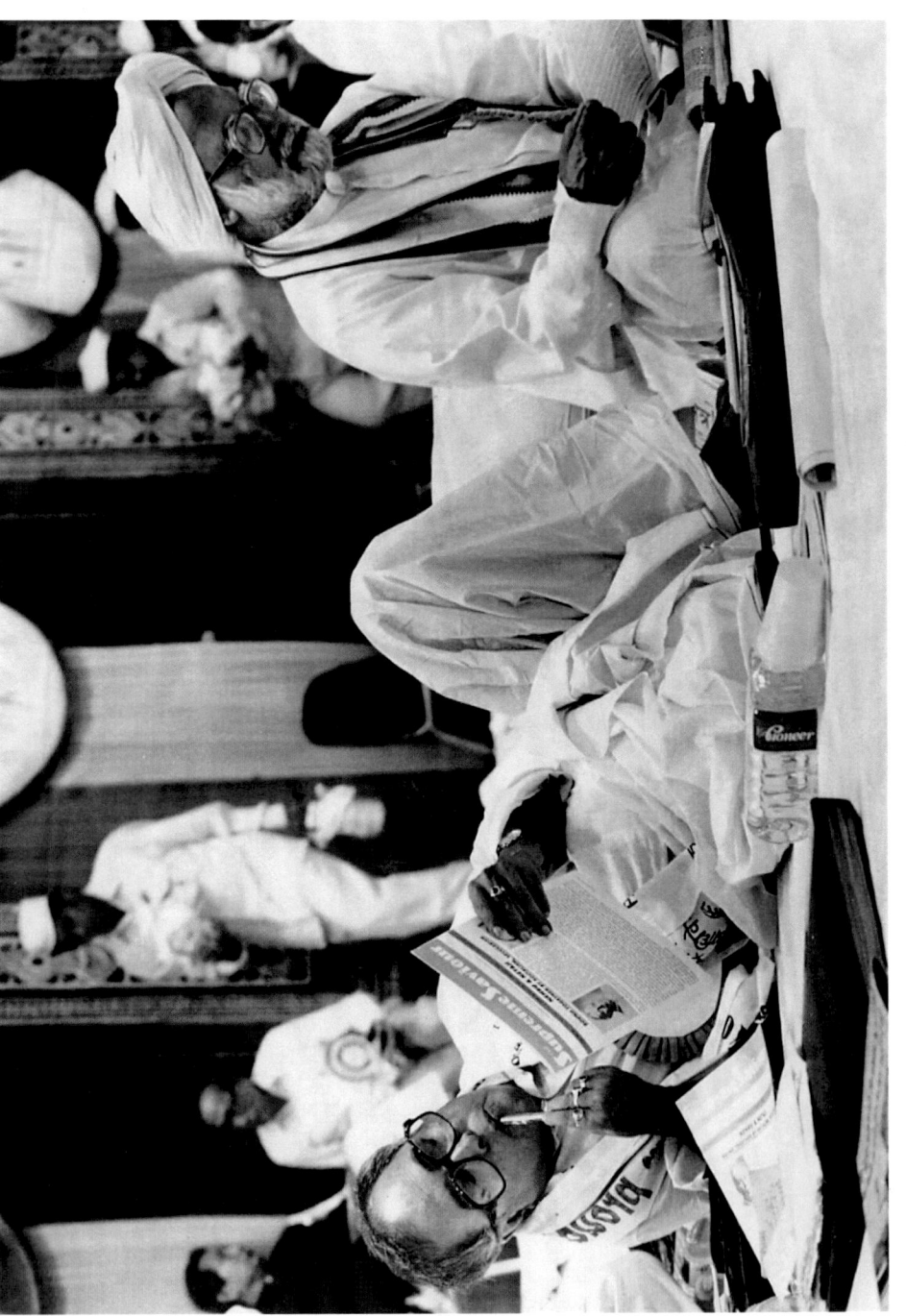

3. *August 1997: Pranab Mukherjee and Dr Manmohan Singh at the 80th Plenary Session of the Congress in Calcutta.*

4. *August 1997: Pranab Mukherjee with Somen Mitra and Sitaram Kesri at the 80th Plenary Session of the Congress in Calcutta.*

5. *March 1998: Sonia Gandhi, Pranab Mukherjee, Arjun Singh and Ghulam Nabi Azad at a Seva Dal function in New Delhi.*

6. March 1998: Sonia Gandhi with Sitaram Kesri in New Delhi.

7. February 1999: Sonia Gandhi, Pranab Mukherjee, Dr Manmohan Singh and Sharad Pawar at the CPP meeting in New Delhi.

8. *February 1999: Pranab Mukherjee with Sharad Pawar and Ajit Jogi in New Delhi.*

9. *May 1999: Congress leaders at the AICC Session in New Delhi.*

10. *March 1999: Pranab Mukherjee greets Sonia Gandhi on her completion of one year as Congress President.*

11. *May 2000: Congress MPs meet Prime Minister Atal Bihari Vajpayee.*

12. *May 2002: Pranab Mukherjee with Sonia Gandhi and other Congress leaders at the AICC Session in New Delhi.*

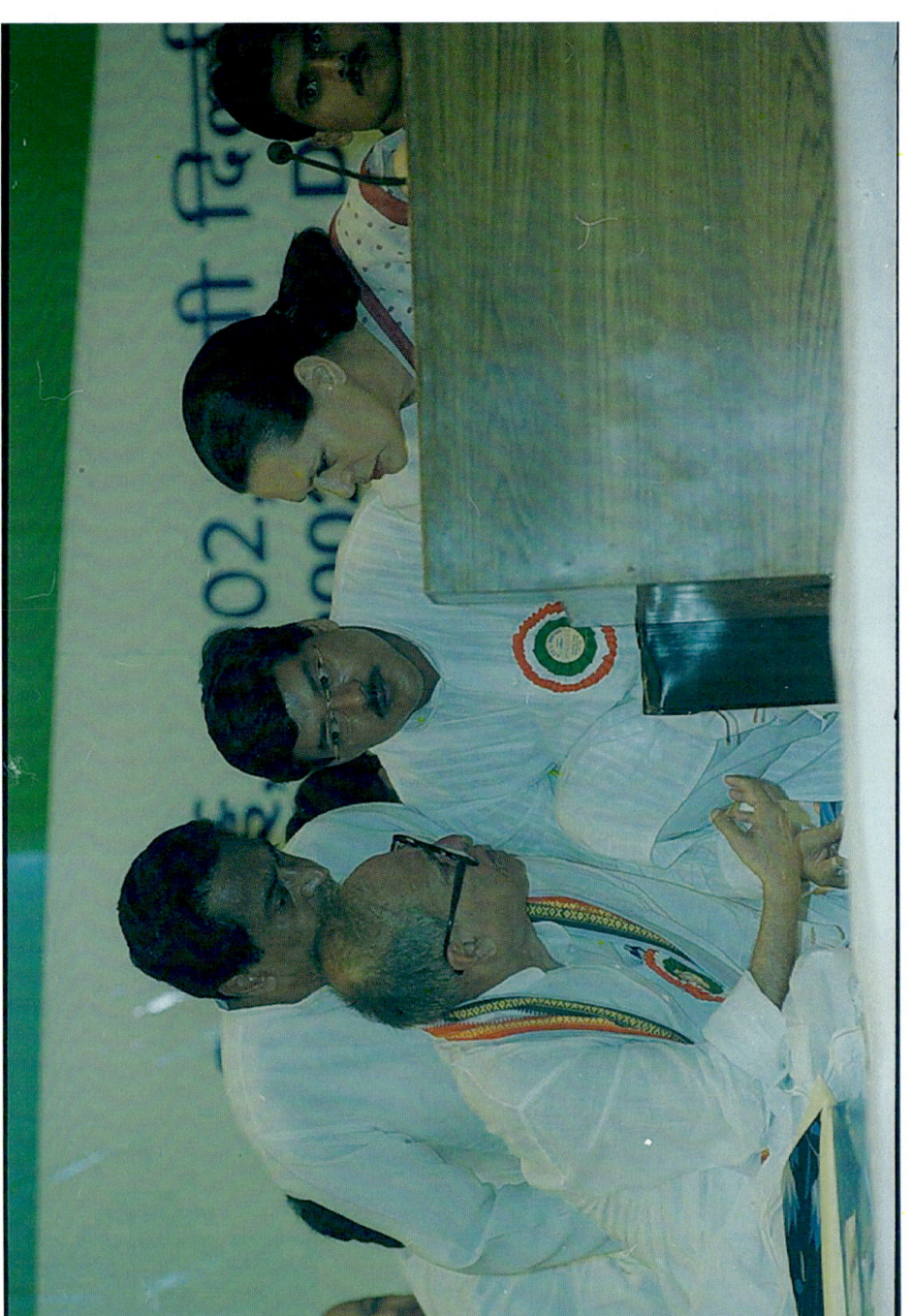

13. May 2002. Pranab Mukherjee with Sonia Gandhi and other Congress leaders at the AICC Session in New Delhi.

exit from the party in 1999.

Naturally, this statement by three senior leaders created a furore as it was a direct attack on Sonia Gandhi. She called some of us and told us firmly that she was going to resign.

At the CWC meeting on 17 May, Sonia Gandhi said:

> You are all well aware of the background of this meeting. I also received the same letter. The letter deals with matters directly concerning myself. I feel I should recuse myself and perhaps Pranabji could conduct the meeting... I have penned down a statement. I am also leaving a copy of the statement with Pranabji.[53]

She then left the meeting.

In her statement, Sonia Gandhi expressed her anguish that her sense of duty and loyalty to the party and nation, and indeed, the people of India, was being questioned. She maintained that India is her motherland and that is where her loyalties lie. With that, she tendered her resignation.

The CWC unanimously rejected her resignation, and a few of us rushed to her residence to get her to see reason. The crisis was averted when she withdrew her resignation a few days later.

1999 ELECTION

The Congress's performance in the 1999 elections was no better than that in the previous two elections. The strength of the Congress in the Lok Sabha came down from 232 to 140 in 1996 under P.V. Narasimha Rao and 141 in 1998 under Sitaram Kesri. In 1999, the Congress under Sonia Gandhi could obtain only 114 seats. Sonia herself was, however, elected to the Lok Sabha

---

[53]'India's Congress Party rallies for Sonia Gandhi', CNN, 17 May 1999, http://edition.cnn.com/WORLD/asiapcf/9905/17/india.gandhi.01/

from Amethi. Since then, she has continued to be a member of the Lok Sabha, contesting subsequent elections from the Rae Bareli constituency.

As Congress president, she automatically became the Leader of the Opposition in the Lok Sabha. Madhavrao Scindia was made Deputy Leader and P.R. Dasmunsi became the Chief Whip. Manmohan Singh became the Leader of the Opposition in the Rajya Sabha.

Sonia Gandhi was a proactive leader of the Opposition. When the Parliament was in session, she would hold a meeting of senior Congress parliamentarians every morning so as to discuss the agenda and the strategy for the day.

Many a times, she and I did not agree on every issue. We had differences on the way we should function as the Opposition party in both the Houses.

While she and the Congress members in the Lok Sabha took the obstructionist path, Singh and I held a differing view. We felt that conciliation and engagement would work better. Finally, she told us, 'You manage your way in the Rajya Sabha and I will manage my way in the Lok Sabha.' That put the matter to rest.

I am of the firm opinion that the accident of seating in the Parliament must not stand in the way of nation-building. It was this belief that helped me forge a strong working relationship with Pramod Mahajan, the then Parliamentary Affairs Minister. He was always appreciative of my efforts in the passing of important legislations.

FIRST FULL-TERM NON-CONGRESS GOVERNMENT

Vajpayee's NDA coalition came back with a bang in the 1999 Lok Sabha elections, and was the first full-term non-Congress government in Independent India's history. Adeptly managing the coalition, Vajpayee carried forward the economic reforms agenda laid out by the 1991–96 P.V. Narasimha Rao government. With a stable growth rate of 6 per cent, he enlarged the scope of FDI, increased disinvestment in central PSU's, turned India into a global centre for information technology, and laid the groundwork for the telecom revolution. In addition, there was a big push for infrastructural development.

In foreign policy, Vajpayee continued in his zeal for an Indo–Pak détente, despite the Kargil imbroglio and a series of aggressive terrorist attacks on India. There were many such during this period—the hijacking of the Indian Airlines flight IC 814 in 1999, the bombing of Jammu & Kashmir Assembly in 2001 and of Akshardham Temple in Gujarat in 2002, and the audacious attack on the Parliament in New Delhi just as the Lok Sabha and the Rajya Sabha were in session in December 2001.

In fact, I was in the Parliament House when the attack occurred. As the House had been adjourned, I was talking to Rajya Sabha Chairman Krishan Kant as he was walking towards the exit. Kant left the building and I went back inside thinking I would get myself a balushahi, a sweet I am inordinately fond of. Just then, there was a commotion, the alarm was raised, all doors of the Parliament were shut and security personnel fanned out, with some taking position on the first floor. Pramod Mahajan rushed towards us, warning us not to step out. Though several people had left the building, a number of us were still inside. I then rushed to Manmohan Singh's room, and from there we together went to L.K. Advani's room for an update. We later learnt that the terrorists had planned to gain entry just when gate no. 11 opened for the Vice President's motorcade.

This was a heinous attack, and one which sought to strike at the heart of democracy. To show that we would not be cowed down, we—both in the Lok Sabha and in the Rajya Sabha—

decided that the business of Parliament would not be disturbed. We were determined to carry on with business as usual, and members of both the Houses expressed a strong will to counter any attack on the nation. The solidarity across parties that Prime Minister Vajpayee mentioned in the Parliament was evident from the fact that the leader of the Opposition, Sonia Gandhi, on hearing about the attack, had immediately called him to check on his well-being.

Throughout this period the demand for the construction of the Ram Temple in Ayodhya had been building up. The heightened communal tensions had a distressing fallout in Gujarat which witnessed a communal carnage in 2002. The rioting began at Godhra, a small town in Gujarat, where 58 people were burnt to death in a fire that engulfed a compartment of the Sabarmati Express. The victims were all Hindu Kar Sevaks who were returning from Ayodhya. This provoked widespread riots in many cities of Gujarat. Possibly the biggest blot on Vajpayee's government, it may have been Godhra that cost BJP the next elections.

ATAL BIHARI VAJPAYEE

Atal Bihari Vajpayee was a consummate parliamentarian. With an excellent command over the language, he was a great orator who instantly connected with people and brought them together.

'An uncompromising patriot', he declared India a full-fledged nuclear state, emphasizing that there is 'no compromise on national security; we will exercise all options, including nuclear, to protect security and sovereignty.'[54] At the same time, he was able

---

[54]Prabhu Chawla, 'The Vajpayee Years', *India Today*, http://indiatoday.intoday.in/story/india-today-40th-anniversary-prabhu-chawla-the-vajpayee-years/1/543196.html

to deftly limit the damage that India had to face in the aftermath of the nuclear tests and managed to contain the negative fallout.

Vajpayee's signature in politics was achieving consensus, and in this process, he earned the respect of his party, allies and opponents at home. Abroad, he projected a harmonious image of India, and connected it to the world through his foreign policy outreach.

An empathetic and humble politician, he didn't shy away from giving credit where it was due: 'We are not the initiators of reform. We are carrying forward a process that was started by the Narasimha Rao government, and continued by two United Front governments. But we do take the credit for having broadened, deepened and accelerated the reform process.'[55] He didn't take political rivalries personally.

His nature can be understood by a couple of interactions I had with him.

After the Emergency, the Janata government set up the Shah Commission to investigate the alleged excesses of the Emergency. On 14 November 1977, I was summoned by the Commission. However, I took a principled stand and refused to give evidence. After meeting with the Commission, I went to the Parliament where I met Raj Narain and Vajpayee. Raj Narain sarcastically asked me, '*Darr se bhaag gaye?*' Before I could say anything, Vajpayee quipped, '*Kyun darr se bhaagenge? Yeh apne baap ke bete hai.*' I think at a personal level he appreciated my stand.

Another instance showcases his humility. During the tenure of the NDA, I aggressively criticized George Fernandes for a comment he made about China. Vajpayee, who was the prime minister then, came to my seat in the Rajya Sabha and said,

---

[55]Prabhu Chawla, 'The Vajpayee Years', *India Today*, http://indiatoday.intoday.in/story/india-today-40th-anniversary-prabhu-chawla-the-vajpayee-years/1/543196.html

'*Bechare George ko chor deejiye.*' I folded my hands and told him that as he was my senior he should have called me rather than coming to me with the request. However, I carried on with my criticism of Fernandes, though slightly muted in deference to the request from the Prime Minister.

L.K. ADVANI

L.K. Advani personally requested me to be the chairman of the Parliamentary Standing Committee on Home Affairs. I had numerous interactions with him, though most of them resulted in heated discussions. I particularly remember our exchanges on the repeal of the Illegal Migrants (Determination by Tribunals) Act or IMDT Act. Applicable only to the state of Assam, the Act provided that anybody settled in the state before 25 March 1971 was a legal citizen. Significantly, for the rest of India, the cut-off date for acquiring Indian citizenship is 19 July 1948.

Advani and other BJP leaders continuously demanded the repeal of the IMDT Act and had brought a bill in the Parliament to scrap it. As chairman of the Standing Committee, I had several discussions with various groups in Assam and submitted my report. However, Advani insisted that '[The] Congress for the sake of vote bank politics had delayed the bill through the then Chairman of the Parliamentary Standing Committee, Pranab Mukherjee.' In response, I asked Advani about the delay in making amendments to the Act based on the recommendations of the Committee even after two sessions of the Parliament.

Notwithstanding our differences in the political arena, I always looked up to Advaniji for wise counsel and friendly advice. When I moved to Rashtrapati Bhavan we drew closer as we both share interest in books and often enjoyed the music recitals at the Rashtrapati Bhavan's Indra Dhanush programme.

CHAPTER 5

2004

The 2004 general election was due in October. Just a year ahead of this, nine states went into Assembly elections—four in February and five in November 2003. As the results poured in, it was clear that the year didn't start off too well for the BJP. The Congress won in Himachal Pradesh, formed coalition governments in Meghalaya and Nagaland, while the Left Front retained Tripura. The BJP had improved its numbers in Nagaland but only by seven seats.

Winds changed for the BJP with the next set of Assembly elections in November 2003. They won decisively in Madhya Pradesh, Rajasthan and Chhattisgarh (Hindi heartland), the Mizo National Front (MNF) retained power in Mizoram. However, the BJP lost in Delhi, which went to the Congress with a two-thirds majority. There was cheer within the BJP at the resounding victory in important states. However, there were some who advised caution in interpreting these results as a marker of broader national sentiment.

> ...it is important to remind ourselves of what this verdict of the assembly elections is *not*. It is not, first of all, a sign of a nationwide wave in favour of the BJP. The BJP's

victory in Rajasthan and Chhattisgarh was much narrower than the number of seats might suggest. While it did win a comprehensive victory in Madhya Pradesh, it also faced a comprehensive defeat in Delhi, more sweeping than the number of seats would suggest. The defeat faced by Congress in two states out of three was small and is by no means irreversible. In any case, whatever the margin of victory and defeat in each state, it is not clear if that has much relevance for other states.[56]

The five-year term of the government was scheduled to come to an end in October 2004. This meant that elections to the 14th Lok Sabha should have been held at that time. However, the BJP decided to make use of this moment of strength and brought forward the general election by six months to April 2004.

PREPARING FOR THE GENERAL ELECTION

With elections looming large, all parties went into planning mode. The Congress held a party conclave at Shimla from 7 to 9 July 2003, to formulate its election strategy. At the conclusion of this conclave, which was attended by about 250 members, Sonia Gandhi said:

> Taking into account the present political scenario, the Congress would be prepared to enter into appropriate electoral coalition arrangements with secular parties on the basis of mutual understanding but without compromising on its basic ideologies... No sacrifice would be too great to ensure the defeat of the BJP and its allies in the forthcoming polls.[57]

---

[56]Yogendra Yadav, 'Open contest, closed options', http://www.india-seminar.com/2004/534/534%20yogendra%20yadav.htm
[57]Purnima S. Tripathi, 'Coalition offer, with a rider', *Frontline*, July–August 2003,

The Shimla Sankalp[58] urged every Congressperson to work towards defeating religious fundamentalism of all kinds and the communal forces led by the BJP. It also outlined the party agenda of economic and social reform, rural development, transparency in governance and the decriminalization of politics.

The issue of being open to forming a coalition was definitely a change of tack from the Pachmarhi Conclave where we had agreed that 'Coalitions will be considered where absolutely necessary.' At Shimla, inputs of all delegates were sought and heard. Most of them, including Sonia Gandhi and Manmohan Singh, seemed convinced that the Pachmarhi strategy had to change. I was the lone voice stating a contrarian view as I believed that sharing a platform and/or power with other parties would undermine our identity. I maintained that the party should not forsake that identity for the sake of forming a government; there was no harm in sitting in the opposition, should that happen. I remain consistent with that view even today.

The Shimla Sankalp was adopted unanimously, and with that programme of action we went into election mode against the BJP-led NDA, which had pulled out all stops for its 'India Shining' campaign.

I CONTEST MY THIRD LOK SABHA ELECTION

I decided to contest the Lok Sabha elections from Jangipur (Murshidabad) in 2004. I had contested elections to the Lok Sabha twice before—from Malda in 1977 and from Bolpur in 1980—and was unsuccessful both the times.

There were a number of reasons why I contested these elections. One was the fact that I wanted to follow the principle

---

http://www.frontline.in/static/html/fl2015/stories/20030801004502100.htm
[58]Appendix 3: Shimla Sankalp July 9th, 2003.

espoused by Nehru—that any Rajya Sabha member who becomes a minister should get himself elected to the Lok Sabha at the earliest opportunity. It is with this thought that I had contested earlier too. Two, since 1984, I had been the chairman of every national campaign committee. This raised the pertinent question, at least in my mind—should the chairman of the campaign committee himself not face the court of the people? Third, while this question was burdening my mind, the state Congress workers became increasingly vocal in their demand that I contest the elections.

It was Adhir Chowdhury, now PCC President, who finally prevailed upon me to contest from Jangipur. After the defeat in Bolpur in 1980, I did not contest any Lok Sabha elections. In 1981, I was elected to the Rajya Sabha from Gujarat and then came to the Rajya Sabha from West Bengal in 1993 and 1999. Adhir, along with other local leaders, insisted that I contest from Jangipur, which is a rural constituency.

I was, however, aware that I might not win. I contested the Lok Sabha elections even though the Congress President had assured me of my re-nomination to the Rajya Sabha once my current term expired.

'You need not worry; we will be able to bring you from some other place if we don't have enough strength in West Bengal,' she had assured me.

Nobody, including myself, had the confidence that I would win in 2004. My opponent was Abul Hasnat Khan, a two-term CPI (M) MP with strong influence over the beedi workers of the area, who were a significant support base. However, I had the full support of the local Congress and we campaigned from village to village in the scorching heat. I was determined to be third time lucky.

Though the election campaign was intense and had its share

of difficult moments, two heartwarming incidents stand out clearly in my memory. We were driving on a kutcha road, not far from the Bangladesh border, towards our next campaign stop. I was standing on the jeep so as to take stock of the areas we were travelling through when one of my colleagues said that we had just passed a lady who had been waiting there to meet me. I asked for the jeep to reverse, and we got out as the dust settled. I walked to where the lady was standing along with a young girl. As soon as I reached her, she said to me in Bengali, 'Why are you taking so much trouble going from village to village in this heat? We will all vote for you anyway!' I laughed and was grateful at this simple, unilateral vote of confidence, even more so when she uncovered a small bowl and offered me rasgullas. 'Eat these, it will be good for you in this heat.' Fond as I am of anything sweet, I took one even as she insisted that I take more. I was touched to the core by this concern.

Another time, we were campaigning in a CPI (M) stronghold. It was late afternoon and we had been campaigning since early morning. The plan was to head to another village but as I was bone-tired, I decided to take a break while the rest carried on. I got off the car and sat in the shade of a mango tree. Not too long after, I saw a young boy peeping at me from behind some trees. He had a roll of papers under his arm. When I beckoned him insistently, he came forth hesitatingly and asked, 'Are you Pranab Mukherjee? Are you the one contesting elections from our area?' I answered him, and enquired about the papers he was carrying under his arm. He sheepishly told me that they were CPI (M) posters which his uncle had given him to distribute, telling him that if he came across the Congress party people or Pranab Mukherjee, 'You will neither look at them nor hear them.' I laughed at his innocent admission and, probably a little more at ease, he shot out another question, 'If you win, will you build an embankment?' When I asked why he wanted an embankment, he told me that every year his house was destroyed by the floods and an embankment would ensure that his family, along with others, did not have to suffer the annual tragedy.

I was struck by the extent of the prevalent hardship, and promised him that I would definitely start work on the embankment if I won. I am happy to say that I did keep my promise, and the embankment was commissioned soon after we came to power. On my first visit back to the constituency, I made it a point to go to the boy's village so that I could meet him. However, his uncle, the CPI (M) activist, came and told me that the boy was too scared to come and meet me—the Defence Minister of India!

With the campaign done, it was now time for the election day. Ahead of the counting, I returned to New Delhi to attend to the responsibilities assigned to me by the Congress President. When I informed her that I would need to go back to the state for the counting of votes, her cryptic comment was, 'You need not wait till you are sure you've lost; return immediately.'

Counting took place on 13 May. Thanks to the EVM machines, results poured in quickly. I knew by one o'clock that I was likely to win hands down. Television channels started announcing my lead in Jangipur. Both Ahmed Patel and Sonia Gandhi, joyous and amazed, called to congratulate me and asked about my return. I told them that I would leave for Kolkata as soon as I received the certificate and would reach Delhi the following day by an early morning flight.

It so happened that I won by a margin of around 36,000 votes. The larger significance of it was that I had won from all seven Assembly segments. In one Assembly segment, my margin was only 1,900 and in another just 2,100 votes. But in the remaining five segments, it was 6,000-plus votes.

As my Lok Sabha constituency was spread over three subdivisions, it was almost 9 p.m. by the time official results could be declared. As I had promised to return to Delhi immediately, I left for Kolkata the very same night after receiving the certificate. Somen Mitra was with me as he had come to Jangipur to witness the counting, he had also decided to return with me. We reached Kolkata around 3 a.m. and were at my residence at 3.45 a.m. Even at that unearthly hour, I found people waiting to greet me!

I spoke to them, rested a little and boarded a flight to Delhi early next morning. As soon as the plane took off, I went into deep slumber and did not wake up even after landing. The airhostess had to shake me vigorously to wake me up. I smiled at her half-asleep and deplaned. At my Delhi residence, there was a huge crowd as well. Many eminent people had also come to meet me. Eventually, I managed to take some rest and received a number of congratulatory calls.

On the same evening, Atal Bihari Vajpayee tendered his government's resignation to the President.

I went to my party office in the evening, but there was not much work as election results were still pouring in. Some people—I particularly remember Ahmed Patel—were involved in deliberations with various political parties. After some discussions amongst ourselves, I returned to my residence around 7.30 p.m., and had to deal with various state leaders and the media who were curious to know whether I would join the government and, if so, which portfolio would be assigned to me.

The Lok Sabha results brought the Congress back to power. Many were surprised by the victory of the Congress and other non-BJP parties. Several psephologists had predicted a clear victory for the NDA. As late as 9 February 2004, an INDIA TODAY-ORG-MARG opinion poll had predicted a clear victory for the Vajpayee-led alliance. The magazine, interpreting the opinion poll, wrote: 'Riding on the crest of the Prime Minister's popularity and economic boom, the BJP-led alliance appears set for a sweep in the forthcoming elections.'[59]

The confidence of the NDA had been shaken. Its 'India Shining' campaign had spawned the opposite outcome and cast a pall of gloom over the BJP. It led Vajpayee to ruefully comment that he could never understand the mood of the voter.[60]

SONIA GANDHI ELECTED LEADER OF CPP

The Congress had contested these elections in some sort of alliance with 19 parties and got the largest number of seats. These were later brought together to form the United Progressive Alliance (UPA). The CPP met in the Central Hall of the Parliament at 11 a.m. on 15 May and unanimously elected Sonia Gandhi as the leader of the Congress Legislature Party (CLP). Manmohan Singh was to propose her name first and then it was to be seconded by me. I took the microphone and began by saying, 'I welcome the members of the Congress Parliamentary Party; perhaps as the oldest Congress Member in the Parliament and one of the newest Members in the Lok Sabha.' I could not conceal my joy at having finally entered the Lok Sabha after two unsuccessful attempts. Everyone laughed.

I continued, 'I propose the name of Sonia Gandhi for the Leader of the Congress Party in the Parliament.' Everybody applauded and expressed unanimous support. Thereafter, I gave

---

[59]'Atal Wave', *India Today*, 9 February 2004, at http://indiatoday.intoday.in/story/vajpayee-bjp-set-for-landslide-win-in-forthcoming-2004-elections/1/197000.html

[60]Ramashray Roy, Wallace Paul, *India's 2004 elections: Grassroots and National Perspectives,* Sage Publications, 2007, p 10.

the microphone to Sonia Gandhi who gave a brief analytical account of the political situation, and then thanked everyone.

On 16 May, the very next day, the UPA and its supporters elected Sonia Gandhi as the coalition's prime ministerial candidate. On 18 May, she declined this offer. She said:

> Throughout these past six years that I have been in politics, one thing has been clear to me. And that is, as I have often stated, that the post of prime minister is not my aim... Power in itself has never attracted me, nor has position been my goal. I was always certain that, if ever I found myself in the position I am in today, I would follow my inner voice. I humbly decline the post. I request that you accept my decision; it is my inner voice, my conscience. My aim has always been to defend the secular foundation of our country and the poor of our country...[61]

Following the announcement, scores of newly elected Congress MPs shouted and appealed to Ms Gandhi to change her mind. I heard of this announcement from Ahmed Patel, following which I rushed to 10 Janpath along with Manmohan Singh and Ghulam Nabi Azad. We met Sonia Gandhi and insisted that she was the electorate's choice for the post of prime minister. It was a responsibility that she could not shun. We impressed upon her the need to reconsider her decision and accept this responsibility. She told me that she did not want to be the reason for sharp divisions in society because of her elevation to the position of prime minister.

Other leaders too, including Shibu Soren, K. Chandrashekhar Rao, Natwar Singh, Harkishan Singh Surjeet and Lalu Prasad

---

[61] George Wright and Agencies, 'Sonia Gandhi declines Indian prime ministership', *The Guardian,* 18 May 2004, https://www.theguardian.com/world/2004/may/18/india.georgewright

Yadav tried to dissuade her. Finally, it was left to her to choose the prime minister.

There was intense speculation in the party and the media about her choice.[62] Within the Congress party, the consensus was that the incumbent must be a political leader with experience in party affairs and administration. Finally, she named Dr Manmohan Singh as her choice and he accepted.

The prevalent expectation was that I would be the next choice for prime minister after Sonia Gandhi declined. This expectation was possibly based on the fact that I had extensive experience in government, while Singh's vast experience was as a civil servant with five years as a reformist finance minister.

The media speculation and frenzy began. Some media commentators reported that I would not join the government because I could not work under Manmohan Singh, who had been my junior when I was the finance minister. The fact was that I was reluctant to join the government, and informed Sonia Gandhi accordingly. She, however, insisted that I should join the government since I would be vital to its functioning, and also be of support to Dr Singh. As it turned out, Dr Singh would talk to me on all important issues and seemed to depend on me. We shared out a good working relationship.

COALITION CONSULTATIONS

Meanwhile, consultations with other parties were in full swing. I was informed by Ahmed Patel that I should initiate talks with Sharad Pawar, Lalu Prasad Yadav, Ram Vilas Paswan, Shibu Soren, K. Chandrasekhar Rao (K.C.R.) of the TRS, and a few others. Sonia Gandhi met the leaders of the Left (Harkishan Singh

---

[62]Randeep Ramesh, 'Uproar as Gandhi says: I won't be PM', *The Guardian*, 19 May 2004, https://www.theguardian.com/world/2004/may/19/india.randeepramesh1

Surjeet and Jyoti Basu); after which Ahmed Patel and I took the discussions forward.

The formula which I worked out in the presence of Sonia Gandhi, Manmohan Singh, Natwar Singh and Ahmed Patel, was that political parties with a minimum of five Lok Sabha seats would get a Cabinet rank minister. An exception was made in the case of Ram Vilas Paswan for his strength was only four seats. He had been a Cabinet minister earlier, and was an important scheduled caste leader. He had also acted as the leader of the Lok Sabha at some point.

I told Shibu Soren that his party would get one Cabinet rank minister, and he was given the Coal Ministry. He asked for another ministerial berth, which I declined.

In the context of TRS's participation, K.C.R. told me, 'Pranabji, you know my ambition; I want a separate Telangana. Which portfolio you give to me is not important. Whatever you give, I will gladly accept. But for God's sake, please consider a separate Telangana.'

The Congress had already decided to retain the four major portfolios of Defence, Home, External Affairs and Finance. I anticipated that Sharad Pawar would stake claim to one of the four. But he surprised me by saying that he would not join the government and instead, suggested other names from his party. I insisted that he join the government and pointed out that if the government was to survive a full term, it could not start with an inherent weakness. My approach was that basic principles should not be compromised merely to form the government. Sharad Pawar said he would accept Agriculture and asked for an additional MoS, which we readily agreed to.

Lalu Prasad Yadav wanted one of the four big portfolios, preferably Home. I told him very clearly that these four were out of the question. It was conveyed that if Raghuvansh Prasad

Singh[63] wanted to join, he would be given an important portfolio. Ultimately, Sonia Gandhi offered him Rural Development.

I asked Sonia Gandhi to speak to Karunanidhi. She passed on the job to Manmohan Singh, who in turn requested Kamal Nath. After the discussion with Karunanidhi, it was decided that Dayanidhi Maran would get Communications & IT, while T.R. Baalu would be given Shipping, Road Transport & Highways, and A. Raja was made minister for Environment & Forests.

Sonia Gandhi and Manmohan Singh discussed likely ministers from the Congress. In that context, Sonia called me and asked which of the four portfolios I would prefer to take. Her inclination was for me to take up Finance. However, I told her that I would not like to be charged with Finance due to my ideological differences on economic policy with the Prime Minister-designate. I also told her that I would prefer Home over External Affairs—I had worked as the chairman of the Standing Committee on Home Affairs for over six years and was conversant with the ministry—and that I had no experience in Defence. She heard me out, making no commitment, nor indicating a decision other than saying that Defence was a world in itself and the Defence Ministry would offer me maximum autonomy, taking into account my seniority.

It was at the swearing-in that I got to know that I was to be the minister for Defence.

The media speculation on the reasons for Defence being given to me saw no respite. Many stories circulated, with one being that a senior Congress leader had blocked me from the Home Ministry. The media also said that the Congress President was keen that I hold the Defence portfolio as it had, under my predecessor and

---

[63]Raghuvansh Prasad Singh, a mathematics scholar, is a brilliant man. I was told that when he taught in class, there would be pin-drop silence. He could teach even complicated subjects like applied mathematics in Hindi.

the Gandhi family baiter, George Fernandes, become embroiled in several controversies. She had reportedly concluded that I would unearth many of them. A leading journalist, Shekhar Gupta, was to later write that, 'When Congress unexpectedly returned to power in 2004, it was desperate to find something on NDA's defence "scandals".[64]

I was not able to fathom what exactly was in the mind of the Congress President when she chose me to be the Defence Minister. However, I chose not to give credence to any of the rumours.

Manmohan Singh was keen on either Montek Singh Ahluwalia or P. Chidambaram for the job of Finance Minister. Although Chidambaram was not from Congress (he represented Tamil Maanila Congress, but had fought the election on a Congress ticket), he was chosen. Shivraj Patil was made Home Minister and Natwar Singh was the External Affairs Minister.

Then the question of Deputy Chairman, Planning Commission came up. Two rounds of talks were held. Sonia wanted me to hold dual responsibility, as I had done under P.V.—a major ministerial portfolio and Deputy Chairman, Planning Commission. I suggested other names. Manmohan Singh wanted Montek. Finally, Manmohan Singh's views prevailed and Montek was assigned the position.

Once the portfolios were allocated, the second challenge was to finalize seating arrangements. Manmohan Singh was No. 1 and I was no. 2. Lalu wanted to be no. 3, but the decision was to have the Home Minister as no. 3. Lalu was hence designated no. 4, with Sharad Pawar at no. 5. I told Lalu, 'I am putting all ex-CMs together. I am not going by any other seniority; former

---

[64]Shekhar Gupta, 'Guns Thieves and Ghosts', *Business Standard*, 7 May 2016, http://www.business-standard.com/article/opinion/shekhar-gupta-guns-thieves-and-ghosts-116050600882_1.html

chief ministers in the Cabinet would sit side-by-side.'

SHARAD PAWAR

Sharad Pawar started his career with the Youth Congress at the age of twenty-four, and became a member of the Maharashtra Legislative Assembly in 1967. Initially mentored by Y.B. Chavan and Vasantdada Patil, he matured into an ambitious and astute politician and has been a long-time parliamentarian for seven terms from 1984, four times chief minister of Maharashtra, and the Union minister responsible for various portfolios such as Defence, Agriculture, Consumer Affairs, Food and Public Distribution and Food Processing.

His role and position in Maharashtra politics notwithstanding, probably one of Pawar's lasting regrets has been that he has always often been the bridesmaid, never the bride, when it came to national politics. This is in spite of the fact that he is a strategic and clever politician with excellent organizational capabilities. The latter characteristic is also evident in the crises Pawar has ably handled, be it the 1993 serial blasts in Mumbai or the Latur earthquake where he personally oversaw the relief work in the affected areas. Not satisfied with mere relief operations, I remember Pawar coming to me with a request for technological support, with an eye for its future prosperity.

It was the period just after Rajiv Gandhi's assassination that saw Pawar take up the gauntlet for the top job in national politics. It was at this point that he made his prime ministerial ambitions apparent, but clearly to no avail. P. V. became prime minister and also the Congress president. Soon thereafter, in 1993, the challenger returned to Maharashtra as chief minister (though the Congress lost Maharashtra just two years later).

Sharad Pawar came back to national politics in 1996, and

chose not to return to state politics, though he nurtured and mentored the second-rung leadership. In pursuance of his national agenda, Pawar made an abortive move to challenge Sitaram Kesri's election to the Congress presidency in 1997. This was an ill-judged move. Unable to assess the mood within the party, he lost miserably and Kesri got more than 80 per cent of the votes.

Once Sonia Gandhi donned the mantle of Congress president in the year 1998, he attempted to rock the boat again. He was the prime mover in the Sonia Gandhi foreign origin issue. I am still not sure what his reasons were—maybe he thought that she would not be able to rally the party and get the requisite numbers in the next general election; or maybe he just had larger ambitions.

Later, when the UPA formed the government in 2004, Sharad Pawar and his NCP were an important constituent. I was surprised that he didn't make a pitch for one of the four major ministerial portfolios. Instead, he asked for Agriculture. My surprise apart, he was perhaps one of India's best Agriculture ministers, who applied his innovative ideas and thoughts on the national scale. His pragmatic policies led to a revival in the nation's agricultural sector. A man of progressive thoughts, modern outlook and professionalism, Pawar has always been committed to rapid development.[65]

CHOOSING THE SPEAKER

After the formation of the government, we started the exercise of identifying the Speaker. A.R. Antulay expressed interest; but there was some speculation about Shivraj Patil, even though he was not a member of the Lok Sabha. Meira Kumar's name also

---

[65] Aditi Phadnis, *Business Standard Political Profiles of Cabals and Kings*, BS Books, 2009.

came up. My choice lay elsewhere, and I said, 'Let us persuade Somnath Chatterjee.' While everyone agreed to this suggestion, we were unsure if the CPI (M), and Somnath himself, would agree. The Left had decided not to join the government, and I felt that giving them the Speaker's position would ensure they remained committed to the coalition. Fortunately, I had a good rapport with both Harkishan Singh Surjeet and Jyoti Basu. I persuaded them and also spoke to Somnath Chatterjee who, after initial hesitation, agreed.

COMMON MINIMUM PROGRAMME

With the positions settled and the government formed, I shifted the focus on the draft of the Common Minimum Programme. Every party in the coalition was asked to give their views and inputs for the agenda. On behalf of the Left, who were extending their support from the outside, Sitaram Yechury, A.B. Bardhan and Debabrata Sarkar were involved. Once all parties were heard, Jairam Ramesh, myself and a team of people collated and presented the draft for approval to the UPA partners. Even though we had diverse partners and some with specific demands—such as TRS asking for an independent state of Telangana—this exercise was, surprisingly not contentious. The Common Minimum Programme was released at the end of May that year.

MANMOHAN SINGH

A strong nationalist, a man of courage and conviction, Manmohan Singh was certainly not an 'accidental prime minister'. I am convinced that the future will judge Manmohan Singh in a different light as P.V. is assessed today.

For his role in the 1991 economic liberalization, Singh can

rightly be called the 'father of reforms'. At a time when the country was on the verge of default, he took on the challenge and initiated strong correctives. With the clear mandate from Prime Minister P.V. Narasimha Rao, Singh started the dramatic restructuring process. With an able team in place, he virtually abolished industrial licensing through industrial and trade policy reforms; opened up the private sector while also reducing the obstacles to foreign investment; liberalized interest and exchange rates, and cut tariffs and taxes. In an instant, the economic landscape was transformed, laying the groundwork for an economically sound India in an increasingly globalized world.

It was with this legacy and in-depth experience that he became prime minister. Notwithstanding the debate regarding his appointment as prime minister, there could have been no one more experienced in economic policymaking than Manmohan Singh. An apolitical person, he held national interest above all else, had the courage to stand firm on his convictions, and was able to build consensus when needed through his persuasive nature.

His tenure marked significant achievements which I have detailed in subsequent chapters, but the highlight would be the firmness with which he handled the Indo–US nuclear deal. As he himself said later:

> [The] best moment for me was when we were able to strike a nuclear deal with the United States to end the nuclear apartheid which had sought to stifle the processes of social and economic change and technical progress of our country in many ways.[66]

It was with tenaciousness that Manmohan Singh handled the

---

[66]Press Information Bureau, Government of India, Prime Minister's Office, 3 January 2014, http://pib.nic.in/newsite/PrintRelease.aspx?relid=102296

stiff opposition from the Left, one of the government's coalition partners, lending support from outside. Singh firmly refused to go back on the international commitment even when faced with a No-confidence Motion on the Indo–US nuclear deal as a result of the Left's withdrawal of support. He was steadfast and won the confidence motion.

Manmohan Singh had to manage a diverse coalition, and this required skills that not many can boast of—particularly when faced with a few adversarial partners. He did this with aplomb, and empowered his senior ministerial colleagues to do their jobs. I say this out of personal experience, of the prime ministers I have worked with—Indira Gandhi and Narasimha Rao—I got the maximum autonomy when I worked with Manmohan Singh.

> History will be kind to Manmohan Singh. It will remember him as the finance minister who launched India's economic reforms in 1991, and the Prime Minister who presided over 8.5% GDP growth for most of a decade.[67]

---

[67]Swaminathan Anklesaria Aiyar, 'History will be kind to Prime Minister Manmohan Singh', 15 May 2014, *The Times of India*, http://timesofindia.indiatimes.com/news/History-will-be-kind-to-Prime-Minister-Manmohan-Singh/articleshow/35136406.cms

CHAPTER 6

IN DEFENCE

My appointment as defence minister came with its challenges. Barely four years had passed since the Kargil conflict of 1999, which had laid bare the critical shortages of equipment in the Indian Armed Forces. It had evidently prevented the armed forces from effectively ejecting Pakistani soldiers from Indian soil. There was much speculation about the poor state of our equipment. A Carnegie publication, for instance, wrote that '... because of the rudimentary bomb sights, the inaccuracy of their unguided weapons and the ruling against crossing the LOC, MiG-21, MiG-23 pilots typically achieved limited effectiveness when attempting to provide close air support against enemy point targets.'[68] Something had to be done and fast, to adequately equip our forces. Hence, if there was a single issue that I had focused on during my stint as the defence minister, it was the modernization of the forces and the need to establish systems for it.

---

[68]Benjamin Lambeth, 'Airpower at 18,000': The Indian Air Force in the Kargil War', Carnegie Endowment for International Peace, 2012, p 8, http://carnegieendowment.org/2012/09/20/airpower-at-18-000-indian-air-force-in-kargil-war

MODERNIZATION OF FORCES

The evidence of outdated systems was hard to ignore. The obsolescence of several systems had resulted in an increasing number of accidents in the armed forces. Just months before I took over, in February 2004, an MIG-23 aircraft crashed near Jaisalmer, killing the pilot. In the same month, a Jaguar of the Indian Air Force crashed in the same area due to a technical fault and its pilot was also killed. The frequent crashes of MIG-21 planes, which had already claimed the lives of 170 pilots since 1970, earned the aircraft the opprobrium of 'flying coffin'.[69]

These accidents did not bode well for our security and underscored the need for immediate remedial measures to upgrade our defence equipment. It reinforced my assessment that the neglect of defence procurement was something our nation could ill afford. I was bolstered in my resolve to accord utmost priority to the modernization of our equipment.

Whatever may have been the cause of the accidents, I was determined not to allow any more deaths of our young pilots. I issued instructions for taking necessary technical and remedial steps to prevent further accidents. At the same time, I felt compelled to consider the steps needed to ensure that our armed forces were equipped with the best armaments.

As for the MIG-21 aircraft, the adoption of new safety measures brought down crashes significantly, and eventually I decided that those aircrafts would be phased out by 2017.

Too many scandals had dented the morale of the armed forces. To make things worse, Gohar Ayub Khan, a former Pakistan foreign minister claimed in his autobiography that an Indian Army brigadier had sold war plans to Pakistan in 1965 for

---

[69]Kabir Taneja, 'The Trouble With India's Mig-21 Fighter Jets', *The New York Times*, 8 August 2013.

₹20,000. In an interview to *The Telegraph*, Gohar Ayub said his father 'had accessed the plans for the 1965 war from a brigadier of the Indian Army's DMO in 1957.'[70]

Naturally, the Indian Army was deeply concerned by this allegation. The Army Headquarters and the Chief of Army Staff, General J.J. Singh, held a series of meetings to ascertain the veracity of these allegations. I was also in a dilemma. It was difficult to comprehend that an Indian Army brigadier would betray his country. In any case, I was not going to be influenced by any effort of an adversary to tarnish the reputation of a senior Indian officer. Lacking evidence, I did not give much credence to such allegations. The allegations, in any case, referred to an event that had taken place 30–35 years ago, and I was unwilling to divert attention to such unsubstantiated claims.

FUNDING ACQUISITIONS

When I took over the reins of the Ministry of Defence, the bleak picture of the state of our armed forces unfolded before me. The past decade had hardly witnessed any major acquisitions. The scandals and allegations of corruption had scared bureaucrats into what can be termed as 'non-action'. The political leadership, on the other hand, appeared more intent on unearthing the wrong-doings of the preceding government. Search for ammunition in the political arena took a heavy toll on acquiring ammunition from armed forces.

The Tenth Five-Year Plan (2002–07) had made an attempt to address some of the shortcomings in India's war-fighting capability. Despite serious intent, the defence outlay had not been finalized until then. It became a constraint on the expansion

---

[70]'Probe into Gohar claim', *The Telegraph*, 1 June 2005, https://www.telegraphindia. com/1050601/asp/nation/story_4812827.asp

and modernization of our forces.

Some of the strategies under consideration were also not workable. The NDA had proposed a rolling fund in the Defence Ministry. The rationale was that defence acquisition, being an elaborate and lengthy process; it was often not feasible to complete the acquisition process within the planned financial year. Invariably, unexpected delays pushed many acquisitions into the following financial year.

I could not, however, either accept the proposal of the rolling fund or consider it since it would have been unconstitutional to do so. The constitutional provision was clear: all expenditure should have the approval of the Parliament for every financial year.

What weakened the proposal further was that the funds allocated for the modernization of the armed forces in the three previous years had not been fully utilized. In any case, a non-lapsable fund would have had the undesirable effect of encouraging the accumulation of funds without any attendant pressure or compulsion to expedite acquisitions. Effectively, it would have the cumulative effect of encouraging further delays in the acquisition process.

The Kargil conflict had already impressed upon me that defence outlays had to be substantially enhanced in order to safeguard national security. I required little persuasion on this account.

BUDGETARY ALLOCATIONS

I was convinced that capital acquisitions required maximum attention. I was also of the firm opinion that defence allocation had to be increased on a sustained basis. Thus, budget allocations and acquisitions became my primary focus. Sporadic bursts of sharp increase in the aftermath of crises did not serve the real security needs of the nation. The reality is that we raise our defence budgets sharply in the aftermath of wars, when we are struck by the gravity of the immediate situation, and then reduce the outlays once the memory of the war begins to fade.

This was nothing new. We did it in the aftermath of the 1962 War, increasing the defence budget from ₹309 crore in 1961–62 to ₹474 crore in 1962–63, and to ₹816 crore in 1963–64. Similarly, faced with the Bangladesh crisis, we increased the budget from ₹1,199 crore in 1970–71 to ₹1,525 crore in 1971–72 and ₹1,652 crore in 1972–73. Following the 1971 War, our budget witnessed an average increase of 20.15 per cent for the period 1972–73 to 1976–77. For the next two years, we witnessed single digit growth once again. This pattern was repeated. During the year of the Kargil War (1999–2000), our defence expenditure jumped by 18 per cent to ₹47,071 crore over ₹39,897 crore in the previous year (2000–01), only to slip back to an average growth of 2.66 per cent in the following three years (2001–02 to 2003–04).

I was certain that the approach being followed was irrational. There had to be a departure from the ad hoc treatment of the issue of modernization of defence forces. I firmly believed that we needed to be prepared for war to prevent one.

Determined not to repeat the mistakes of the previous governments, I set up a special meeting with Finance Minister P. Chidambaram at South Block on 17 June 2004 to apprise him of the fact that Defence Ministry's requirement of funds would be much higher as compared to previous years, and that he should make adequate provisions for it.

During the meeting, I explained to the Finance Minister the critical gaps in our armament strength. As an illustration, I informed him of the irony that we now had a smaller and older submarine fleet as compared to the fleet in 1998. I explained to him that even if we implemented future projects as planned, we would still struggle to maintain a credible force of underwater vessels. I elaborated in the context of P-75I, the submarine-building project that aimed to construct 12 such platforms.

The P-75I project had been lying dormant for several years despite the rapidly declining strength of the fleet. Even if P-75I were implemented immediately, I explained, we would hardly be able to attain the level prevalent a decade ago.

In the meeting that lasted almost 90 minutes, I convinced the Finance Minister to fork out almost ₹12,000 crore more than the previous year's budget, which was nearly 18 per cent increase in outlay. I also persisted in my demand that defence allocations should match the annual budget estimates and this ministry should be spared the usual cuts that North Block applied on demands.

This led to first of a kind action. It was virtually the first time that the estimates of the Defence Ministry escaped the sharp scissors of the Finance Ministry.[71] More importantly, I was able to increase the capital outlay in 2004–05 to ₹31,486 crore, an increase of 59 per cent over the previous year. In the following year too, I ensured that there was an increase in the defence budget to guarantee revenue expenditure—critical for keeping the equipment at battle readiness and enable capital procurement to acquire new equipment. The overall defence budget rose by 8 per cent to ₹85,000 crore, and allocation for capital expenditure climbed to ₹34,375.14 crore, registering an increase of 9.1 per cent over the previous year. The effort was to make up for what was termed as the 'lost decade of defence modernization'.[72]

Not only did I ensure increased budgetary provisions, I also personally monitored the progress of acquisitions in the Defence

---

[71]'India's Military Budget', GlobalSecurity.org, http://www.globalsecurity.org/military/world/india/budget.htm
[72]Ibid.

Acquisition Council (DAC) meetings. The lessons of the Kargil War were fresh in my mind and I was determined to set new standards in the ministry and put an end to the wide gaps between Budget Estimates (BE) and Revised Estimates (RE), which reflect faulty planning and inefficient project implementation. Similarly, my effort was also to reduce the gap between RE and actual expenditure. Consequently, we were able to achieve minimal revision at the RE stage and the capital head. The figures spoke for themselves and the difference between BE and RE for the two years of 2004-05 and 2005-06 was a narrow 3.8 per cent when compared to a difference of 24.9 per cent between the BEs and REs of the two previous years (2002–03 and 2003–04).

Through close monitoring, we were also able to bridge the gap between BE and 'surrender'. While for the two years, 2002–03 and 2003–04, there was a total surrender of ₹10,547.93 crore, that is, 24.9 per cent of the total BE under capital head, the figure for the next two years was drastically reduced to ₹3,526.3 crore, that is, 5.1 per cent of the BE. We were able to achieve this though there was a 61.26 per cent increase in the BE of 2004–05 and 2005–06 over that of 2002–03 and 2003–04.

In order to address the contentious issue of coastal security, I increased the allocation to ₹742 crore. This would be used for surveillance of coastal areas and for programmes for special maritime police stations.

MORALE OF THE ARMED FORCES

I was acutely concerned about the need to ensure substantial remuneration so that the morale of our forces remained high. It is the nation's duty to make provisions that enable troops, especially those in the lower ranks, to lead a decent life post-retirement. With this in mind, I increased the pension of ex-servicemen up to the rank of Havaldar by ₹400 to ₹500 per month.

Several years later, in 2008, as the Chairman of the Ministerial Committee constituted by the government to examine and address the pay concerns of armed forces personnel in the Sixth Central Pay Commission (CPC) report, I recommended placement of Lieutenant Colonels or those of equivalent ranks in Pay Band (IV). This recommendation, along with other demands regarding service conditions, pension and allowances, was accepted and implemented by the government.

Another important step was to increase the compensation paid to the families of the soldiers killed in battle. The problem came to the fore when an Indian peacekeeper lost his life in Northern Congo, fighting Ugandan rebels. I decided that the government would provide full benefits to Indian Army casualties of UN peacekeeping operations.

DEFENCE PROCUREMENT PROCEDURE

Within weeks of taking charge as the defence minister, I realized that one of the main reasons for delays and scams was the absence of a well-formulated and rational Defence Procurement Procedure (DPP). The existing procedure was last revised in 2002 and it evidently had several drawbacks. There were gaps in the procedure that gave too much discretion to authorities, leaving enormous scope for allegations, many of which established nothing, but served only to delay the acquisition process.

Apart from these gaps, the procurement procedure was also not equipped to handle large acquisitions. Therefore, I focused my attention on the need for the ministry to radically revise the procedure and make it rule-based. The aim was to achieve the twin objectives of greater transparency and accountability in the acquisition process, and reduction in the acquisition time cycle. After several consultations, a revised and streamlined procedure was announced in June 2005.[73] It ushered in several changes.

One of the most significant changes was the introduction of the 'mandatory integrity pact' for all contracts over ₹300 crore.[74] It was a decisive move to avoid both unsubstantiated criticism and unethical practices in defence procurement.

Another equally significant introduction was the incorporation of the provision of 'offsets' in defence contracts. It was expected that this compensatory arrangement would help the indigenous defence industry to grow. According to the provision, all foreign companies that won contracts above ₹300 crore had to mandatorily invest 30 per cent of the value of the contract in the country as direct offsets.[75] To avoid delays, which were the bane of the ministry, a set of timelines were prescribed for each step in the acquisition process.

A slew of new reforms was introduced in the procedure to make it more efficient. They included the linking of the acquisitions to the Services Long Term Perspective Plans, making all capital acquisitions in conformity with the Staff Qualitative Requirements (SQRs). The goal of transparency was further promoted by removing the provision of waiver for SQRs. Further, single vendor acquisitions were strongly discouraged.

---

[73]Ministry of Defence, 'Defence Procurement Procedure', 2005, https://www.google.co.in/url?sa=t&rct=j&q=&esrc=s&source=web&cd=1&ved=0ahUKEwi2vJqi_rrNAhWBqY8KHUyWCEgQFggeMAA&url=http%3A%2F%2Fwww.buylawsindia.com%2FDPP%2520(2005).pdf&usg=AFQjCNExjm0LWUTkFmSCZXS9KvLF8KXbkwhttps://www.google.co.in/url?sa=t&rct=j&q=&esrc=s&source=web&cd=1&ved=0ahUKEwi2vJqi_rrNAhWBqY8KHUyWCEgQFggeMAA&url=http%3A%2F%2Fwww.buylawsindia.com%2FDPP%2520(2005).pdf&usg=AFQjCNExjm0LWUTkFmSCZXS9KvLF8KXbkw

[74]'Future Defence deals to contain no-bribe clause', *Hindustan Times*; 9 June 2005.

[75]Ibid.

The effectiveness of the new procedure encouraged me to further improve and amend it in August 2006. Under the new procedure:

- All major decisions pertaining to the procurement process were to be taken simultaneously to reduce the timeframe for acquisitions.
- To strengthen transparency, all generic requirements of the services were to be uploaded on the Defence Ministry website and were to generate vendor registration through the Internet.
- An 'integrity pact' was made compulsory for all contracts above ₹100 crores; and an 'offset' obligation for all contracts above ₹300 crores.

An agency to facilitate implementation of offsets, called Defence Offset Facilitation Agency (DOFA), was established in the Department of Defence Production. It was tasked with providing assistance in monitoring offset provisions, promoting exports of defence products and services, and offering advisory clarifications on policy and procedures.

The revision was also motivated by the need to encourage and provide a boost to 'self-reliance'. The objective was to assist the indigenous industry to develop appropriate technologies as well as the capability to undertake upgrade of systems indigenously. To achieve this, a first of its kind 'Make' procedure for the development of systems based on indigenous research and design was prescribed.[76] The import (buy) and transfer of technology

---

[76]Ministry of Defence, 'Defence Procurement Procedure', p 136, 2006, https://www.google.co.in/url?sa=t&rct=j&q=&esrc=s&source=web&cd=2&ved=0ahUKEwi2vJqi_rrNAhWBqY8KHUyWCEgQFggkMAE&url=http%3A%2F%2Fwww.buylawsindia.com%2FDPP%2520(2006).pdf&usg=AFQjCNEXoed3Ym2kdkGWCI_2H4RtDtD8lw

(buy and make) procedures were also streamlined and made transparent. Importantly, necessary changes were implemented in the procedures to provide a level playing field for indigenous industries vis-à-vis their foreign counterparts.

The Prime Minister's Office (PMO) played a significant role in clearing major defence acquisitions like the Scorpene submarines and the Jaguar fighter aircraft.

THE NAVAL WAR ROOM CASE

Just as things appeared to be improving, we were confronted with what came to be known as the 'naval war room leak case'. In October 2005, it was reported that over 7,000 documents had been leaked from the Directorate of Naval Operations in New Delhi.[77] A few of these were intercepted by the Air Force Intelligence from the house of Wing Commander S.L. Surve. Further investigations revealed that an arms dealer, Abhishek Varma, and a few armed forces officers were involved in the leak of these documents, which dealt with Indian defence purchases and future plans of the navy.

Although most of the leaked documents were primarily commercial in nature, the very fact that they had been ferreted out from a secure naval computer, was unsettling. Irrespective of the nature of the information that had been leaked, the sheer criminality of the act had to be established. The truth had to be unearthed and I was not willing to compromise on that. I, therefore, took the decision to refer the matter to the CBI, which registered a case on 20 March 2006.[78]

---

[77]'Defence minister asks CBI to probe navy war room leak', *Outlook,* 19 February 2006, http://www.outlookindia.com/newswire/story/cbi-probe-into-war-room-leak-in-navy-hq-deceptive-fernandes/356533

[78]'Charges framed against 6 in naval war room case', Rediff.com, 31 July 2014,

Unfortunately, one of the prime accused in the naval war room leak case was Ravi Shankaran, a former naval officer and a relative of the wife of the then Chief of Naval Staff, Admiral Arun Prakash, a decorated naval aviator and a man known for his high integrity and professionalism. Shankaran owned a company called Shank Ocean Engineering and was involved in the business of naval supplies. He had allegedly used his relations with officers in the naval directorate to acquire information.

Confronted with this revelation, Admiral Arun Prakash, in the true tradition of a man in uniform, called on me and submitted his resignation in August 2006.[79] Though I appreciated his expression of propriety, I was unwilling to accept his resignation without there being any prima facie evidence against him. I was influenced in my decision by the dictum that every individual is responsible for his or her own action, and the relatives of an accused do not have to bear the burden of any criminal or improper act unless there is some evidence to the contrary. And to this day, I feel vindicated about the decision I took since nothing has even remotely surfaced so far, linking Admiral Prakash to any wrong-doings of his relative.

I was, however, determined to convey to the armed forces that there is a compelling need to maintain secrecy and integrity in matters relating to the security of the nation. A message had to be sent out that there would be zero tolerance in matters relating to breach of security. I made this clear in unequivocal terms in the annual address of the Naval Commanders Conference

---

accessed: 21 June 2016 http://www.rediff.com/news/report/charges-framed-against-6-in-naval-war-room-leak-case/20140731.htm

[79]'Cover up begins', *Outlook*, 10 July 2006, http://www.outlookindia.com/magazine/story/cover-up-begins/231798

on 2 May 2006. The armed forces had to follow 'a zero defect system to ensure secrecy'.[80]

EMERGENCE OF THE CIS AND BUILDING BRIDGES WITH THE US

Even after the end of the Cold War, India's dependence on Russia for defence systems continued. However, the situation was now different. The dismemberment of the erstwhile Soviet Union posed, in its wake, new problems. Many of the famed defence industries of the erstwhile superpower were established in the Commonwealth of Independent States (CIS) countries. Consequently, not only were there enormous delays bedevilling the implementation of projects concluded with the former Soviet Union, but even servicing and sourcing of spare parts had also become very difficult.

I had already spent over a year in External Affairs Ministry in the mid-1990s. As the minister in charge of foreign affairs, I was one of the strong votaries of building bridges with the US in the aftermath of the Cold War. Consequently, when I became the defence minister in 2004, I was well aware that in the long term, India's dependence on Russia for her security requirements had to be reduced. Further, the dismantling of the Cold War military blocs reduced past differences between India and the US. Both were democracies and at the fundamental level, there was more confluence than divergence of interests. The time had come to engage with the US and I directed the ministry to work towards building closer ties with the Pentagon.

---

[80]'Defence Minister takes Navy to task', *The Tribune*, 2 May 2006.

PRELUDE TO US VISIT

My visit to the US was preceded by a brief interaction with former US Secretary of State, Henry Kissinger, at South Block, in 2004. During the meeting, he commented on the robust trade relations established between the two nations during the tenure of US Secretary of Commerce, Ron Brown, and questioned the lack of comparable synergy and substance in the defence relationship. In my reply to his question, I stated categorically that Indo–US defence relations had suffered due to a complete trust deficit. I reminded him of the US decision to block the critical cryogenic deal, which was of supreme national interest to India. It had impelled India to indigenize. 'If the US could not subscribe to India's national interest, why should we subscribe to your national interest and forge deeper defence ties?' I responded. Subsequently I discussed the issue in detail with Dr Singh who asked me about the rather unexpected outburst during the meeting with Kissinger. A few days after Kissinger's return from India, I was informed by our Ambassador to the US, Ronen Sen, about American media reports regarding the possibility of a defence partnership between the two nations.

Soon institutional mechanisms were put in place and India's willingness to establish strategic ties with the US was emphasized in the 6th meeting of the US–India Defence Policy Group held in India on 1–2 June 2004.[81] This was followed by the much anticipated visit of Secretary of Defence, Donald Rumsfeld, to New Delhi on 8 December 2004.[82] We discussed the general scope of our bilateral relations and I used this opportunity to open dialogue on the possibility of a defence partnership with

---

[81]Statement by Defence Minister in Lok Sabha on 22 August 2004, http://164.100.47.192/Loksabha/Questions/QResult15.aspx?qref= 53584&lsno=14
[82]'Rumsfeld to visit India on December 8', *The Tribune*, 2 December 2004.

the US. During the media interaction, I expressed deep concern about the repercussions of the US arms supplies to Pakistan and stressed on the demand to immediately de-hyphenate the Indo–Pak equation. I was also asked about my plans to visit the US at the invitation of Secretary Rumsfeld. I mentioned that the visit was under consideration. On the completion of our interaction, Secretary Rumsfeld once again urged me to consider his invitation for a US visit.

The following year in June 2005, I visited the US. My objective was clear. As defence minister, I was determined to take our defence relationship with the US to a higher level. I publicly acknowledged India's desire to establish closer security partnership with the US. Addressing the Carnegie Endowment for International Peace in Washington on 27 June, I suggested that the security threats in South Asia could be countered by the two largest democracies in conjunction. I said, 'Today, more than ever, the US and India realize that they share common values and security concerns; and that there is an objective convergence of interests.'[83]

DEFENCE FRAMEWORK AGREEMENT

On the subsequent day, 28 June 2005, Donald Rumsfeld and I signed the historic 'New Framework for US–India Defence Relations', building on the Agreed Minutes of 1995.[84] It was a roadmap for establishing closer defence relations between the two nations in the coming decade. The framework articulated how India and the US had entered a new era, transforming their relationship

---

[83]Carnegie Endowment for International Peace on India's strategic perspectives, 27 June 2005, speech delivered by Pranab Mukherjee, http://carnegieendowment.org/files/Mukherjee_Speech_06-27-051.pdf
[84]New Framework for US–India Defence relations, p 4, 2005, http://library.rumsfeld.com/doclib/sp/3211/2005-06-28%20New%20Framework%20for%20the%20US-India%20Defence%20Relationship.pdf

to reflect our common principles and shared national interests in the new international order.[85] The framework also reflected the common objective in combatting terrorism, religious extremism and the spread of weapons of mass destruction. One other salient provision in the framework was the establishment of a 'Defence procurement and production group' to broaden the scope of the existing security cooperation group and intensify interactions.[86]

The Defence Framework signalled a positive change in India–US bilateral relations. The visit also opened up the US as a potential source of advanced defence equipment and technology, increasing our options and leverage, vis-à-vis suppliers in the acquisition of defence technology. It also aimed at the promotion of cooperation with the US to enhance the capabilities of India's armed forces, strengthen its defence industries and increase our strategic manoeuvrability in international affairs without committing to any specific actions that would be detrimental to the country's national interest.[87] It signalled a level of trust between the two nations that had not existed since independence.

Even during the run up to the visit, I had advised the senior officers of the ministry that I was not looking for a buyer-seller relationship with the US. I had emphasized the need to evolve a mechanism to facilitate the transfer of technology from the US and in the long-term open vistas for defence co-production. The need was to highlight the fact that the cost of production in

---

[85]New Framework for US–India Defence relations, 28 June 2005, p 1, http://library.rumsfeld.com/doclib/sp/3211/2005-06-28%20New%20Framework%20for%20the%20US-India%20Defence%20Relationship.pdf

[86]'Defence Minister Pranab Mukherjee in the US', USA News, *India Review*, 1 July 2005, p 4.

[87]Statement by Defence Minister in Lok Sabha on, 27 August 2005, http://164.100.47.192/Loksabha/Questions/QResult15.aspx?qref=15449&lsno=14

India was low and we had highly trained manpower operating in a world-class environment.[88] Perceiving India's requirements, on 20 April 2005, General Jeffrey Kohler informed the Ministry of Defence that the US was willing to jointly develop and produce 'futuristic weapons systems in India.'[89]

Not all in India were, however, happy about the strengthening India–US defence partnership. We came in for severe criticism from the Left parties. The main thrust of their criticism was that the government was jettisoning its independence and non-alignment policy. Prakash Karat and other Left leaders even asked Prime Minister Manmohan Singh 'not to go further' with the deal and 'dump it'.[90] The unrelenting criticism forced me to go into damage control mode. On 4 July 2005, I held a press conference and reaffirmed that India would not abandon its independent foreign policy.

I reiterated this position on 2 August 2005, when I said that 'as a trustee of the legacy of Independence, secularism, non-alignment and autonomy and independence of our domestic and foreign policies, we have the self-confidence to recognize and resist anything that is not in our national interest.'[91]

Looking back after more than a decade, I feel vindicated that we were able to sow the seeds of closer Indo–US strategic relations with particular emphasis on security and defence and pave the way for subsequent joint development and coproduction of defence equipment.

---

[88]'India wants US to ease space, Ntech curbs', *The Tribune*, 29 June 2005.
[89]Satish Kumar, *India's National Security*, Knowledge World Publication, New Delhi, 2006 p 34.
[90]'Cancel Defence pact with the US, left tells govt', *Hindustan Times*, 8 July 2005.
[91]'US pact in India's interest', *Hindustan Times*, 2 August 2005.

BUILDING INDIGENOUS CAPACITY

As the defence minister, I became critically conscious of the fact that we were hopelessly dependant on external sources to fulfil India's defence needs. I also shared this view in Parliament. Replying to a question on 1 December 2005, I declared that as a matter of policy, priority would be accorded to sourcing all defence equipment indigenously. Defence items would only be imported when the armed forces required wares of a particular technology and within a defined time frame, and when it was not possible to source them locally. Even while taking a decision to import a particular defence equipment, its local manufacture under transfer of technology would be explored.[92] With this objective in view, I resisted all attempts to import platforms where an effort could be made to make the same in India. Thus, when the issue of building an aircraft carrier came up, I was quite resolute in my opinion that the 37,500-tonne platform called 'indigenous air defence ship' be built in the Kochi shipyard.[93]

I also encouraged DRDO to undertake special projects to augment India's nuclear capabilities. Though India is a 'reluctant nuclear power' operating on the principles of 'minimum credible deterrence' and has a 'no-first use' policy (NFU), it has to build a credible arsenal. Addressing a press conference after the inauguration of the Aero India 2005 air show in Bangalore, I announced the launch of project 'Sagarika', India's first submarine-launched ballistic missile under the aegis of the DRDO. This step was taken because the sea leg of India's nuclear triad was the weakest and the most vital. 'For a nation that has limited land

---

[92]Statement by Defence Minister in Lok Sabha on 1 December 2005, http://164.100.47.192/Loksabha/Questions/QResult15.aspx?qref=20893&lsno=14
[93]'India to build aircraft carrier', *The Tribune*, 23 March 2005.

and air-launched nuclear weapons, comparatively rudimentary delivery systems and a declared NFU policy, the strengthening of this leg is of paramount importance.'[94]

DEALING WITH SCAMS: COFFINGATE

Under the NDA regime, the defence ministry was rocked by several scams. One particular scam consumed considerable time of the MoD. It related to the procurement of coffins during the Kargil War and came to be known as the 'coffin scam'. A commission that was set up under Justice S.N. Phukan to probe the allegations did not yield much result. Several related issues refused to die down and the matter reached the Supreme Court.

A controversy was created after an affidavit was filed by the MoD. Later, at a press conference, my predecessor George Fernandes claimed that he was given a clean chit in the affidavit. I was not aware of the affidavit, which was sent without my approval. At the same time, I was not inclined to capitalize on the situation to derive political mileage from the crisis.

Law Minister H.R. Bhardwaj had also claimed that the views of his ministry had been ignored and the report that was submitted by his ministry through the services of the Attorney General, had been changed. The fact of the matter, however, was that the first draft of the report, along with its changes, had been vetted by the Attorney General. I shouldered complete responsibility for the contents of the affidavit though I had to reprimand my secretary for not having submitted the file to me.

My two-and-a-half years in the Defence Ministry were as exciting as they were challenging. I must confess that I was

---

[94]Dr Thomas Mathew, 'Signs of the Emerging Third Leg: Strengthening of India's Triad'. Institute of Defence Studies and Analyses, *Journal of Defence Studies*, Vol. 2, No. 1, 2008.

not without trepidation when I was informed by the Congress President of her decision to allot the defence portfolio to me. But the apprehensions did not last very long. Within weeks into the new assignment, I started enjoying the pressures of this complicated ministry. I was also suddenly faced with a situation where sitting on the opposite side of North Block (which I had occupied as finance minister and the chief advocate of restricted spending), I would now have to reverse my role and seek larger outlays for defence.

I was reminded of this transformation when the Chief of Naval Staff, Admiral Madhvender Singh, in lighter vein, referred to the change. In 1983, he had in fact accompanied the then Chief of Naval Staff Admiral O.S. Dawson who had met me for additional outlays for the Navy, which did not elicit any encouraging response. I was not even willing to part with an additional ₹25 crore.

It was at a conference where I enquired from the three Chiefs of their defence acquisition plans. I had apparently, maybe enthusiastically, asked if they required additional funds to which they all replied in the affirmative. I assured them that no effort would be spared to enhance their allocations. At this point, Admiral Madhvender Singh, noticing the sudden transformation in me said, 'Sir, you seem to have happily given up the baggage of the other side.' I broke into a laughter which puzzled the Army and Air Force Chiefs for it was a secret that only the Chief of Naval Staff and I shared in a context that only the two of us were privy to.

FROM DEFENCE TO FOREIGN AFFAIRS

Just as I had begun to make changes in the Defence Ministry and enjoying my role, I was also called upon to assume some of the responsibilities of the External Affairs Minister, subsequent to the resignation of Natwar Singh on 6 December 2005.

Some Foreign Service Officers seemed to have been more informed than me. When I was in New York to attend the United Nations (UN) General Assembly meeting, some even hinted that I would soon be shifting to the Ministry of External Affairs (MEA). At that juncture, I was more inclined to dismiss these as mere speculations, but on my return I realized how wrong I was. On arrival, I was informed that I would move to the External Affairs Ministry and A.K. Antony would succeed me in Defence.

It was not that I was unhappy to move from Defence to External Affairs. I was simply disappointed that I had made several changes in the Defence Ministry, secured budgets beyond their expectations and was leaving my plans only partially executed. To confess, I was rather enjoying the positive changes that I had brought about in this important ministry.

CHAPTER 7

MANAGING THE EXTERNAL
ENVIRONMENT

I assumed charge of the Ministry of External Affairs (MEA) in October 2006,[95] and was assisted by two MoS—E. Ahamed and Anand Sharma—throughout my tenure. Having been at the helm of this ministry earlier, the nature of the task was familiar. I also had the experience of other ministerial portfolios—Finance, Commerce and Defence—which provided me a holistic understanding of an integrated approach to foreign policy issues.

I have always held the view that foreign policy has to facilitate India's developmental processes, leveraging our international partnerships to the best possible effect. Thus, my aim was to make foreign policy play a major role in India's economic renaissance. With this in mind, I sought to significantly upgrade our economic relationship with Southeast Asia, East Asia, Latin America and Africa, build new investment-driven partnerships with the US and the European Union (EU) and nurture a web of cooperative energy security networks in Asia and with new suppliers in

---

[95]Profile of the President: Official Biography of Shri Pranab Mukherjee, The President of India, http://presidentofindia.nic.in/Images/pdf/president-profile.pdf

West Africa, Central Asia and Latin America. Additionally, given the increasing security concerns, I emphasized on promoting an environment of peace and security in the region and beyond—a prerequisite for development—and was particularly motivated to expand the South Asian Association for Regional Cooperation (SAARC).

About 20 days after assuming office, I had the opportunity to spell out my vision for India's foreign policy in a speech made to the 46th National Defence College Course on 15 November 2006. The speech was titled 'Indian Foreign Policy: A Road Map for the Decade Ahead.'

In that speech, I pointed out that India's foreign policy was a product of its history, geopolitical setting and the needs and aspirations of its people as distilled by its democratic institutions. I said:

> This policy is inspired by the vision of our founding fathers, in particular Pandit Nehru, and is nourished by a tradition of continuity and consensus... India is set resolutely on a path of economic growth of at least 8 per cent per annum. In a decade from now, it is slated to be the third largest economy in the world... I foresee Indian foreign policy playing a major role in this economic renaissance... There is a range of foreign policy instruments available to advance our economic interests... We need to creatively add to this tool box and in fact, retune mindsets so that our entire approach to a bilateral relationship is premised on that relationship's contribution to our economic well-being... The primary task of our foreign policy has to remain the facilitation of India's developmental processes, leveraging our international partnerships to the best possible effect. Our focus in the coming decade should be on promoting trade and investment flows, in assisting

the modernization of infrastructure, in assuring predictable and affordable energy supplies and in securing the widest possible access to technologies... Maritime security, WMD proliferation, energy security and terrorism are important and emerging issues with a bearing on the security of our region. We have to promote an environment of peace and security in the region and beyond which is a pre-requisite for development.

I called for a significantly different set of relationships in the neighbourhood and asserted that India, as the largest country in South Asia, had to assume greater responsibility for the region's challenges. I reiterated:

> I want India's Foreign Policy to pay particular attention to each and every one of our bilateral relationships in the neighbourhood, from Myanmar to Afghanistan, and provide them with depth and diversity of mutually beneficial interaction... In more ways than simply economic, the future of the Indian sub-continent depends upon whether this open mindedness prevails over the more traditional mind-sets. On its part, India has extended its hand in all directions and is willing to go the extra mile for a better future.

I concluded stating that in the coming decade, India's foreign policy would have to contend with intensified engagement with not only the major powers, but also emerging power centres as well as our immediate and extended neighbourhood. I said:

> Demographic trends, policy choices and India's inherent societal strengths have come together to put India among the key players of this century. While we still have many challenges in addressing the basic needs of our people, the world's perception of India, its capacities and its strengths

have changed irreversibly. This is both a challenge and an opportunity for our foreign policy. We have to act, and more quickly than before, from a platform of increased self-assurance and responsibility to ensure that India continues to enjoy a peaceful and supportive environment for pursuing her development goals as well as to ensure that the world's expectations of India are met and we are able to contribute, as our forefathers have always wanted, to the fashioning of a better world based on universal human values.

FOCUS ON THE NEIGHBOURHOOD

The prospects in our immediate neighbourhood called for more imaginative initiatives given that we were committed to ensuring a peaceful periphery. Peace was a requirement not only for India's continued growth, but also for the larger good of the region.

Hence, we stepped up our bilateral engagements while seeking to make SAARC a broader and more open organization. At its 14th Summit meeting in New Delhi in April 2007, we welcomed Afghanistan as a member, and China, Japan, the US, the EU and South Korea as associated observers. Combatting terrorism, including its financing, was another major focus of the summit.[96] Our vision of stronger regional cooperation and harmony had led us to boldly address even difficult historical problems with a view to finding long-term solutions.

The summit agreed to improve intra-regional connectivity through physical, economic and people-to-people linkages. In case of physical connectivity, an important decision was to extend the SAARC Regional Multimodal Transport Study to

---

[96]Declaration of the 14th SAARC Summit, New Delhi, http://www.satp.org/satporgtp/countries/india/document/papers/sarc14ind.htm

Afghanistan. For economic connectivity, the SAARC countries committed themselves to early operationalization of the SAARC Development Fund (SDF) and implementation of trade facilitation measures.[97] The Heads of governments agreed to strengthen the security network by sharing of information, increased frequency of meetings between security chiefs and consider India's proposal to work towards finalizing the Agreement on Mutual Legal Assistance in Criminal Matters.[98]

That period was one of the most productive that SAARC has ever known. The impetus provided by India during the 14th SAARC Summit was largely responsible for the gradual and irreversible transition of SAARC from the declaratory to the implementation phase. This phenomenon was further complemented by India's commitment to discharge its responsibilities in an asymmetric and non-reciprocal manner, coupled with the increasing needs of other member states to look to SAARC to find solutions for their domestic developmental challenges.

The increasing vitality of the grouping was evident. The SDF was operationalized before SAARC's permanent premises was established, which was due in Bhutan in 2010. India's financial commitment of $189.9 million to the SDF was met in full.

The progress made on the establishment of the South Asian University (SAU) in New Delhi was very encouraging. The total cost of establishing the SAU was estimated at $308.91 million. India offered to contribute $229.11 million to the project, including 100 per cent of the capital cost.

There was significant movement in the area of trade

---

[97]Declaration of the Fourteenth SAARC Summit, Press Information Bureau, 4 April 2007, http://pib.nic.in/others/saarc_car_rally/D_F_SAARCSummit.pdf
[98]Opening statement of External Affairs Minister, Shri Pranab Mukherjee at the end of 14th SAARC Summit Press Conference, http://pib.nic.in/newsite/erelcontent.aspx?relid=26649

cooperation. The South Asian Free Trade Agreement showed tangible progress, though it has now been overtaken by other events.

India took the initiative to convene important meetings using the SAARC platform. New Delhi hosted the 8th meeting of the SAARC environment ministers from 19–21 October 2009. The Bhutan Government proposed climate change as the theme of the 16th SAARC Summit scheduled to be held in April 2010. In the meeting, the Delhi Statement on Cooperation in Environment was issued. It called upon SAARC member states to pursue environment-related projects on the basis of concept notes submitted by India. The meeting also considered the setting up of 50 weather stations in member states for installing advance storm warning systems. Through India's efforts in establishing a framework for cooperation in the field of environment—a draft regional environment treaty was also circulated by us— the SAARC member states were ready for greater engagement. The growing convergence of interests among member states culminated in the presentation of a 'Cooperative Position on Climate Change' to the United Nations Framework Convention on Climate Change (UNFCCC) Secretariat prior to its summit in Copenhagen in December 2009.

There was also renewed vigour in people-to-people engagement. In 2009, India hosted the Third SAARC Bands Festival and the Second SAARC Festival of Literature in New Delhi, while the Second SAARC Folklore Festival was hosted in Chandigarh.

India pursued her engagement in the region with a non-reciprocal approach, funding projects in sectors such as telemedicine, solar rural electrification, rainwater harvesting and seed-testing laboratories. We followed the hub-and-spoke model—India being the hub with member states as spokes.

On the whole, there was confidence that if growing economic

interdependence could be developed further, SAARC would emerge as a platform for economic cooperation in South Asia.

REGIONAL BILATERAL RELATIONSHIPS

The expansion of the SAARC framework automatically helped India consolidate one-to-one regional ties. I had the opportunity to visit all of our South Asian neighbours immediately after taking over as External Affairs Minister. This was with the purpose of inviting the Heads of states to the SAARC summit at Delhi.

BHUTAN

I visited Bhutan on 2–3 December 2006, just a week before Jigme Khesar Namgyel Wangchuck took over as the fifth king of the country (though he was crowned in 2008). This was also the time that transition to democracy had commenced there in the country, thus raising the possibility of some change in the Indo–Bhutan relationship.

Relations between the two countries had thus far been governed by the Indo–Bhutan Friendship Treaty of 1949, which essentially looked after the interests of both the nations—Bhutan enjoyed the security of protection from any external aggression and India got a neutral buffer between China and itself.

However, with the ushering in of democracy and a changing geopolitical situation, Jigme Singye Wangchuck (fourth King of Bhutan) discussed the revision of the Treaty with me. Bhutan now wanted sovereignty over its foreign policy and would not require India's permission over arms imports. I was not in favour of that and told him, and that if we revisited this Treaty then Nepal may also raise a similar demand. But he stated that my predecessor, Natwar Singh, had indicated to him that the MEA would not have any objection to a revision of the Treaty. There was a detailed discussion as Dr Singh and I were keen to maintain the status quo. The King remained persistent, but also said that the spirit of cooperation would continue to underline our relationship. It was in that spirit that the following clause was included:

> In keeping with the abiding ties of close friendship and cooperation between Bhutan and India, the Government of the Kingdom of Bhutan and the Government of the Republic of India shall cooperate closely with each other on issues relating to their national interests. *Neither Government shall allow the use of its territory for activities harmful to the national security and interest of the other.*[99]

On 8 February 2007, the revised Treaty was signed in New Delhi. I signed on behalf of India, while the Crown Prince signed on behalf of Bhutan, though it was his father who had negotiated the terms of the agreement. The amendments were reflected in Articles 2 and 6, giving Bhutan autonomy to pursue its foreign policy and in the purchase of non-lethal military equipment as long as such decisions did not damage India's vital strategic interests. Following the signing of the Treaty, King Namgyel Wangchuck said, 'From a guiding role upon Bhutan's first step to modernization, we now stand as close friends and equal partners in the global arena.'[100]

While India welcomed Bhutan's move to democracy in 2008, with the country holding its first free elections in that year, India's rising concern was the possibility of Bhutan tilting towards

---

[99] India–Bhutan Friendship Treaty, 2007, Ministry of External Affairs, New Delhi, https://mea.gov.in/Images/pdf/india-bhutan-treaty-07.pdf
[100] Amit Baruah, 'India, Bhutan update Friendship Treaty', *The Hindu*, 9 February, 2007, http://www.thehindu.com/todays-paper/India-Bhutan-update-friendship-treaty/article14718182.ece

China. That concern notwithstanding, the relationship continued on solid grounds of mutual trust and collaboration.

I have had great personal equations with both the kings. On one of my trips, I took with me as a gift for King Jigme Singye, a scarf that my wife had knitted for him. Immensely touched, he wanted to send for her an exquisite piece of jewellery, which I refused to accept and laughingly added that I would have to deposit it into the state treasury.

On 16–17 May 2008, Prime Minister Manmohan Singh visited Bhutan during which he addressed the first session of their democratically elected Parliament. During the visit, Dr Singh announced that India will double the target of hydropower development in Bhutan to 10,000 MW for export to India by 2020; Government of India's assistance for construction of the first rail link between India and Bhutan; and setting up of the prestigious Nehru–Wangchuck scholarship for Bhutanese students.

Over the years, I have maintained a strong, personal relationship with Bhutan's royal family. I invited King Jigme Khesar Namgyel Wangchuck and Queen Jetsun Pema to India immediately after their royal wedding in 2011. In 2013, King Namgyel Wangchuck was the chief guest at the 64th Republic Day celebrations. The royal couple stayed at the Rashtrapati Bhavan and visited other parts of India during this visit.

NEPAL

India and Nepal have historically shared a unique relationship based on a long tradition of cultural and kinship ties between its people. The bedrock of Independent India's relationship with this land-locked country has been the India–Nepal Treaty of Peace and Friendship of 1950. Over a period of time, this treaty has remained a subject of debate in Nepal, through the churn the country's polity has seen over the years. There have been frequent changes in the political system in Nepal from monarchy to panchayat democracy and constitutional democracy, injecting some level of political instability. That notwithstanding, a pro-democracy Maoist insurgency gained strength during the 1990s and early 2000s.

It was in that background of political and social strife that on 1 February 2005, King Gyanendra dismissed the government and assumed all executive functions, thus restoring absolute monarchy.[101] That became a worry for India.

> The principal concern driving the Indian Government's policy towards King Gyanendra is not democracy but how his palace putsch is going to affect the Royal Nepal Army's counter-insurgency operations against Maoist rebels.
>
> There is anxiety about the future of multi-party democracy there and even consternation over the fate of political leaders, but these are largely derivative—not ideological—concerns. What bothers New Delhi most of all is the likelihood that now that the King has cast aside the protective buffer the political parties provided him, the Maoists are likely to increase their influence.[102]

Nepal-India relations then took a turn for the worse.

I visited Nepal on 17 December 2006, and here too I extended an invitation to the King for the SAARC Summit.

The year 2006 was a turning point in Nepal's history, as a multi-party democracy was restored in April.[103] Subsequently, a

---

[101]'Nepal's King dismisses Government, assumes power', *The Hindu*, 2 February 2005, http://www.thehindu.com/2005/02/02/stories/2005020206700100.htm

[102]Siddhartha Varadarajan, 'India's Nepal stand driven by concern for Maoist danger', *The Hindu*, 4 February 2005, http://www.thehindu.com/2005/02/04/stories/2005020413041100.htm

[103]Susan I. Hangen, *Indigenous Nationalities Movement, The Rise of Ethnic Politics in Nepal: Democracy in the Margins*, Routledge, p 37, 2009.

Comprehensive Peace Agreement was signed by the Government of Nepal and CPN (Maoist), which formally brought to an end the armed insurgency. The agreement laid down a roadmap for further steps—promulgating the interim constitution, initiating the process of arms management and constituting an interim Legislature, with the inclusion of CPN (Maoist) in January 2007 the process of arms management was initiated, the interim Constitution promulgated, and an interim Legislature, with the inclusion of CPN (Maoist), constituted in January 2007.

These developments were significant steps in Nepal's journey towards a settled constitutional order to enable its people to realize their aspirations for peace and prosperity. India extended its full support to the Government of Nepal and its people at this important juncture of their history.

In the elections held in April 2008, the Maoists won a clear majority. After the restoration of democracy, Nepal's Prime Minister Pushpa Kamal Dahal 'Prachanda' made his first official foreign visit to India from 14–18 September 2008. During the visit, both Prime Ministers held talks, and India conveyed its commitment to support Nepal's democratic and economic transformation. As agreed by both sides, several high-level bilateral consultation mechanisms were also reactivated. It was in this year that Indo–Nepal ties got a further boost with an agreement to resume water talks after a four-year hiatus.

I visited Nepal that November and met Prachanda, Finance Minister Baburam Bhattarai and the Foreign Affairs Adviser to Prachanda, Hira Bahadur Thapa, and discussed Nepal's political situation, the peace process and the army's integration with the Maoists.

Over time, I had become a sort of an unofficial adviser to a multitude of Nepalese politicians and leaders, and had come to understand the dynamics of the country's politics. With this understanding, I handled this relationship myself during my tenure rather than leaving it to one of my MoS.

SRI LANKA

India and Sri Lanka have had deep cultural and linguistic ties. Ironically, it is these deep ties—represented by the Tamils on either side of the ocean—that have caused a certain friction in the relationship in the past.

> The complexities of domestic politics have played a significant role in deciding the direction of bilateral relations between India and Sri Lanka. According to Sivarajah (1990), the nature of Tamil minority in Sri Lanka affects India's domestic politics as much as that of Sri Lanka's politics, because there are nearly seventy million Tamils in the state of Tamil Nadu who belong not only to the same ethnic stock as Tamils in Sri Lanka, but also speak the same language and follow the same cultural patterns. Whenever communal riots between the Sinhalese and the Tamils take place, the seventy million Tamils in the Indian state of Tamil Nadu press the government of India to take up the matter with Sri Lanka and to do something or redress the injustice done to their brethren in that country.[104]

Sri Lanka faced a protracted civil war for over two decades since the 1980s. Led by the Liberation Tigers of Tamil Eelam (LTTE), a predominantly Tamil Hindu population of northern Sri Lanka started a movement demanding an independent state.

---

[104]Asantha Senevirathna, 'India–Sri Lanka Relations: Examining Domestic Factors and External Influences on State Behaviour', 8th International Research Conference 2015, http://www.kdu.ac.lk/proceedings/irc2015/2015/dss-009.pdf

India, on the request of the Sri Lankan Government, sent a peacekeeping force (1987–90) to restore normalcy.[105] However, the Indian forces were unsuccessful in achieving the desired objective, and returned home. While a ceasefire was declared in 2001, hostilities resumed soon after.

Sri Lankan President Mahinda Rajapaksa visited India in November 2006, followed by Prime Minister Ratnasiri Wickremanayake in January 2007. I visited Colombo in January 2007 to hand over the SAARC Summit invitation to the Sri Lankan President. In all our interactions with Sri Lankan leaders, we conveyed the need for a negotiated political settlement which met the legitimate aspirations of all communities while respecting the unity, sovereignty and territorial integrity of Sri Lanka.

In 2008, I made a suo moto statement in Parliament reiterating the Indian Government's stand that the deteriorating humanitarian situation in the northern part of Sri Lanka was of serious concern, and that we were troubled by the plight of the civilians caught in the hostilities and the growing number of internally displaced people. I emphasized that there could be no military solution to the ethnic conflict and that the Government of Sri Lanka should continue to nurture the democratic process in the Eastern Province as well.[106]

It was a difficult situation. We had to balance the sensitivities on either side of the border. So, every trip I made to Sri Lanka

---

[105]Data extracted from 'A Bloodied Accord', *India Today*, 15 November 1987, http://indiatoday.intoday.in/story/after-16-days-of-bloody-battle-ipkf-finally-captures-ltte-stronghold-jaffna/1/337703.html and 'Rajiv Gandhi's Sri Lanka policy led to his death: Natwar Singh', *The Hindustan Times*, 1 August 2014, http://www.hindustantimes.com/india/rajiv-gandhi-s-sri-lanka-policy-led-to-his-death-natwar-singh/story-0JLTRSHTUF92n32q904rnL.html

[106]Appendix 4: Suo Motu Statement by Minister of External Affairs Mr Pranab Mukherjee in Lok Sabha on Foreign Policy-related Developments.

was preceded or succeeded by a visit to Chennai as well.

BANGLADESH

India and Bangladesh are not just neighbours, but are bound by an umbilical connection of ethnicity and kinship. India always attaches highest importance to bilateral relations with Bangladesh because of our shared history, heritage, culture, language, physical proximity and also the role which the two nations can play together for the development and prosperity of the entire subcontinent and beyond. The bedrock on which the edifice of this unique relationship stands is the unwavering faith of both the countries in democratic values, principles of liberalism, egalitarianism, secularism, and respect for each other's sovereignty and integrity.

Bangladesh has faced many ups and downs in its short history as a nation state. In late 2006, violent protests broke out in the country when Prime Minister Khaleda Zia's term was coming to an end and a decision needed to be taken on a caretaker administration till the next elections. As a result, President Iajuddin Ahmed assumed the caretaker role till the elections, which were announced for January 2007. However, just before the elections (in January 2007), President Ahmed declared a state of Emergency and installed a caretaker government headed by Bangladesh Chief Adviser, Dr Fakhruddin Ahmed.

During this period all prominent political leaders were imprisoned. Sheikh Hasina too was jailed on charges of bribery and corruption.[107] While India continued to engage with the caretaker government we stressed the need for full restoration

---

[107]'Sheikh Hasina arrested, sent to jail', *The Times of India*, 16 July 2007, http://timesofindia.indiatimes.com/world/rest-of-world/Sheikh-Hasina-arrested-sent-to-jail/articleshow/2206776.cms

of democracy through peaceful, credible, free and fair elections.

Dr Fakhruddin Ahmed visited India to attend the 14th SAARC Summit in New Delhi. Subsequently, I visited Bangladesh on 1 December 2007 in the aftermath of the severe cyclone which had struck Bangladesh in November that year. I expressed India's solidarity with the people and the Government of Bangladesh and reiterated our readiness to assist in the relief as well as rehabilitation work in the cyclone affected areas. I said:

> On hearing of the calamity, India has already rushed some immediately required relief assistance like medicines, ready-to-eat meals, blankets, tents and portable water purifiers worth about Taka 11 crore. In response to Bangladesh Government's request, India has also announced a waiver of ban on exports of rice to Bangladesh for 50,000 tons. In addition, 20,000 tons of rice is being sent by sea to Chittagong. In fact, India's total relief assistance to Bangladesh this year so far amounts to more than Taka 270 crore.[108]

In February 2008, Bangladesh Army Chief Moeen Ahmed came to India on a six-day visit. He called on me too. During the informal interaction, I impressed upon him the importance of releasing political prisoners. He was apprehensive about his dismissal by Sheikh Hasina after her release. But I took personal responsibility and assured the General of his survival after Hasina's return to power. I also sought an appointment with the US President George W. Bush to request his intervention in the matter and ensure the release of both Khaleda Zia and Sheikh Hasina. With my intervention

---

[108] Arrival statement by H.E. Mr. Pranab Mukherjee Minister of External Affairs of India on his visit to Bangladesh on December 1, 2007, https://www.mea.gov.in/Speeches-Statements.htm?dtl/2049/Arrival_statement_by_HE_Mr_Pranab_Mukherjee_Minister_of_External_Affairs_of_India_on_his_visit_to_Bangladesh_on_December_1_2007

through the then National Security Advisor M.K. Narayanan, I ensured the release of all political prisoners and the nation's return to stability. Several years later, I also facilitated General Moeen's treatment in the US when he was suffering from cancer.

Sheikh Hasina had been a close family friend, and when I was the External Affairs Minister, India tried to help her cause by building adequate international pressure for free and fair elections after the caretaker government. In fact, when some Awami League leaders deserted her at the time she was in jail, I rebuked them for their stand and told them that to leave someone when they are down is unethical.

General election was held in December 2008, and Sheikh Hasina won with a thumping majority.[109]

Thereafter, India and Bangladesh worked to strengthen the bilateral relationship and engagement. Sheikh Hasina visited India in January 2010. It was a landmark visit and the subsequent Joint communiqué was comprehensive, forward-looking and path-breaking. I reiterated that we were firmly committed to implementing the vision when I visited Bangladesh in August 2010 to sign the $1 billion Line of Credit Agreement—the largest given by India to any country—between EXIM Bank and Government of Bangladesh.

Politics in Bangladesh has always been extremely virulent, marking a clear departure from West Bengal's political culture. The genesis of this phenomenon can be traced to the fact that all revolutionary leaders were recruited from middle-class Bengali Hindu families residing in East Bengal. This created a lasting impact on the people of the country. Another reason for the continued political violence in Bangladesh is the failure of military leaders

---

[109]Sheikh Hasina, Bangladesh Telecommunication Regulatory Commission, Government of the People's Republic of Bangladesh, http://www.btrc.gov.bd/content/sheikh-hasina

to resolve basic problems like poverty and unemployment.

PAKISTAN

As the Minister for External Affairs, I visited Pakistan in January 2006 to invite its President for the SAARC Summit. The Mumbai blasts of July 2006, which had cross-border linkages, had resulted in the postponement of Foreign Secretary-level talks. When Prime Minister Dr Manmohan Singh met President Pervez Musharraf in Havana in September 2006, it was decided to institute a joint anti-terror mechanism and resume the Composite Dialogue. The joint anti-terror mechanism was set up during Foreign Secretary-level talks in November 2006.

The Composite Dialogue Process with Pakistan entered its fifth round in 2008–09. The Dialogue had been premised, since its resumption in 2004, on the commitment made on 6 January 2004, that Pakistan would not permit territory under its control to be used to support terrorism in any form.

Notwithstanding some achievements in segments of the Composite Dialogue Process, terrorism and non-implementation of the 6 January 2004 commitments by Pakistan eroded the fundamental premise of this initiative. Terrorist attacks in India and on the Indian Embassy in Kabul in July 2008, increase in ceasefire violations and continued infiltration across the Line of Control (LoC) placed a strain on the dialogue process in particular, and India–Pakistan relations in general. Finally, the terrorist attacks on Mumbai on 26 November 2008 and concrete evidence of the involvement of elements in Pakistan in the attack led to the suspension of the dialogue process.

26/11

On 26 November 2008, Pakistani Foreign Minister Shah Mehmood Qureshi was in India at my invitation for official bilateral discussions. Normally, the Indian Foreign Minister hosts a lunch or dinner for his counterpart on the first day of the visit at Hyderabad House in New Delhi. In the normal course, discussions should have been followed by the dinner.

But the Pakistani Foreign Minister excused himself from the dinner as he had scheduled an engagement with his country's High Commissioner. He suggested that we could have lunch together the next day at Chandigarh. I agreed. He was invited, along with delegates from Pakistan's farming community, for a roundtable discussion at Chandigarh organized by the Centre for Research in Rural and Industrial Development, headed by Dr Rashpal Malhotra. Manmohan Singh was one of the founders of this centre. Enhancement of cooperation between India and Pakistan in the agriculture sector was the agenda for discussion.

After discussions with the Pakistani Foreign Minister, I left Hyderabad House for North Block. It was known to everybody in my office that I worked till late in the night and did not leave office before 8.30 or 9 p.m. At around 9 p.m., some of my staff members informed me about the news of a terrorist attack in Mumbai. We immediately switched on the TV in my office. I was shocked to see the audacity and scale of the attack, which took place at different locations. I came home at around midnight but could hardly take my eyes off the TV.

The next day, I received a situation report from both the Intelligence Bureau and Home Ministry. Home Minister Shivraj Patil, along with his team, had reached Mumbai at midnight. Then they returned to Delhi to file the report. Every news channel gave varying interpretations, estimating the number of people inside the hotels (Taj and Oberoi) and other details like the arrival of the terrorists through sea, their departure from Karachi Port, the capture of an Indian fishing vessel and the killing of its crew.

Then the question of continuing with Foreign Minister Qureshi's visit arose (I had already cancelled my visit in Chandigarh). The Foreign Secretary prepared a speaking note for me. The Pakistan High Commission informed us that their Foreign Minister was in the midst of a press conference with a group of women journalists. I interrupted the press conference through a journalist I knew personally and asked her to inform the visiting Foreign Minister that the Indian Foreign Minister wanted to talk to him urgently. When the Minister came on the line, I read out the note and concluded by adding:

> Mr Minister, no purpose will be served by your continuing to stay in India in these circumstances. I advise you to leave immediately. My official aircraft is available to take you back home whenever you find convenient. But it would be desirable if a decision is taken as quickly as possible.

After some time, the Pakistan High Commission informed me that their Foreign Minister had expressed his gratitude for the offer. I was told that a Pakistan Air Force aircraft would take him back home. On his return to Pakistan, the Minister told the media that he was extended all courtesies and diplomatic privileges in India. Though my note contained a strong message, I had remained courteous during the entire conversation.

Subsequently, there was a lot of speculation in the media about Indo–Pak relations. As usual, Pakistan was in denial mode and some Pakistani leaders maintained that the terrorists were non-state actors. My response was sharp and strong. When asked by the media, I asserted 'non-state actors do not come from heaven. They are located in the territory of a particular country.'

In this case, we had evidence that the terrorists came from Karachi port. They were dropped in mid-sea with a smaller vessel. They captured an Indian fishing vessel, killed the crew and finally killed the pilot, upon reaching Mumbai coast. All these records were available and in the possession of Indian authorities.

After the incident, the first call (of the many I received) was from the US Secretary of State, Condoleezza Rice. She was concerned about the fallout. I told her, 'The situation is grave. I do not believe in romanticizing relations or indulging in any sort of adventurism, but there is a limit to one's patience. We are truly concerned.' I also insisted that the US exert pressure on Pakistan to stop cross-border terrorism. I took strong exception to the sale of sophisticated arms and equipment to Pakistan by the US. I refused to buy their argument that these weapons were supplied to Pakistan for limiting the threats from terrorist groups like al-Qaeda and Taliban, and pointed out that they were actually being used against India.

I knew that time was of essence for the success of our diplomatic initiative to reach out to world leaders and expose Pakistan's nefarious designs. Over the next three days, I spoke over the telephone to foreign ministers of more than 100 countries across different time zones. Everybody expressed their solidarity with us and condemned the attack. They were concerned about the growing menace of terrorism. There were no takers for Pakistan's 'non-state actors' excuse. I did not seek support from Israel since it carried the risk of isolating 54 Islamic countries that backed India. The reaction from China was along expected lines. Though the leadership was very prompt in conveying its condolences to India, they did not accept the fact that the strikes were carried out by elements based in Pakistan. This cautious approach was managed largely by Pakistan. But the leadership did acknowledge the report on the attacks submitted by me.

Naturally, the reaction in the Indian Parliament was sharp. Amid heated debates within the Cabinet, there was a demand for military intervention which I rejected. I made an observation which was quoted frequently later:

> I do not believe there is any scope of romanticism in external relations. Similarly, I do not indulge in any sort of adventurism in guiding the foreign policy of the country... Dialogue is the only course available for resolution of all problems; unfortunately this process has been disrupted by this totally condemnable act of Pakistani terrorists. The proposed comprehensive dialogue between India and Pakistan is suspended till a conducive atmosphere is created.

One of the few lighter moments around this time was a particular incident which led to the Pakistan Air Force being put on alert and the armed forces ordered to meet any eventuality.

A call was allegedly made from my office to President Zardari threatening him of dire consequences. I heard about this from my office as I landed in Kolkata. On the way from the airport to my residence, I was told that the US Secretary of State was frantically trying to contact me. I called her as soon as I reached home. She enquired about the status of the situation and the veracity of the information that I had warned Pakistan of dire consequences. Though she did not tell me that she had been informed by Pakistani authorities, other sources told me that the information had indeed been provided to her by the Pakistani leadership who seemed to have genuinely panicked.

I told her 'If there was any such eventuality, do you believe that the Foreign Minister of the country would be 1,200 km away from the capital? I am in Kolkata and I am planning to go to my constituency, another 250 km away from the capital tomorrow. Whatever you have heard is nothing but rumours.'

Later, Pakistani newspaper, *Dawn,* reported that a hoax call was made to President Zardari's office by a person who was in a Pakistani jail.[110] He called the President's office and pretended that he was speaking from Pranab Mukherjee's office. The entire episode provided some comic relief in an otherwise tense situation.

FROM PATIL TO CHIDAMBARAM

This was also a time when several people came under heavy for criticism, one of them being Shivraj Patil.

A CWC meeting was held on 29 November during which the post-attack scenario was discussed. During this meeting, P. Chidambaram was stridently vocal against Shivraj Patil and advised a change of the Home Minister. I tried to bring the sentiment down a bit by saying that we should not blame an individual; we all have our weaknesses. Throughout this discussion Shivraj Patil remained stoically silent.

I got a call from Dr Singh on the morning of 1 December and he suggested that I meet him as soon as possible. I left for Race Course Road immediately. As I was driving in, I noticed that Shivraj Patil was driving out, but at that time I had no inkling of what was to happen. As soon as I was ushered into Dr Singh's office, he told me that Shivraj Patil had resigned, and that Sonia Gandhi had suggested that I take over as Home Minister. He went on to say that he advised Ms Gandhi against this as I was handling a war-like situation as the External Affairs Minister and that the ministry could not afford the change at this time. Hence, it was decided that P. Chidambaram would replace

---

[110]'A hoax call that could have triggered war', *Dawn,* 6 December 2008, https://www.dawn.com/news/333312/a-hoax-call-that-could-have-triggered-war

Shivraj Patil. It was at about this time that Chidambaram too joined the meeting, and we discussed the transition.[111]

DEBATE IN PARLIAMENT

There was a full-fledged debate in both the Houses of Parliament on the Mumbai attacks. The debate began with a suo moto statement by the Home Minister.[112] Members from all parties condemned the terrorists and Pakistan in the strongest of terms.

Intervening in the debate to point out the external factors and elements associated with this attack, I told Parliament that the epicentre of this attack, and the series of attacks prior to this, was located in a neighbouring country.

> Since November 26, more than 16 Heads of States and Governments have spoken to our Prime Minister over telephone and expressed their concern. Almost every Head of State and Head of Government has sent written messages and I have received a large number of calls from my counterparts all over the world... We are not provoked. We have no intention to be provoked... Yes, we should build up an international campaign against terrorism and explain to all the countries concerned that this is not an India–Pakistan issue... This is an issue which is part of the whole issue of global terrorism.[113]

---

[111]'Home minister Shivraj Patil quits, Chidambaram to take over', *The Times of India*, 30 November 2008, New Delhi http://timesofindia.indiatimes.com/india/Home-minister-Shivraj-Patil-quits-Chidambaram-to-take-over/articleshow/3775666.

[112]Appendix 5: Text of Home Minister P. Chidambaram's Speech in the Lok Sabha on the Mumbai Terror Attacks.

[113]Text of External Affairs Minister Mr Pranab Mukherjee's oral intervention in the Lok Sabha during the debate on the Mumbai Attacks, Embassy Archives, Embassy

I spelt out the demands I had conveyed to the Pakistani Foreign Minister on 28 November 2008, which urged that action be taken against organizations indulging in terrorist activities and against fugitives who have taken shelter in Pakistan. I stated Pakistan must completely dismantle infrastructure facilities available to facilitate terrorist infiltration and terrorist attacks in India. However, organizations have continued to be active in Pakistan even after they were banned by simply changing names and signboards.

India has suggested to Pakistan several times, in international and bilateral fora through dialogue and communication that they should deny sanctuary to terrorists. Pakistan has assured us of positive steps in the direction. But mere expression of intent is inadequate. Pakistan, during telephonic discussions with the Prime Minister, initially offered that ISI's director general would visit India, but this was later denied. There are internal problems such as this in Pakistan, but it is not going to help India. We have to deal with Pakistan. We cannot change our neighbour; neither can we live with them in perpetual tension. The issues will have to be addressed.

Following the debate in the Parliament, on 11 December 2008, the Lok Sabha decided in a solemn resolution that 'India shall not cease in her efforts until the terrorists and those who have trained, funded and abetted them are exposed and brought to justice.'

Our efforts internationally to seek justice and ensure that such attacks do not recur resulted in the UN Al-Qaeda and Taliban Sanctions Committee listing individual entities based in Pakistan, including leaders of the Lashkar-e-Taiba (LeT), under Security Council Resolution 1267. The Jamaat-ud-Dawa

---

of India, Washington DC USA, https://www.indianembassy.org/archives_details.php?nid=941

(JuD) was also listed as an alias of the LeT. On 12 February 2009, the Indian High Commissioner in Islamabad was formally informed of Pakistan's response to the dossier that India had made available on 5 January linking the terrorist attacks on Mumbai to perpetrators in Pakistan. In their response, Pakistani authorities admitted that elements in Pakistan were involved in the Mumbai attacks. Pakistan also sought further information and material relating to the investigation.

On 13 February 2009, I made the following suo moto statement in the Parliament on 'Follow-up to Mumbai terrorist attack.' In this statement, I said:

> Hon'ble Members will appreciate that Government has constantly been guided by the two objectives of ensuring that the perpetrators who planned, organized and trained the terrorists in Pakistan are brought to justice, and that the infrastructure of terrorism which exists in Pakistan is dismantled so that we prevent a recurrence of such attacks. The international community has also worked with us, using its influence on Pakistan to ensure that the terrorist infrastructure and the support provided to such elements is put to an end, since terrorism emanating out of Pakistan is a threat not only to us, but to the world. We will continue to review the situation including Pakistan's responses and will take further steps that we deem necessary in order to protect our people.
>
> The threat of terrorism from Pakistan has emerged as a global menace and cancer. The major onus of responsibility to eliminate this threat rests on the Government of Pakistan. It is imperative that it acts with sincerity and acts effectively against the licence that terrorist groups enjoy on its territory. It is essential that the assurances given to us repeatedly at

the highest level by Pakistani leaders are implemented as solemn commitments.

We are at a point in our relationship where the authorities in Pakistan itself have to choose the kind of relationship that they want with India in the future. Much depends on actions in the Mumbai case reaching their logical conclusion. I must underline that we have no quarrel with the people of Pakistan. We wish them well and we do not think that they should be held responsible or face the consequences of this situation. We have, therefore, consciously and after due deliberation, not thought it necessary or fit to curtail people to people contacts, trains and road links.[114]

My stay in the External Affairs Ministry was an eventful one with several significant developments on the foreign policy front. We geared up to deal with the increasingly challenging global landscape by strengthening our own mechanism. During my tenure, there were several important initiatives that deserve a mention. The Passport Seva project was initiated to make the issue of passports to citizens more transparent, accessible, timely and reliable. The project began after the National Institute for Smart Government, Hyderabad, commissioned to study the IT aspects of this initiative, submitted its report in 2007. The issue of manpower at the headquarters, missions and posts of the Ministry of External Affairs was addressed. An expansion plan was sanctioned by the Cabinet, authorizing the creation of 514 posts over a 10-year period beginning 2008. The decision to re-establish the famed Nalanda University was also taken. The

---

[114]External Affairs Ministry's Suo Motu statement in the Parliament on Follow Up to Mumbai Terrorist Attack, New Delhi, 13 February 2009, http://mea.gov.in/in-focus-article.htm?927/EAMs+Suo+Motu+statement+in+Parliament+on+Follow+Up+to+Mumbai+Terrorist+Attack

ancient seat of learning was renowned for its internationalism. Hence, the proposal was shared with the leaders of East Asia at its Summit in Cebu, Philippines, in January 2007. Today, Nalanda University is fully functional.

CHAPTER 8

INDIA–US CIVIL NUCLEAR COOPERATION AGREEMENT

One of the most satisfying achievements of my tenure as the Minister of External Affairs was the signing of the Indo–US Civil Nuclear Agreement in October 2008. This was not merely because the deal went through a challenging procedural maze of enactments and agreements, which we successfully managed to overcome, but also because the government, having been fully convinced of its benefits for the country, took a principled stand to see the process through. We achieved this despite stiff political resistance from opposition parties, including the Left who were part of the ruling coalition. The UPA government not only faced the acid test of convincing the nation at large of the utility of such an agreement, it also had to withstand a No-confidence Motion in the Lok Sabha after the withdrawal of support by the Left parties. The Congress-led UPA government not only won the trust vote and remained in power, but also came back in power after the 2009 general election to form the government again. This election verdict was a vindication of our stand on the Indo–US Civil Nuclear Cooperation Agreement, besides the numerous programmes and initiatives taken by the UPA government that were bearing fruit.

BACKGROUND

Before I delve into the action that surrounded the nuclear deal, a background would be in order. An international legal architecture had existed for almost four decades to prevent the spread of nuclear weapons and technology, and promote cooperation in the use of nuclear energy for the purpose of peace. This was the Treaty on the Non-Proliferation of Nuclear Weapons, or commonly known as the Non-Proliferation Treaty (NPT). The principle bargaining standpoint of this Treaty was that the NPT states would never acquire nuclear weapons and, in exchange, the nuclear-weapon states would share the benefits of peaceful nuclear technology with them.

The NPT came into force in 1970. India refused to sign it and has remained outside its ambit, as have some other UN member states such as Pakistan, Israel and South Sudan.

India's refusal is based on the principled stand that this treaty is unfair. It divides nations into two groups: the 'nuclear haves' and the 'nuclear have-nots'.[115] The NPT allows some states to legally possess nuclear weapons—those which tested them before 1967—thus creating this division. In effect, these 'privileged' nations are free to own a nuclear arsenal and are at liberty to multiply the same.

India has always insisted on a time-bound action plan for universal and comprehensive non-proliferation towards a nuclear-free world. That our intentions have been honourable as well as rational can be gauged by the fact that India has also adopted

---

[115] *India Energy Policy, Laws and Regulations Handbook*, USA International Business Publications, p 35, 2009.

a voluntary no first use (NFU) policy.[116]

In addition to the NPT framework, there exists a multinational body called the Nuclear Suppliers Group (NSG). It was founded purportedly in response to the nuclear tests conducted in May 1974 by India, which showed that certain nuclear technology meant for peaceful purposes could be used for weapons' development. The NSG operates on guidelines for export control of nuclear material, equipment and technology. These guidelines allow nuclear exports after meeting stringent conditions relating to the safeguards by the International Atomic Energy Agency (IAEA). The safeguards basically ensure that a country does not switch nuclear energy from peaceful to weapons use. India is yet to be admitted as a member of the NSG despite the support from countries like the US, the UK and France.

In a scenario where India found herself outside the boundary of the global nuclear structure, it was not only expedient but also compelling to develop indigenous resources for nuclear power generation and reactor technology. But the challenges were many. India had envisaged reaching a nuclear power generation capacity of 20,000 MW by the year 2020. In 2007, we had a capacity of about 3,700 MW. However, the amount of nuclear fuel needed for power generation of this magnitude was very high. Our estimated uranium reserves that accounted for a mere 1 per cent of the known uranium reserves in the world were grossly inadequate. It was clearly evident that the restrictions imposed by the NSG would restrain our intended growth in nuclear power generation capacity. Hence, it was felt that cooperation in the sphere of energy with the US and other nuclear resource-rich nations would help us secure a steady

---

[116] *India Energy Policy, Laws and Regulations Handbook*, USA International Business Publications, p 35, 2009.

supply of fuel to meet our domestic energy requirements.

It is equally true that the US saw a window of opportunity for their industry to secure enhanced business cooperation with India. Nuclear isolation had driven India to expand her nuclear programme with indigenous technology. Through the ingenuity of her scientists, India had become proficient in fast-breeder technologies. There was a realization in the West particularly in the US, that by limiting India's access to nuclear technology, it was in effect preventing itself to achieve the desired legroom to access India's nuclear technological developments. The international sanctions imposed on us after the nuclear tests at Pokhran in May 1998 did not have any major impact on the economy. In fact, the GDP growth rate which was 5 per cent[117] in 1997–98, accelerated to 5.8 per cent[118] and 5.9 per cent over the next two years.[119] Consequently, sanctions were dropped by the US in 2001. In its place, a strategic partnership between India and the US had evolved.

As mentioned earlier, I had, as Defence Minister in June 2005, signed the 'new framework for the US–India defence relationship for the next ten years' with my US counterpart, US Secretary of Defence, Donald Rumsfeld. The new framework provided opportunities in areas such as technology transfer, co-production and research and development. The major agreement was on expansion of defence trade. It stressed that the defence relationship would support and be part of the larger evolving bilateral strategic partnership.

---

[117] Economic Survey 1997-98, Government of India: Ministry of Finance, http://indiabudget.nic.in/es97-98/chap111.pdf

[118] Economic Survey 1998-99, Government of India: Ministry of Finance, http://indiabudget.nic.in/es98-99/table12a.htm

[119] Economic Survey 1999-2000, Government of India: Ministry of Finance, http://indiabudget.nic.in/es99-2000/table12.htm

Earlier in January 2004, the Next Steps in Strategic Partnership (NSSP) initiative was launched under which India and the US agreed to expand cooperation in the areas of civilian nuclear activities, civilian space programmes and high-technology trade. Over the next one and a half years, the two governments worked together to conclude the NSSP. The conclusion of this initiative coincided with the visit of Prime Minister Manmohan Singh to the US. An India–US Joint Statement was made on 18 July 2005 after Singh met with US President George Bush.[120] The statement recognized the significance of civilian nuclear energy for meeting growing global energy demands in a cleaner and more efficient manner.

President Bush told Dr Singh that he would work to achieve full civil nuclear energy cooperation with India as the US realizes India's goals of promoting nuclear power and achieving energy security. He said he would seek agreement from the US Congress to adjust their laws and policies. The US would work with friends and allies to regulate international regimes to enable full civil nuclear energy cooperation and trade with India. Dr Singh conveyed that India would reciprocally agree that it would be ready to assume the same responsibilities and practices and acquire the same benefits and advantages as other leading countries with advanced nuclear technology.

Civil nuclear cooperation between India and the US promised enormous strategic and economic benefits to both the countries, particularly energy security, a more environment-friendly energy source and robust non-proliferation efforts. Keeping this in perspective, between June 2006 and July 2007, five rounds of negotiations between India and the US were held. Finally, on the successful conclusion of the negotiations, Condoleezza Rice

---

[120]Appendix 6: India–US Joint Statement.

and I issued a joint statement on 27 July 2007:[121]

> The United States and India have reached a historic milestone in their strategic partnership by completing negotiations on the bilateral agreement for peaceful nuclear cooperation, also known as the '123 Agreement'. This agreement will govern civil nuclear trade between our two countries and open the door for American and Indian firms to participate in each other's civil nuclear energy sector... This achievement reinforces the growing bilateral relationship between two vibrant democracies. We are committed to the strategic partnership outlined by President Bush and Prime Minister Manmohan Singh, and look forward to working together to implement this historic initiative.

The completion of negotiations of the 123 Agreement was followed by further discussions. The next steps included India negotiating an India-specific safeguards agreement with the IAEA. India also needed support from the 45-member NSG (it has 48 members now) for a modification of their guidelines to enable NSG to enter into nuclear cooperation and trade with India. The US, in accordance with the July 2005 joint statement, would work with friends and allies in the NSG to drive the desired change. Once these processes were complete, the text of the 123 Agreement would have to be submitted to the US Congress for approval. But before the next steps could be initiated, there were several challenges in store for us on the domestic turf.

MANAGING THE COALITION

The 123 Agreement had evoked mixed reactions from the political

---

[121]'Joint Statement', *Outlook*, 27 July 2007, https://www.outlookindia.com/website/story/joint-statement/235172

class, policymakers, scholars and scientists. The Left parties, who were part of the UPA coalition but not part of the government, made their stand clear through a statement on 7 August 2007 in which they opposed the Agreement. They contended that since the Nuclear Cooperation Agreement was an integral part of the July 2005 joint statement that had political, economic and strategic aspects, it was 'not possible to view the text of the bilateral 123 Agreement negotiated with the US as a separate and compartmentalized entity without considering its implications for India's independent foreign policy, strategic autonomy and the repercussions of the US quest to make India its reliable ally in Asia.'[122]

While it may not be possible to outline in minute detail every aspect that the Left parties were opposed to, given below are some of the major points of their contention:

- The Hyde Act, though an internal law of the US, would apply to the 123 Agreement which legitimizes the US to abide by its national laws. The Hyde Act could be invoked to terminate the 123 Agreement if India tests a nuclear device or if India does not conform to US foreign policy.
- As per the terms in the Hyde Act, 'full civil nuclear cooperation', which found mention in the 123 Agreement, would not be possible as cooperation or access would be denied in any form to fuel enrichment, reprocessing and heavy water production technologies. The denial would extend to transfers of dual use items that could be used in enrichment, reprocessing or heavy water production

---

[122]Prakash Karat, A.B. Bardhan, Abani Roy, Devarajan, 'Unable To Accept The Agreement', *Outlook*, 7 August 2007, https://www.outlookindia.com/website/story/unable-to-accept-the-agreement/235261

facility. Fast-breeder reactors under the Agreement would be treated as part of the fuel cycle. Any technology required for this would come under dual-use technology and hence would be denied.

- Though the Agreement spelt out India's acceptance of safeguards in perpetuity, the linkage of such safeguards with fuel supply in perpetuity remained unclear. While there was the US assurance to enable India to build a strategic fuel reserve as a guard against disruption of fuel supply during the lifetime of the nuclear reactors, the continuance of fuel supply after cessation or termination of the Agreement would depend solely on the US Congress. Under the Hyde Act, the US would work with other NSG countries to stop fuel and other supplies to India if the 123 Agreement is terminated under the US laws. Thus, fuel supply from the US would cease not only in case the US decides to terminate the Agreement, but it would also be incumbent on the US under the Hyde Act to work with the NSG to block all future supplies.
- As far as the energy dimension is concerned, nuclear energy can never be central to India's energy security. Even if the nuclear power generation capacity of 20,000 MW is achieved in two decades, it can at best meet 7 per cent of India's energy requirement. On the cost dimension, the cost of power from imported reactors ranges from ₹4.60 to ₹5 per unit as against power from coal-fired units that ranges from ₹2.20 to ₹2.60 per unit.

On the day the Hyde Act was passed by the US Congress, I had clarified that 'there are prescriptive provisions in respect of the Hyde Act which are not applicable to us and we will not accept it. If the US wanted to impose the conditions of

14. May 2004: Pranab Mukherjee with Sonia Gandhi and Abdul Mannan Hossain during an election campaign in Murshidabad.

15. May 2004: Pranab Mukherjee, Prime Minister Dr Manmohan Singh and Sitaram Yechury share a light moment as Jaipal Reddy and Shish Ram Ola look on, after the swearing in ceremony at the Rashtrapati Bhavan.

16. December 2005: Defence Minister Pranab Mukherjee with Army Chief General J.J. Singh (L), and Air Force Chief Air Chief Marshal S.P. Tyagi (R) during Vijay Diwas celebrations in New Delhi.

17. *October 2006: Defence Minister Pranab Mukherjee interacts with officers and jawans in the Siachen Glacier.*

18. January 2007: External Affairs Minister Pranab Mukherjee meets Pakistani President Pervez Musharraf in Islamabad.

19. February 2007: Crown Prince of Bhutan Jigme Khesar Namgyel Wangchuck and External Affairs Minister Pranab Mukherjee exchange the agreement of the 2007 MoU of India–Bhutan friendship in the presence of Dr Manmohan Singh in New Delhi.

20. *March 2008: External Affairs Minister Pranab Mukherjee meets United States President George W. Bush at the White House in Washington.*

21. May 2008: *External Affairs Minister Pranab Mukherjee and Sitaram Yechury CPI(M) leader after the UPA-Left meeting on the Indo–US civil nuclear deal.*

22. June 2008: *External Affairs Minister Pranab Mukherjee and Foreign Minister of Pakistan Makhdoom Shah Mahmood Qureshi at delegation level talks in New Delhi.*

23. October 2008: External Affairs Minister Pranab Mukherjee with US Secretary of State Condoleezza Rice prior to a meeting at Hyderabad House in New Delhi.

24. September 2008: Dr Manmohan Singh, Sonia Gandhi and Pranab Mukherjee at the meeting of the Extended CWC in New Delhi.

25. November 2008: External Affairs Minister Pranab Mukherjee with Foreign Ministers of Nepal, Bhutan, Sri Lanka, Myanmar, Bangladesh and Thailand at the second summit of the Bay of Bengal Initiative for Multi-Sectoral Technical and Economic Cooperation (BIMSTEC) meeting in New Delhi.

the Hyde Act or if they wanted to link their cooperation with India with reference to the Hyde Act, it would constitute a breaking point.' I maintained that we would never compromise on our independent foreign policy. We scrupulously avoided any prescriptive provision in the Agreement and informed officials negotiating on behalf of India to be careful on this count. The Hyde Act generated a lot of debate in the Parliament and we explained the position. As the leader of the House (Lok Sabha), it was my responsibility to maintain communication and share our views in the matter.

JOINT UPA–LEFT COMMITTEE

Nevertheless, due to the concerns raised by the Left parties, the government, on 30 August 2007, announced that a mechanism would be established to evaluate their objections. Thus, a Joint UPA–Left committee was constituted. The Congress was represented by P. Chidambaram, Kapil Sibal, Salman Khurshid and Veerappa Moily. From the Left, A.B. Bardhan and Sudhakar Reddy represented the CPI, Prakash Karat and Sitaram Yechury brought forth the views of the CPM, while Debabrata Biswas and Chandrachoodan and Abani Roy were members of the group from the Forward Bloc and Revolutionary Socialist Party (RSP), respectively. I was made the convener of this group.

It was decided that the committee's findings would be taken into account before the operationalization of the civil nuclear cooperation.

The complete absence of a convergence of interests between the two sides meant that tempers ran high in every meeting of the committee. These meetings, conducted at my residence, were followed by a joint press briefing by Sitaram and myself. Prakash Karat was absolutely clear that the Left would not support any agreement with the US. In my assessment, Karat also believed that Sonia Gandhi would call off the deal owing to the stiff opposition from the Left. But I was determined to pursue it, despite this resistance, with a view to bolster our country's ever-increasing energy requirements.

The committee met nine times between September 2007 and June 2008. The Left parties submitted six notes and rejoinders on the issues examined by the committee. The UPA, in response, submitted five notes, including one response to two rejoinders sent by the Left parties on the same day.

In our response to the Left parties we mentioned:

> 'Hyde Act does not apply to India. India's commitment will arise from the 123 bilateral cooperation agreement which once approved by the US Congress will become law. The 123 agreement as the prevailing law will then delineate the specific rights and the responsibility of the US and India that govern and control the agreement's implementation.'[123]

The Agreement is not circumscribed by the various US laws and stands on its own since customary international law (Articles 26 and 27 of the Vienna Convention on the Law of Treaties, 1969) would ensure that the Hyde Act does not apply to India or override the agreement. Besides, the US Constitution provided for the treaties made under the authority of the US Government to be the supreme law of the land.

SOVEREIGN RIGHT TO TEST

The 123 Agreement provided for full civil nuclear energy

---

[123]'Left stand on civil nuclear deal—Notes exchanged in the UPA-Left Committee on the India-US Civil Nuclear Cooperation', Progressive Printers, https://cpim.org/upa/2008_nuclear-notes.pdf

cooperation covering nuclear reactors and aspects of the associated nuclear fuel cycle, including enrichment and reprocessing. It provided for nuclear trade; transfer of nuclear material, equipment, components and related technologies; and for cooperation in nuclear fuel cycle activities. The Agreement also provided specifically that India's strategic nuclear programme, three-stage nuclear programme and R&D activities would remain unhindered and unaffected. This aspect was earlier highlighted by Dr Singh in the Parliament on 17 August 2006.

It was emphasized as questions were raised about whether India would retain her right to undertake nuclear tests once the civil nuclear agreement with the US came into force. I had already made a statement in the Parliament (16 August 2007) to dispel any misperception in this regard. I reiterated that India retained the sovereign right to test and would do so if it was necessary in national interest. The only restraint would be our voluntary unilateral moratorium on nuclear testing, declared by the previous government and being continued by the successive government. I went on to assure everyone that there was nothing in the bilateral Agreement that would tie the hands of future governments or legally constrain their options. I hoped to have laid this doubt to rest.

A COSTLY SOURCE OF POWER?

The Left parties seemed to have doubts on the need for a civil nuclear cooperation. They suggested that nuclear power was not only expensive as compared to other sources, it was also unlikely to be a major component in our nation's energy mix. This proposition needed to be examined from the standpoint of the energy deficit the country was likely to face in the future.

It was projected that the energy deficit taking into account all sources—thermal, hydel, petrol, diesel and even non-conventional sources—would be to the tune of 1,50,000 MW by 2030. The deficit would further rise to 4,12,000 MW in 20 years time. Assuming we begin to seriously expand our nuclear power capacity starting in 2008, some studies suggested that we could produce about 40,000 MW annually between 2012 and 2020. This had the potential to reduce the energy deficit to only 50,000 MW by 2030 and 7,000 MW by 2050.

As regards to the comparative cost of power, some studies suggested a cost advantage for nuclear power generation. A 2005 study, 'Economics of Light Water Reactors in India' had shown that at 5 per cent real discount rate, the levelled cost of generation in paise/kWh was 114 for nuclear power, 160 for domestic coal (at 800 km from pithead), 162 for imported coal at port, and 179 for gas. Of course, it is not easy to do a comparative costing of different energy sources as several other factors are also involved. For instance, the future cost of traditional sources of energy like hydrocarbons will be an important input as India is heavily dependent on hydrocarbon imports.[124]

THOSE IN FAVOUR

In an open letter to MPs, which was carried in *The Indian Express* on 15 November 2007, former military chiefs, bureaucrats and scientists argued that the Agreement with the US was absolutely essential not only from the point of removing existing constraints on our nuclear programme, but also for India to evolve as one of the principal powers in the community of nations.[125] As regards

---

[124]'Left stand on civil nuclear deal—Notes exchanged in the UPA-Left Committee on the India-US Civil Nuclear Cooperation', Progressive Printers, https://cpim.org/upa/2008_nuclear-notes.pdf p 44–45.

[125]'The question is can we get a better n-deal? No', *The Indian Express*, 15

the charge that the Agreement would make India subservient to the US, the letter stated that 'international relationships are shaped by strength, the stronger you are the greater your freedom of action. We believe India is more vulnerable to foreign pressures without this agreement than we would be by increasing our strength through an intelligent use of it to put through various development programmes which currently falter.' Earlier, roughly two months after the negotiations had begun, nine nuclear scientists—all former heads of nuclear-related institutions in India—had issued an appeal to the MPs that was carried in *The Hindu* on 15 August 2006.[126] The scientists called the initiation of the nuclear agreement with the US 'a most welcome initiative of the UPA government.'

NEGOTIATIONS WITH THE IAEA ON THE SAFEGUARDS AGREEMENT

In a meeting of the Joint UPA–Left Committee held on 16 November 2007, it was decided that the government should start negotiations with IAEA on a safeguards agreement. It was further agreed that the outcome of the negotiations would be presented to the Committee for its consideration, and that their findings would be taken into account before operationalization of the Indo–US civil nuclear cooperation agreement. At the seventh meeting of the committee held in March 2008, the outcome of the talks with IAEA was reported, but a copy of the text of the safeguards agreement was not provided. This became the subject

---

November 2007, www.indianexpress.com/news/the-question-is-can-we-get-a-better-ndeal-no/239308/0

[126]'Appeal to parliamentarians on nuclear deal', *The Hindu*, 15 August 2006, http://www.thehindu.com/todays-paper/tp-opinion/appeal-to-parliamentarians-on-nuclear-deal/article3090406.ece

of much consternation amongst the Left parties.

We explained that we could not share the text because of varied country protocols regarding methods of treating documents. IAEA used the phrase restricted and de-restricted. Officials said that they could not bind any sovereign country with their documents, except the agency itself. Therefore, we informed the Left parties that we would have to wait for the text to be circulated as an agenda for the approval of the Board of Governors of IAEA before it was made available.

When the discussions veered towards the likely fate of the IAEA safeguards agreement at a press conference in Delhi on 8 July in the context of the imminent pull-out of support for the government by the Left parties, I stated that I could not bind the government if we lost our majority. What I essentially meant was that if the government had to prove a majority in the Lok Sabha and failed to do so, it would not be in a position to go ahead with the Agreement. Taking the India-specific safeguards agreement to the IAEA Board for approval was not tantamount to signing the Agreement, and hence, it could be taken to the Board by us even before a trust vote.

The Left parties interpreted my statement differently. They held that the government would send the safeguards agreement to the IAEA Board only if we won the trust vote in the Parliament.

On the same day, Dr Manmohan Singh was attending the G-8 summit in Japan as an observer. There, he made a remark that the government would submit the India-specific safeguards agreement to the IAEA Board very soon. In the light of the Prime Minister's remark, the Left parties accused us of going back on our commitment—ostensibly given by me—and withdrew support to the UPA.

I tried to reason with the Left and sought the intervention of Jyoti Basu, who was convinced about the merit of the nuclear deal. Jyoti Basu spoke to Prakash Karat and suggested that there might be value in Karat meeting me. Karat did meet me, but remained vehement in his opposition, and maintained that the Left would join hands with the BJP to vote the UPA out. His open defiance of Jyoti Basu and the Bengal lobby was quite surprising. I believe that Ramachandran Pillai and K. Balakrishnan incited Karat to lead the Left agenda.

THE LEFT WITHDRAWS

I had convened a meeting of the Joint UPA–Left Committee on 10 July (its 10th meeting) to consider the draft report of the Committee so as to finalize the findings that could be taken into account by the government. But the Left parties had already decided to withdraw their support to the UPA government.

In the letter of withdrawal of support addressed to President Pratibha Patil on 9 July, the Left Front requested the President to direct the UPA government to seek a Vote of Confidence in the Parliament.[127] The Bahujan Samaj Party (BSP) had earlier (on 21 June) withdrawn support of its 17 MPs, accusing the Congress-led UPA coalition of supposedly neglecting and adopting a negative approach towards UP. To my mind, the reasons were deeper and probably stemmed from their unreasonable expectation of getting a clean chit in the Taj Corridor case, which had Mayawati embroiled in it. Now with the withdrawal of support of 59 MPs belonging to the Left Front parties, the UPA government was likely to become a minority government.

However, on the very same day, within hours, the Samajwadi Party (SP) submitted a letter to President Patil pledging the support of its 39 members in the Lok Sabha to the UPA alliance.

---

[127]'Letter of withdrawal by Left parties to President Pratibha Patil, 9 July 2008, Rashtrapati Bhavan, New Delhi.

CPI (M) General Secretary Prakash Karat read out his letter to me, through which the Left Front planned to approach the President to submit the list of MPs withdrawing support. The last line of that letter mentioned that '...the time has come to withdraw support.' The time in India was 12.30 hours then, but the time in Vienna (where the safeguards agreement would be sent to the IAEA Board as agenda) was only 09.00 hours. The next course of action (that is, the submission of the text of the agreement to the IAEA Board and its release thereafter), had happened subsequent to the withdrawal of support and not before. Hence, there was no question of betrayal of the Left partners in any way!

VOTE OF CONFIDENCE

The UPA government now had to seek a Vote of Confidence in the Lok Sabha. At a meeting with President Pratibha Patil on 10 July, Dr Singh expressed the desire to seek a trust vote at the earliest. The Cabinet Committee on Political Affairs met on the morning of 11 July to recommend the dates, which was later endorsed at a meeting of the full Union Cabinet. On 11 July, the UPA government sent a communication to the President to recommend the convening of a special session of the Lok Sabha on 21–22 July to enable it to seek a Vote of Confidence.

When Dr Manmohan Singh moved the Motion of Confidence in the Lok Sabha on 21 July, he also expressed that the exercise was wholly avoidable. He remarked:

> I had repeatedly assured all political parties, including the Left, that if the Government was allowed to complete the negotiations with the IAEA on its safeguards agreement, and after the decision of the Nuclear Suppliers Group (NSG), I would myself come to the Parliament and seek its

guidance before operationalizing the Civil Nuclear Energy Cooperation Agreement, which we intended to enter into.[128]

The first to speak on the motion was the leader of the Opposition, L.K. Advani, who said that we did not follow the coalition dharma. CPI leader Gurudas Dasgupta, who spoke later in the evening that day, accused us of 'aggressive unilateralism'. It did not seem proper to them to recognize what we had been doing: carrying all UPA constituents all along through the common minimum programme.

The coalition government of the UPA was formed in 2004 with outside support of the Left parties. It was a convenient arrangement for them as they could take credit for the achievements of the UPA and duck the brickbats. Was it really unilateralism that the UPA government practised vis-à-vis the Left parties? What about the Joint UPA–Left Committee established as an instrument for holding consultations with the Left parties before arriving at any decision over the nuclear cooperation agreement? In any case, the parties opposed to the motion were trying to do their best to embarrass the government over trivial issues.

After L.K. Advani and CPI's Mohammad Salim spoke on the motion, I decided to intervene. I submitted certain facts and figures with regard to the strength of the UPA and its supporters. Prior to the withdrawal of support by the BSP and the Left parties, the total strength of the UPA government along with its supporters was 317—UPA: 234, CPI(M): 43, CPI: 10, RSP: 3, Forward Bloc: 3, Kerala Congress: 1, BSP: 17, Rashtriya Lok Dal: 3, Independents/Unattached: 3. With the withdrawal of BSP+ (19) and Left Front (61), our strength came down to 237.

---

[128] PM's reply to the debate on the Motion of Confidence in the Lok Sabha, 22 July 2008, http://archivepmo.nic.in/drmanmohansingh/pmsinparliament.php?nodeid=32

However, with the Samajwadi Party's 39 members, the strength of the government rose to 276, which was more than the number required for a simple majority in a House whose effective voting strength at that time was 541. I asserted that the government could not become a minority unless proven otherwise. I also highlighted the imperative of signing the civil nuclear cooperation agreement and the various procedural formalities that required to be fulfilled. On a point raised by L.K. Advani about seeking parliamentary approval before signing important international agreements, I said that the constitutional position, since 26 January 1950, had been that the authority to sign international agreements rests with the Executive. I cited the example of an important agreement, the Indo–Soviet Treaty of Peace, Friendship and Cooperation in 1970, where the Parliament came to know of it after the agreement had been signed. But in the case of the civil nuclear cooperation agreement, numerous statements had been made by both the Prime Minister and myself in the Parliament and several debates had already taken place on this subject. I really did not understand why L.K. Advani raised this issue making it seem as if the Executive branch of the government had tried to overlook the Parliament.

The facts spoke otherwise. Though we were not required to seek parliamentary sanction on the civil nuclear cooperation agreement, which is an international treaty, we had taken the Parliament into confidence and had frequently informed it about various developments. We told our Left partners to allow us to go through the negotiating process after which we would seek parliamentary approval prior to operationalizing the nuclear agreement.

The debate went on till 10 p.m. after which the Lok Sabha was adjourned till 11.00 hours the next morning. The next day, 48 MPs spoke before Dr Singh stood up to say:

The nuclear agreement that we wish to negotiate will end India's nuclear isolation, nuclear apartheid and enable us to take advantage of international trade in nuclear materials, technologies and equipment. It will open up new opportunities for trade in dual use high technologies opening up new pathways to accelerate industrialization of our country. Given the excellent quality of our nuclear scientists and technologists, I have reasons to believe that in a reasonably short period of time, India would emerge as an important exporter of nuclear technologies, and equipment for civilian purposes.

Thereafter, the House went for a vote. The UPA won the trust vote by 275 votes against 256 and remained in power for the remainder of the five-year term.

We were confident of proving our majority in the Lok Sabha on 22 July. Hence, we simultaneously prepared our strategies to face the IAEA and then the NSG. The government set up an eight-member, high-powered team to tour the 45 member nations of the NSG to make them favourable towards the Indo–US civil nuclear agreement. The team comprised Union ministers—Prithviraj Chavan, Anand Sharma and Kapil Sibal; National Security Adviser M.K. Narayanan; government interlocutor on the India-US nuclear agreement, Shyam Saran; Foreign Secretary Shiv Shankar Menon; and two senior officials from the Ministry of External Affairs.

On 1 August 2008, the Board of Governors of the IAEA approved the India-specific agreement for the application of safeguards to civilian nuclear facilities. The safeguards agreement, of course, recognized the three basic imperatives for India in respect of her nuclear programme: one, that India attaches significance to civilian nuclear energy as an efficient, clean and sustainable energy source for meeting global energy demand, in particular for meeting India's growing energy needs; two, India is committed to the full development of its national three-stage nuclear programme to meet the twin challenges of energy security and environment protection; and three, India has a sovereign and inalienable right to carry out nuclear research and development activities for the welfare of its people and other peaceful purposes.

After the deal at the IAEA, the next stage was to get an exemption from the NSG for India from its guidelines to allow complete nuclear cooperation and trade. A plenary meeting of the group was to be held in Vienna on 4 and 5 September 2008. On the eve of the meeting, on 3 September, *The Washington Post* carried a report of a secret correspondence between the US State department and the US Congress indicating that the US would stop nuclear fuel supply to India if we conducted a nuclear test.[129] No doubt, there was opposition to the Indo–US nuclear deal not only in India but also in the US. It appeared that such opponents released this letter, ostensibly written in January, to the media in September 2008 to thwart India's efforts to seek NSG's approval for which discussions were at the final stages.

The disclosure took us by surprise, but more than that, it revived a political battle for a government that barely a month ago had successfully overcome a No-confidence Motion in the Lower House of Parliament. The government had always maintained a bona fide position that India had the sovereign right to undertake a nuclear test and would do so if it was expedient in national interest. In the light of this report, there was a huge uproar led by the Opposition, which insisted that

---

[129] Glenn Kessler, 'In Secret Letter, Tough U.S. Line on India Nuclear Deal', *The Washington Post,* 3 September 2008, http://www.washingtonpost.com/wp-dyn/content/article/2008/09/02/AR2008090202733.html

the government had made false assurances to the Parliament and that it should resign for the alleged deceit.

In an official statement released on 3 September itself, the government countered the news report stating that while its attention had been drawn to that particular report, it did not, as a matter of policy, comment on internal correspondence between different branches of another government. We reiterated that the government would continue to be guided solely by the terms of the bilateral agreement between India and the US, the India-specific safeguards agreement with IAEA, and the clean waiver from the NSG, which it hoped would be forthcoming in a two-day meeting. On the issue of testing, the statement confirmed the known position of the government, that of a unilateral moratorium on testing which was also reflected in the India–US Joint Statement of 18 July 2005.

We knew that we were in a position to defend our stance against the Opposition's charges on a technical level. We briefed the media and quoted the pertinent clauses from the text of the 123 Agreement to prove that there was no contradiction between the government's stand on nuclear testing and the obligations it would assume as part of the nuclear deal with the US.

But what worried us more was our ability to deal with a potentially explosive political situation that had developed after the news report. It was again a battle of perception, like it had been throughout the 'making of the deal'. Through a proactive stance that involved the government engaging with the people at large and explaining the nuances and benefits likely to accrue from the deal, we were again able to turn the popular opinion in favour of the Agreement. This time, too, the gathering storm eventually subsided. But it threatened to delay the process at the all-important platform at the NSG where a grant of waiver to India in respect of the NSG guidelines was being discussed.

Scepticism gained ground for a while at the NSG forum due to the events back home. There were reservations expressed by countries like Austria, Ireland and New Zealand. Some members asked for clear assurances from us to the effect that India would desist from nuclear testing and from selling enrichment and reprocessing technologies to other countries. We had said repeatedly that India would not relinquish its sovereign right to test owing to any deal. It was feared that the members could ask for more time to deliberate on the waiver proposals rather than approve them within the scheduled dates of the plenary meeting.

Any delay at the NSG would have been costly for the entire deal. As presidential elections in the US were round the corner, and general election in India was due the following year with the nuclear deal certain to be a major poll issue, even a temporary hold-up in the passage of the waiver at the NSG could have derailed the nuclear deal. It would have extended to a new US administration and a new government in India, if not a new party in government. The situation had become tricky, and I was certain that the US would call off the deal. However, Dr Singh was extremely confident of the unwavering support of the Bush administration.

To reiterate India's stand on disarmament and non-proliferation, I made the following statement on 5 September 2008:[130]

> A Plenary meeting of the Nuclear Suppliers Group to consider an exception for India from its guidelines to allow for full civil nuclear cooperation with India is being held in Vienna from September 4–5, 2008.

---

[130]Statement by External Affairs Minister of India Shri Pranab Mukherjee on the Civil Nuclear Initiative, 5 September 2008, Ministry of External Affairs, Government of India, http://mea.gov.in/in-focus-article.htm?18806/Statement+by+External+Affairs+Minister+of+India+Shri+Pranab+Mukherjee+on+the+Civil+Nuclear+Initiative

India has a long-standing and steadfast commitment to universal, non-discriminatory and total elimination of nuclear weapons. The vision of a world free of nuclear weapons, which Shri Rajiv Gandhi put before the UN in 1988, still has universal resonance.

We approach our dialogue with the Nuclear Suppliers Group and all its members in a spirit of cooperation that allows for an ongoing frank exchange of views on subjects of mutual interest and concern. Such a dialogue will strengthen our relationship in the years to come.

Our civil nuclear initiative will strengthen the international non-proliferation regime. India believes that the opening of full civil nuclear cooperation will be good for India and for the world. It will have a profound positive impact on global energy security and international efforts to combat climate change.

India has recently submitted a Working Paper on Nuclear Disarmament to the UN General Assembly, containing initiatives on nuclear disarmament. These include the reaffirmation of the unequivocal commitment of all nuclear weapon states to the goal of complete elimination of nuclear weapons; negotiation of a Convention on the complete prohibition of the use or threat of use of nuclear weapons; and negotiation of a Nuclear Weapons Convention prohibiting the development, production, stockpiling and use of nuclear weapons and on their destruction, leading to the global, non-discriminatory and verifiable elimination of nuclear weapons within a specified timeframe.

We remain committed to a voluntary, unilateral moratorium on nuclear testing. We do not subscribe to any arms race, including a nuclear arms race. We have always tempered the exercise of our strategic autonomy with a sense of global responsibility. We affirm our policy of no-first-use of nuclear weapons.

We are committed to work with others towards the conclusion of a multilateral Fissile Material Cut-off Treaty in the Conference on Disarmament that is universal, non-discriminatory and verifiable.

India has an impeccable non-proliferation record. We have in place an effective and comprehensive system of national export controls, which has been constantly updated to meet the highest international standards. This is manifested in the enactment of the Weapons of Mass Destruction and their Delivery Systems Act in 2005. India has taken the necessary steps to secure nuclear materials and technology through comprehensive export control legislation and through harmonization and committing to adhere to Missile Technology Control Regime and Nuclear Suppliers Group guidelines.

India will not be the source of proliferation of sensitive technologies, including enrichment and reprocessing transfers. We stand for the strengthening of the non-proliferation regime. We support international efforts to limit the spread of ENR equipment or technologies to states that do not have them. We will work together with the international community to advance our common objective of non-proliferation. In this regard, India is interested in participating as a supplier nation, particularly for Thorium-based fuel and in establishment of international fuel banks, which also benefit India.

India places great value on the role played by the IAEA's nuclear safeguards system. We look forward to working with the IAEA in implementing the India-specific Safeguards Agreement concluded with the IAEA. In keeping with our commitment to sign and adhere to an Additional Protocol with respect to India's civil nuclear facilities, we are working closely with the IAEA to ensure early conclusion of an Additional Protocol to the Safeguards Agreement.

My statement clarified India's stand on nuclear non-proliferation and allayed misgivings of some members. The negotiations at the NSG were protracted and spilled over into the wee hours of 6 September. The NSG decided to adjust its guidelines to enable full civil nuclear cooperation with India.

Dr Manmohan Singh welcomed it as a forward-looking and momentous decision. He said it was recognition of India's impeccable non-proliferation credentials and its status as a nation with advanced nuclear technology.

As India's Minister for External Affairs, I issued a statement that day on the final outcome of the NSG meeting. I said that the NSG had adopted a statement on civil nuclear cooperation which constituted a major landmark in our quest for energy security. I mentioned that the decision would open a new chapter in India's cooperation with other countries in peaceful uses of nuclear energy and that we looked forward to working with our international partners in realizing the full potential of mutually beneficial cooperation that this decision entailed. I insisted that the NSG outcome was the development of major significance to global energy security as it would contribute to meeting the challenges of climate change. I went on to state that '…the final outcome fully meets our expectations and is consistent with the government policy and the national consensus on disarmament and non-proliferation. The NSG waiver is a unique development that has been achieved in accordance with commitments given to the Parliament and the people of India, and is consistent with India's national interest.' I placed on record the Indian

Government's deep appreciation for the untiring efforts of the US (particularly President George Bush and US Secretary of State, Dr Rice), France, the UK and Russia throughout the process, and also the support received from the then as well as previous Chairs of the NSG—Germany, South Africa and Brazil.

Though members of the Opposition continued to criticize the government's decision to seek waiver from the NSG stating that it had led India into the non-proliferation trap set up by the US, there were several voices of support as well. Brajesh Mishra, who was the national security adviser when Atal Bihari Vajpayee was prime minister, supported the development at the NSG saying that the waiver did not prohibit India from conducting nuclear tests in the future. Former President Dr A.P.J. Abdul Kalam supported the NSG deal asserting that India reserved the right to break its voluntary moratorium on further testing in supreme national interest.

After the NSG waiver, the decks were virtually cleared for India and the US to ink the 123 Agreement. We informed the US about India's intention to source state-of-the-art nuclear technologies and facilities on the basis of the Agreement. The Nuclear Power Corporation of India had already commenced preliminary discussions with the US firms. Post-NSG, the government began moving towards finalizing bilateral agreements with other friendly partner countries. When Prime Minister Manmohan Singh made a trip to the US on 26 September 2008 to celebrate the conclusion of the Agreement with US President Bush (though the Agreement could not be signed then as it was still pending with the US Congress), he also visited France to convey his appreciation of the country's support to French President Nicolas Sarkozy. At a France–India summit held on 30 September 2008, the two countries signed a number of agreements, of which one was a bilateral nuclear cooperation agreement that would form the basis of wide-ranging collaborations in energy and research. Though announced without much fanfare, that agreement, in fact, became the first pact India entered into in the sphere of nuclear cooperation.

Meanwhile, the 123 Agreement which had reached the doorsteps of the US Congress, was passed by the House of Representatives on 27 September. The Senate, on 1 October, also approved the deal with a huge majority. The US Secretary of State Condoleezza Rice came to Delhi on 4 October. The Agreement, which still awaited the signature of the US President to become a law, could not be signed then. Nevertheless, I took the opportunity to compliment Rice for her tremendous role in transforming the India–US relationship and deepening our partnership. In the luncheon that I hosted in her honour, I told her:

> You [have] come to India at a special moment. Our [India–US] relations have never been better. And their prospects continue to improve. The road that we have embarked upon is one of engagement in all the various fields of human endeavour, bringing benefits to our peoples. The civil nuclear initiative which you have personally piloted through the US Congress is the most visible sign of this. We welcome the fact that the Agreement has been approved by the US Congress with overwhelming bipartisan support. This outcome would not been possible without the personal commitment of President Bush and your unremitting efforts. We are now in the last lap. We look forward to cooperating with the US in signing and bringing the 123 Agreement into effect, and moving on to the commercial arrangements.[131]

---

[131]Remarks by External Affairs Minister Shri Pranab Mukherjee at Luncheon in honour of US Secretary of State Dr Condoleezza Rice, Ministry of External Affairs, Government of India, 4 October 2008, http://mea.gov.in/in-focus-article.

President Bush signed the legislation on 8 October to enact the landmark 123 Agreement. I signed the deal on 10 October in Washington DC, along with Dr Rice. In my remarks at the signing ceremony, I mentioned:

> In signing the Agreement between India and the United States of America for cooperation on Peaceful Uses of Nuclear Energy, we have brought to fruition three years of extraordinary effort by both our Governments. The agreement is one more visible sign of the transformed relationship and partnership that our two countries are building together... The significance of this Agreement is that it is the first step to civil nuclear co-operation and trade between India and the USA... We look forward to working with US companies on the commercial steps that will follow to implement this landmark Agreement. It is also the first step to India's cooperation with the rest of the world in civil nuclear energy. By reinforcing and increasing the nuclear element in our country's energy mix, which is vital to sustain our growth rate, nuclear power will directly boost industrial growth, rural development and help us to expand every vital sector of our economy.[132]

I also took the opportunity to express our appreciation and gratitude to President Bush, Dr Rice, the US Congress, and the Indian-American community, whose enthusiasm and support

---

htm?18800/Remarks+by+External+Affairs+Minister+Shri+Pranab+Mukherjee+at+Luncheon+in+honour+of+US+Secretary+of+State+Dr+Condoleezza+Rice

[132] Remarks by External Affairs Minister Shri Pranab Mukherjee at the signing ceremony of the 123 Agreement between India and USA in Washington, 10 October 2008, Ministry of External Affairs, Government of India, http://www.mea.gov.in/in-focus-article.htm?18799/Remarks+by+External+Affairs+Minister+Shri+Pranab+Mukherjee+at+the+signing+ceremony+of+the+123+Agreement+between+India+and+USA+in+Washington

sustained us through the arduous process.

There was a sense of jubilation that the exercise which started more than three years ago finally bore fruit after some extraordinary efforts. But there were sounds of disapproval too. One dissenting opinion seemed to suggest that the NSG consensus, was attained as a result of my commitment given on India's voluntary moratorium on nuclear testing, thereby effectively bringing India within the ambit of the NPT and Comprehensive Nuclear Test Ban Treaty (CTBT). One cannot disagree enough on this ludicrous proposition. The government had reiterated time and again that India's right to test, if necessary in its national interest, would not be affected by the nuclear agreement. There was no mention of testing in the Agreement. However India, as a responsible nuclear state, would continue to observe its voluntary unilateral moratorium on testing and its policies of credible minimum deterrence and NFU.

Nevertheless, after the signing of the nuclear deal with the US, I decided to make a suo moto statement on 'India's Civil Nuclear Energy Initiative' in the Parliament on 20 October, 10 days after signing the deal. I spoke about the imperative of the agreements, consensus and waivers resulting in India obtaining leverage in the nuclear energy sector. Some of the points I mentioned included the following:[133]

- The IAEA approval and the NSG decision provide us the passport which allows us to engage in civil nuclear cooperation with our international partners. We are now in the process of getting visas by engaging with our

---

[133]Suo-Motu Statement by Shri Pranab Mukherjee, Minister of External Affairs, on 'India's Civil Nuclear Energy Initiative' in Parliament, Ministry of External Affairs, Government of India, 20 October 2008, http://www.mea.gov.in/in-focus-article.htm?18798/SuoMotu+Statement+by+Shri+Pranab+Mukherjee+Minister+of+External+Affairs+on+Indias+Civil+Nuclear+Energy+Initiative+in+Parliament

international partners to negotiate and finalize bilateral cooperation agreements.
- The bilateral agreements would provide for cooperation in various aspects of nuclear fuel cycle. They include the fuel supply assurances, which are the basis of our civil nuclear initiative as well as our right to build our strategic fuel reserves, to ensure the uninterrupted operation of our civil nuclear reactors under IAEA safeguards.
- Taken together, the India-specific safeguards agreement, the NSG decision and the bilateral cooperation agreements would provide the basis for us to engage in international cooperation in civil nuclear energy on a long-term and sustainable basis with interested international partners.
- When the enabling bilateral cooperation agreements are brought into force, they would provide the legal framework to negotiate and finalize commercial arrangements to source nuclear fuel for our strategic fuel reserve as well as other nuclear equipment and technologies covering the nuclear fuel cycle.

I then elaborated on why the government considered this initiative a historic contribution to our nation-building effort. The reasons are:

- First, it enhances our development options. We are all aware that the availability of clean, affordable and sustainable sources of energy is a critical requirement if we hope to maintain healthy economic growth and abolish poverty. Today, the shortage of energy hampers our efforts to rapidly develop our economy. Hon'ble members are well aware of the strain put on our economy and on the daily lives of the people by the rise in the global prices of crude oil earlier this year. We must develop and utilize energy sources which are clean and do not contribute to climate change or global warming. We are and will continue to develop renewable sources of energy such as bio-fuels, solar and wind energy as well as other sources like hydel power. Nuclear energy offers us an economically and environmentally viable alternative. With the international cooperation that is now available, we will be in a position to bring additional generating capacity through nuclear power into our energy mix. It will also help our indigenous nuclear programme to grow rapidly. Today, we have about 4,000 MW of installed capacity in nuclear power. Even the existing plants are operating at a much lower level than their capacity due to a shortage of uranium. With the opening up of international nuclear trade and commerce, we will have new opportunities to expand our nuclear power capacity.

- Today, our total power generation capacity is about 1,45,000 MW. If we wish to sustain an annual GDP growth rate of 9–10 per cent, then by 2030, our projected energy deficit would be 150,000 MW. If we go a little more in the future, that is by 2050, our energy deficit would be 412,000 MW. In working out these figures, we have taken into account thermal power, coal, petrol and diesel, hydel power and non-conventional energy sources like wind, solar, etc. Even after their fullest exploitation, the projected deficit would remain. Nuclear power is the only effective way to bridge this gap. As per some studies, if we start work today on nuclear power, to produce 40,000 MW of energy in the period of eight years from 2012 to 2020, then within 22 years, that is by 2030, we will be able to reduce the deficit to only 50,000 MW as against the deficit of 150,000 MW. Thereafter, we will be

able to reduce the energy deficit in 2050 from 412,000 MW to only 7,000 MW.
- This initiative marks the end of the technology-denial regimes that have restricted India for over three decades. These developments are the beginning of a new chapter for India—of engagement as equal partners in civil nuclear energy cooperation with other countries. As we move forward, it will help us to expand high technology trade with technologically advanced countries.
- It is an acknowledgement of the scientific and technological achievements of our scientists whose tireless efforts in the face of adverse conditions laid the basis for this initiative. It is their efforts that have made it possible for the world today to recognize India as a state with advanced nuclear technology. Hon'ble members are aware that the embargoes in the nuclear field that were in place against us had hampered the efforts of our scientists to fully participate in international exchanges. With this initiative they will be able to engage with their counterparts in exchange of scientific ideas and technical know-how and contribute to the global effort to deal with worldwide challenges of energy security and climate change.
- Finally, the initiative is an acknowledgement of India's role as a responsible power in international affairs on the global stage. It is for us to utilize this opportunity with confidence as we pursue our national interests.

As there were questions raised earlier about our ability to maintain the independence of our foreign policy, I thought it appropriate to lay the matter to rest. In my statement to the Parliament, I reiterated that:

We will never compromise on our independent foreign policy. Our foreign policy will be determined at all times by our own assessment of our national interest. This initiative in no way constrains our ability to pursue an independent foreign policy. It does not in any way affect our strategic autonomy. In fact it does the opposite by increasing our foreign policy options. The NSG decision by opening up the possibility for us to engage in civil nuclear cooperation with other countries actually enhances our choices to engage as an equal partner with the international community. The ultimate objective of our foreign policy is to create conditions conducive to our growth so that we can meet our developmental objectives. In this respect, I can say emphatically that this initiative creates more space for us to pursue a foreign policy which serves our national interest.

The Indo–US nuclear deal would not have come to fruition without the strong rapport I shared with Dr Rice. Further, my efforts to reach out to the government in Myanmar, known for its strong anti-US position, were instrumental in securing important concessions for US diplomats and tourists and laid the foundation for a deeper understanding between the two democracies. But it was the steadfast support from President Bush that really clinched the deal. Defying protocol, he went out of the way to meet me several times at the White House and even on the side-lines of the UN General Assembly. The Indo–US nuclear deal was Dr Manmohan Singh's finest hour.

CHAPTER 9

RETURNING TO FINANCE

When the UPA-I government was being formed I was absolutely clear that I did not want the finance portfolio since Manmohan Singh and I held differing views on economic issues. When Sonia Gandhi asked me my preference, all I said was that I would be happy with any portfolio other than finance. She agreed, and I was given the responsibility of defence, after which I shifted to external affairs.

But life has a way of throwing surprises.

In the immediate aftermath of the Mumbai terror attacks, P. Chidambaram was brought into the Ministry of Home Affairs, and Manmohan Singh took over the finance portfolio as additional charge. However, in January 2009, the Prime Minister had to be hospitalized for a heart bypass surgery, and the mantle of finance fell on me. I took over the Finance Ministry in addition to External Affairs.

A Rashtrapati Bhavan communique was issued:

> The President of India, as advised by the Prime Minister, has directed that Pranab Mukherjee, Minister of External Affairs, be assigned the additional charge of Ministry of

Finance from January 24, 2009 until the recovery of the Prime Minister from medical treatment.

It was announced that in the absence of the Prime Minister, I would preside over the Cabinet meetings.[134]

I performed protocol duties of the Prime Minister for the first time when I joined President Pratibha Patil in welcoming Kazakhstan President Nursultan Nazarbayev at the ceremonial reception at Rashtrapati Bhavan during the Republic Day celebrations on 24 January 2009. I also led the delegation-level talks with the Kazakh president at the Hyderabad House the following day. During this visit, a Joint Declaration on Strategic Partnership was adopted which envisaged comprehensive cooperation in all spheres between India and Kazakhstan.

There was some degree of media debate on this issue.

> The Prime Minister's bypass surgery has raised piquant questions about the absence of a chain of command in the government, which should come into effect when the PM is away. Pranab Mukherjee will step into the PM's shoes partially while Manmohan Singh is recuperating, and he cannot be designated as the officiating prime minister.
>
> Congress leaders say there is no constitutional provision for a caretaker PM. So the PM's work has been decentralized and divided, and the decision to do it this way is guided more by politics than by administrative needs or constitutional niceties.
>
> In the last four and a half years, whenever the prime minister was away for a week or a day, a standard procedure used to come into effect, and that empowered Pranab Mukherjee to preside over Cabinet meetings—these were

---

[134]Press Communique, Rashtrapati Bhavan, New Delhi, 23 January 2009.

rare—and the CCPA, to take decisions collectively.

This time however there are two additional aspects of decision-making to contend with. One is the Republic Day celebrations as this is the first time since 1950 that the prime minister will not be present at functions to mark the occasion.

The second aspect of the PM's responsibilities is the additional charge he holds of several portfolios—finance, coal, environment and forests, information and broadcasting, space and atomic energy and personnel.[135]

Further, as the Prime Minister is in charge of the nuclear briefcase, the army officers concerned briefed me in his absence.

THE ECONOMY: THE GOOD YEARS AND THE CRISIS

I was returning to the Finance Ministry after a long gap of 24 years, and the emergent priority was to prepare the interim budget—essentially a full-fledged budget document without taxation proposals.

The first four years of the UPA government witnessed a dream run for the economy with the GDP recording increase of 7.5 per cent, 9.5 per cent, 9.7 per cent and 9 per cent, respectively, from the fiscal year 2004–05 to 2007–08.[136] For the first time, the economy showed sustained growth of over 9 per cent for three consecutive years. With per capita income growing at 7.4 per cent per annum, this represented the fastest ever improvement in living standards over a duration of four years.

---

[135]'Permanent number two', *The New Indian Express*, 26 January 2009, http://www.newindianexpress.com/opinions/2009/jan/26/permanent-number-two-20726.html

[136]Interim Budget: 2009–2010, Speech of Pranab Mukherjee, Minister of Finance, 16 February 2009, http://indiabudget.nic.in/ub2009-10(i)/bs/speecha.htm

During this period, the fiscal deficit had come down from 4.5 per cent in 2003–04 to 2.7 per cent in 2007–08 and the revenue deficit declined from 3.6 per cent to 1.1 per cent. Investment and savings showed significant improvement. The domestic investment rate as a proportion of GDP increased from 27.6 per cent in 2003–04 to over 39 per cent in 2007–08. The gross domestic savings rate shot up from 29.8 per cent to 37.7 per cent during this period. The gross capital formation in agriculture as a proportion of agricultural GDP improved from 11.1 per cent in 2003–04 to 14.2 per cent in 2007–08.

However, this was the time that global financial crisis shook the world, leading to one of the deepest downturns in recent history. This crisis unfolded in 2007, and took a turn for the worse in September 2008 with the collapse of several international financial institutions, including investment banks, mortgage lenders and insurance companies. There was a severe choking of credit subsequently and a global crash in stock markets. The slowdown intensified with the US, Europe and Japan sliding into recession. The prognosis in store for 2009 was much worse.

A crisis of such magnitude in developed countries was bound to have an impact around the world. India was affected too. For the first nine months of the financial year 2008–09, the growth rate of exports climbed down to 17.1 per cent and industrial production fell by 2 per cent on a yearly basis in December 2008.

> The outlook for India, going forward, is mixed. There is evidence of a slowdown in the economic activity. The real GDP growth has moderated in the first half of 2008–09. Industrial activity, particularly in the manufacturing and infrastructure sectors, is decelerating. The services sector too, which has been our prime growth engine for the last five years, is slowing, mainly in the construction, transport and

communication, trade, hotels and restaurants sub-sectors. For the first time in seven years, exports have declined in absolute terms in October 2008. Recent data indicate that the demand for bank credit is slackening despite comfortable liquidity in the system. Higher input costs and dampened demand have dented corporate margins while the uncertainty surrounding the crisis has affected business confidence.[137]

The situation was turning grim. The government provided fiscal stimulus in two packages announced on 7 December 2008 and 2 January 2009, to counter the negative fallout of the global economic slowdown. The primary objective of these packages was to provide tax relief to boost demand and increase expenditure on public projects in order to create employment and public assets. From August 2008 to January 2009 alone, the government approved 37 infrastructure projects worth ₹70,000 crore. These stimulus packages were in addition to the already announced expanded safety net programme for the rural poor, the farm loan waiver package and the payout following the Sixth Pay Commission Report, all of which added to stimulating demand.

Given that I was presenting an interim budget, my initial view was that I would not announce any further economic stimulus measures. However, a further slowdown impelled the announcement of a third fiscal package in February.

As we were headed for elections, in this interim budget, I stated that the new government would need to anchor its policies in a medium-term perspective to achieve the following objectives:

- Sustain a growth rate of at least 9 per cent per annum over an extended period of time.

---

[137]D. Subbarao, 'The Global Financial Turmoil and Challenges for the Indian Economy', Speech at the Bankers' Club, Kolkata, 10 December 2008, p 2–3.

- Strengthen the mechanisms for inclusive growth for creating about twelve million new work opportunities per year.
- Reduce the proportion of people living below the poverty line to less than half from current levels by 2014.
- Ensure that Indian agriculture continues to grow at an annual rate of 4 per cent.
- Increase the investment in infrastructure to more than 9 per cent of GDP by 2014.
- Support Indian industry to meet the challenge of global competition and sustain the growth momentum in exports.
- Strengthen and improve the economic regulatory framework in the country and expand the range and reach of social safety nets by providing direct assistance to vulnerable sections.
- Bolster the delivery mechanism for primary healthcare facilities with a view to improve the preventive and curative healthcare in the country.
- Create a competitive, progressive and well-regulated education system of global standards that meets the aspirations of all segments of society.
- A move towards providing energy security by pursuing an Integrated Energy Policy.

HEADING FINANCE IN UPA-II

The UPA came back to power in the mid-2009 election. I was appointed finance minister and no longer held it as additional charge. In fact, ahead of the appointment, Sonia Gandhi mentioned to me that it was only appropriate that I continue with finance. I agreed.

Thus, just 140 days later, on 6 July 2009, I presented the regular budget for 2009–10. I was ably assisted by my advisers

Ms Omita Paul and Mr Kaushik Basu, who did much of the groundwork. Building on my earlier budget, I reiterated that the government recognized the challenges of our medium-term objectives as I had set out in the interim budget, particularly at a time when the world, and India, were still struggling with an unprecedented financial crisis. I was, however, determined to convert our words into deeds.

My immediate challenge was to bring the economy back to the high GDP growth rate of 9 per cent per annum at the earliest. Growth of income was important in itself, but it was critical for the resources that it would bring in.

The second challenge was to deepen and broaden the agenda for inclusive development; to ensure that every individual, community and region received the opportunity to participate in, and benefit from, the development process.

The third challenge was to re-energize government and improve delivery mechanisms. Our institutions needed to provide quality public services, security and the rule of law to all citizens with transparency and accountability.

I performed my duties as finance minister with these objectives in mind and treated each budget as a continuum, that is, I consciously maintained a link with the earlier budgets and built on them. This effort brought in focus and discipline. This also enforced accountability and transparency.

THE SOCIAL SAFETY NET

I was aware that establishing the social safety net was enormously important, and with that in mind I made handsome allocations for the schemes in my budgets. The government had launched several popular schemes which are now part of public memory. The idea behind them was to further improve on the inclusive growth agenda of the government, which had been the cornerstone of Congress policies in the first term of the UPA government.

The Mahatma Gandhi National Rural Employment Guarantee Act (MGNREGA) of 2005 was hailed as a landmark legislation that created the largest social security net in the world, making all sections of the society equal partners in India's growth story. Putting our experience in UPA-I together with the recommendations of the National Advisory Council (NAC), we developed it as a major social development and anti-poverty programme.

The idea of such a policy was first proposed by Sonia Gandhi. However, Manmohan Singh was not very enthused. Being true monetary economist he did not support what he believed were non-productive benevolent activities.

National Rural Employment Guarantee Act was first promised by the Congress in its 2004 Lok Sabha election manifesto, and was an outstanding success. Notified on 7 September 2005, it 'aims at enhancing livelihood security by providing at least one hundred days of guaranteed wage employment in a financial year to every rural household whose adult members volunteer to do unskilled manual work.'[138] The scheme formed an integral part of the Eleventh Five-Year Plan (2007–12) document and the manifesto of the Congress party in the 2009 Lok Sabha elections. In the manifesto, we pledged 100 days of work at a real wage of ₹100 a day for everyone as an entitlement under the scheme. But MGNREGA was more than just a flagship rural job guarantee scheme. It aimed to create new assets that extended beyond the provision of grants for maintenance and upkeep.

---

[138]Mahatma Gandhi National Rural Employment Guarantee Act, http://www.nrega.nic.in/netnrega/forum/2-MGNREGA.pdf

With the aim of providing a real wage of ₹100 per day, the government decided to index the wage rates to the Consumer Price Index (CPI) for agricultural labour in the 2011–12 budget. These enhanced wage rates resulted in significant enhancement of wages for the beneficiaries across the country.

The scheme has had a positive impact on livelihood security. For the first time, there is an effective floor wage rate for rural workers. Distress migration has reduced, and community assets have been created. Productivity of barren and fallow lands has gone up. The need for improving quality of assets and bringing about greater synergy between MGNREGA and agriculture and allied rural livelihoods was being addressed.

Apart from MGNREGA, the government also started and achieved considerable progress on the ambitious and comprehensive Bharat Nirman programme that aimed to transform rural India. The umbrella scheme included Pradhan Mantri Gram Sadak Yojna, Accelerated Irrigation Benefit Programme, Rajiv Gandhi Grameen Vidyutikaran Yojna, Indira Awaas Yojna, National Rural Drinking Water Programme and Rural Telephony. Implemented and working in tandem, these would effectively ensure expanding and providing irrigation, all-weather roads, houses for the poor, drinking water, electricity for poor families and phone connectivity in all villages.

The government also launched the National Rural Health Mission (NRHM) in 2005, which improved the quality and accessibility of primary health care in villages through the training of Accredited Social Health Activists (ASHAs).

The implementation of the Right to Education Act (RTE) Act was a major success story of both the UPA-II government and Union Minister of Human Resource Development, Kapil Sibal. To harness the nation's demographic dividend, and to achieve the objectives of the RTE, I announced a substantial increase of 24 per cent in the education sector in the 2011–12 budget. While this increased allocation was targeted at strengthening elementary education, the Centre also stressed on the 'vocationalization' of secondary education, which enabled students to pursue job-oriented courses at the plus two level.

While the schemes were launched on a national scale, there were others more regionally focused, such as Bringing the Green Revolution to Eastern India (BGREI). This programme targeted improvements in the rice-based cropping system of Assam, West Bengal, Odisha, Bihar, Jharkhand, eastern Uttar Pradesh and Chhattisgarh. This scheme did particularly well, and resulted in a significant increase in both the production and productivity of paddy, with the eastern states reporting additional paddy production of seven million tonnes in Kharif 2011.

Conscious of the importance of these schemes, my spending on them rose every year. In the 2009–10 budget, I allocated ₹122,345 crore on social sector spending, raising it to ₹151,013 crore in 2010–11, and ₹162,227 crore in 2011–12 and ₹214,400 crore in 2012–13.

The results were significant.

> The fall in unemployment under Current Daily Status (CDS) which measures the employment and unemployment in person-days, is also a reflection of the impact of programmes like MGNREGA which also provide employment in person-days. Unemployment data under CDS measure shows that at the beginning of the MGNREGA in 2005, unemployment was 34.3 million person-days (in 2004–05) and gradually declined since then to 28.0 million person-days in 2009-10 and further to 24.7 million person-days in 2011–12. Poverty in India has also declined (as per Planning Commission estimates using the Tendulkar methodology)

with the poverty ratio in the country coming down from 37.2 per cent in 2004–05 to 21.9 per cent in 2011–12. Along with the growth of the economy, the efforts of the Government through various social sector programmes such as MGNREGA, NRLM, NRHM etc., particularly in rural areas, have helped in poverty alleviation and reduction in unemployment.[139]

FOOD SECURITY BILL

Given that the country had, for long, carried the burden of hunger and malnutrition, we sought to remedy the situation.

Following the sudden rise in food prices in 2009, Manmohan Singh decided to convene a chief ministers' conference on price rise in early 2010 to arrive at a possible solution. Narendra Modi, the then chief minister of Gujarat, was extremely critical of Sonia Gandhi and the Right to Food Bill. I strongly objected to his attempts to politicize the issue. I clarified that the agenda of the conference was not food security, but an attempt to seek advice on ways to control food prices. However, Modi's outburst provided the basis for the Bill. He headed one of the several sub-committees instituted to look into this issue. The comprehensive report prepared by him, which was purely administrative in its content and without any political bias, laid the foundation for the Bill.

It was followed by the announcement in 2010–11 budget that a draft Food Security Bill would be placed in the public domain for discussion. After intense debate, it finally got the presidential

---

[139]Dr H. A. C. Prasad, Dr N. K. Sinha, Riyaz A. Khan, Performance of Major Social Sector Schemes: A Sample Survey Report, http://finmin.nic.in/workingpaper/Performance_MSSSchemes.pdf

nod, interestingly, during my time at Rashtrapati Bhavan.

During the tenure as finance minister, my overarching focus was on reform and institution-building to keep pace with the fast-changing times.

FINANCIAL SECTOR REFORMS

One of the major fallouts of the global crisis was the conscious attempt by countries to critically examine the architecture of their financial systems with an eye to improve their financial stability. I understood that there could not be a one-size-fits-all approach, and while the broad principles were similar, the exact nature of reforms had to be specific to the Indian situation. I have always been a staunch votary of reforms to the financial architecture at international platforms like the G2O and BRICS, particularly since the institutions in place were established in the aftermath of the Second World War.

FINANCIAL STABILITY AND DEVELOPMENT COUNCIL

With a view to strengthen and institutionalize the mechanism for maintaining financial stability, it was decided to set up an apex-level Financial Stability and Development Council (FSDC). FSDC was tasked to monitor macro prudential supervision of the economy, including the functioning of large financial conglomerates, and address inter-regulatory coordination issues. It would also focus on financial literacy and financial inclusion.

While making this announcement in the 2009–10 budget, I reiterated that I had no interest in diluting the powers of existing regulators, and that the FSDC was not a super-regulator. The FSDC would only undertake actions that were missing in the existing setup, and would help us focus on developmental, regulatory, and stability issues in a holistic manner.

DIFFERING VIEWS WITH RBI GOVERNOR

Though Manmohan Singh did not agree with my views on modifying the financial structure, he was very supportive of the initiative of establishing the FSDC. However, the then RBI Governor D. Subbarao did have some reservations. He believed that the 'proposed FSDC structure would create a risk of financial instability transgressing into the domain of monetary and regulatory policies.'[140] I explained to him that India's financial structure was more complex than the arrangement that existed at the time of the RBI's establishment in 1935. There were several gaps between the central bank and the government in areas such as reforms to the institutional set-up and monetary regulatory and promotional institutions, which could be addressed only with the establishment of the FSDC.

I discussed the RBI governor's views with Singh. I pointed out that Subbarao, who was too much of a monetarist, had been thrust upon me. He was given a two-year extension from September 2011, and continued as the Governor till September 2013. The much-publicized standoff between the RBI and the government stemmed from the fact that Rao had limited understanding of autonomy.[141] He maintained that his statutory appointment had authorized him legally to formulate the nation's monetary policy, and that the government had curbed his authority. However, in reality, the governor only enjoyed

---

[140] D. Subbarao, *Who Moved My Interest Rate*, Penguin, 2016.
[141] 'UPA interfered in functioning, pressured RBI to cut interest rates, claims D Subbarao', India TV, 15 July 2016, http://www.indiatvnews.com/politics/national-upa-interfered-in-functioning-pressured-rbi-to-cut-interest-rates-claims-d-subbarao-339530

functional independence. Constitutionally, it was the finance minister alone who was accountable to the people. Ironically, as Secretary of the Department of Economic Affairs (DEA) in 2007, Subbarao had questioned about the functioning of the RBI. I advised him that a change of assignment need not alter one's views on issues.

FINANCIAL SECTOR REFORMS COMMISSION

The other focus of my attention was legislative reforms to the financial sector. In India, this sector is governed by as many as sixty acts, many of which date back several decades, such as the RBI Act of 1934, the Insurance Act of 1938 and the Securities Contract Regulation Act, which was enacted in 1956 when derivatives and statutory regulators were unknown. Over a period of time, innumerable amendments were required to keep pace with developments like establishment of stock markets, opening up of portfolio investments to NRIs, introduction of service tax and the expansion of the financial services sector. As a result, there were gaps and overlaps leading to ambiguity and complexity of regulations in the financial sector. Reforms to regulate this sector were also necessitated by the fact that increasing portfolio investments of NRIs in companies had reduced the effective control of the promoters. The existing controlling mechanism was inadequate to meet the challenging demands of the sector.

As a step towards structural reforms in the financial sector, we focused on rewriting and cleaning up laws and bringing them in line with present-day requirements. The Financial Sector Legislative Reforms Commission (FSLRC) was set up in 2011 by the Ministry of Finance with the mandate to study existing legislation and financial sector regulatory practices and propose improvements.

The Commission, chaired by Retd. Justice B.N. Srikrishna, submitted its report in 2013. It suggested drastic changes to the sector's regulatory architecture. It advised putting in place an Indian Financial Code that would replace a bulk of the existing laws, while creating a single regulator for pension, equity, insurance and the commodity markets. By this time, however, I had moved out of the Finance Ministry and into Rashtrapati Bhavan.

THE FRBM ACT

In my 2011–12 budget, I noted that the experience with the Fiscal Responsibility and Budget Management Act (FRBMA), 2003, both at the Centre and States, showed that statutory fiscal consolidation targets had a positive effect on macroeconomic management of the economy. I promised that in the course of that year the government would introduce an amendment to the FRBM Act, laying down the fiscal roadmap for the next five years. The government introduced the amendments to the FRBM Act as part of Finance Bill, 2012.

THE DIRECT TAXES CODE

The Direct Taxes Code (DTC), envisaged as the existing tax system, was decades old (the current income tax legislation was passed in 1961). Moreover, frequent amendments had made the tax regime complex and sometimes ambiguous. There was an urgent need for the tax system to adapt to the changes in the Indian economy and the ever-increasing demands to meet various expenditures. Thus, the DTC was aimed at establishing an economically efficient, effective and equitable direct tax system which would facilitate voluntary compliance and help increase the Tax-GDP ratio. Another objective was to introduce simplicity in taxation, reduce the scope for disputes and minimize litigation. I believed that the DTC was a positive step towards financial sector reform, stock market regulation and a permanent solution to curb inflation.

The first draft bill of the DTC was released by the government for public comments (along with a discussion paper) on 12 August 2009. Based on the feedback from various stakeholders, a revised discussion paper was released in 2010.

The DTC Bill presented in the Parliament in August 2010 was founded on best international practices. Thereafter, it was referred to the Standing Committee on Finance, which submitted its report to the Parliament on 9 March 2012—a full 18 months later.

While my intention was that the Bill would come into effect by April 2012, it was caught in deep debate. I assured the Parliament that the examination of the report would be expedited and steps to enact the DTC would be implemented at the earliest. However, I incorporated some of the recommendations of the Standing Committee, particularly those relating to General Anti- Avoidance Rule (GAAR).

> Even as the Direct Tax Code (DTC) Bill will miss the target launch date of April 2012, Finance Minister Pranab Mukherjee has announced that many of its provisions will be introduced in the coming financial year. Advance pricing agreement, General Anti Avoidance Rule (GAAR), tax slab changes and reduction in securities transaction tax are among the DTC provisions that are set to be rolled out ahead of the full legislation.[142]

---

[142]'Some DTC provisions debut early', *Business Standard*, 17 March 2012, http://www.business-standard.com/article/economy-policy/some-dtc-provisions-debut-early-112031700072_1.html

GOODS AND SERVICES TAX

The Goods and Services Tax (GST) is a consumption-based tax. The idea is to do away with the complications inherent in the existing system of taxation and replace it with a comprehensive GST regime wherein all transactions would be liable to a single unified tax. Thus, the primary aim then was, and continues to be, the removal of the cascading effect of taxes, that acts as a hidden cost and makes goods and services uncompetitive in domestic and international markets. It is the most potent tool against tax evasion and avoidance of tax, and prevents the levying of double tax by both the Centre and States. In 2003, the Kelkar Task Force recommended GST based on the VAT principle.

The proposal to introduce GST was first mooted by P. Chidambaram in his budget speech of 2006–07. The responsibility of preparing and designing the roadmap for the implementation of GST was then assigned to an Empowered Committee of State Finance Ministers.

In April 2008, the Empowered Committee submitted a report, 'A Model and Roadmap for Goods and Services Tax in India', with broad recommendations about the structure and design of GST.[143] Based on inputs from the Central and State governments, the Empowered Committee subsequently released its first discussion paper on GST on 10 November 2009 with the objective of generating a debate amongst all stakeholders.[144]

In the meantime, on 30 September 2009, I set up a Joint Working Group consisting of officers from the Central as well

---

[143] 'Goods and Services Tax', Empowered Committee of State Finance Ministers, http://empcom.gov.in/content/7_1_GoodsandServicesTax.aspx

[144] 'First Discussion Paper On Goods and Services Tax In India: The Empowered Committee Of State Finance Ministers', New Delhi, 10 November 2009, http://pib.nic.in/archieve/others/2009/nov/gst.pdf

as State governments in order to take the GST-related work further. This group was further divided into three sub-working groups to focus separately on draft legislations required for GST, to process the forms to be followed in the GST regime, and to focus on the IT infrastructure development needed for the smooth functioning of the proposed GST. In addition, an Empowered Group for the development of IT systems was also set up under the chairmanship of Nandan Nilekani. The Thirteenth Finance Commission also made a number of significant recommendations on GST, which contributed to the ongoing discussions.

While the preparatory work for the smooth functioning of the proposed GST was being carried out, I addressed the lack of political consensus on the constitutional amendments needed to provide the legislative framework. I met almost all state chief ministers and held a number of meetings with members of the Empowered Committee so as to evolve a consensus. There was apprehension across states that they would lose the power of taxation. With much heavy lifting across two dozen meetings, there seemed to be a better understanding among stakeholders. I urged the ministers of progressive states like Maharashtra, Karnataka and Tamil Nadu to avoid delaying the passage of the Bill.

However, the states of Gujarat and Madhya Pradesh stood out in active disagreement. Madhya Pradesh Finance Minister Raghavji was completely against the scheme of distribution between the Centre and State. The arrest of former Gujarat Home Minister Amit Shah in July 2010 vitiated the atmosphere even more. The BJP termed the arrest a case of political vendetta. It was no surprise that Saurabh Patel, the state's finance minister, was strongly opposed to the Bill.

On the eve of the Lok Sabha session in 2009, Manmohan Singh invited L.K. Advani, Sushma Swaraj, Arun Jaitley and me for discussions over lunch. On the morning of the lunch, first L.K. Advani and then the other two leaders informed me of their inability to attend the engagement. I insisted that they must apprise the Prime Minister as he was the host. However, their contention was that informing the Leader of the House was adequate. I believe it was the Opposition's attempt to register a protest against Shah's arrest. Singh accepted their decision and acknowledged the fact that the CBI action had complicated matters ever further.

At the CWC meeting, there was no opposition to the GST Bill. In fact, Ghulam Nabi Azad insisted that the Congress support me. However, the GST Bill could not be passed in the Parliament due to lack of support. Moreover, Jitendra Prasada and Maharani Chandresh Kumari wanted to know the reasons for supporting the Bill twice, as it was not passed in the Rajya Sabha.

It was my earnest endeavour to introduce GST along with the DTC in April 2011. For this, the indirect tax administrations at the Centre and the states needed to revamp their internal work processes based on the use of Information Technology. This facilitated the rollout of project ACES (Automation of Central Excise & Service Tax) throughout the country, which imparted greater transparency in tax administration and improved the delivery of taxpayer services. Similarly, a mission mode project for computerization of commercial taxes in states was approved. With an outlay of ₹1,133 crore, of which the Centre's share was ₹800 crore, the project laid the foundation for the launch of GST.

Subsequent to long-drawn interim consultation and discussions with chief ministers and Empowered Committee Members, the Constitutional Amendment Bill was introduced in Lok Sabha on 22 March 2011. It was then referred to the Parliamentary Standing Committee.

Through a time consuming and painstaking process consensus was built and the roadmap was created during the period 2009–12.

P. Chidambaram reiterated the same in his budget speech of 2013, and went on to say:

> It can be seen that the ground work for GST was put in place with full consensus on IT enabled infrastructure during the period 2009–12. The only thing which has been holding back the implementation is Constitutional Amendment Bill which has been pending with the Parliamentary Standing Committee, on which report has been submitted recently to the Lok Sabha. From the table of events, it is clear that 2009–12 was the most eventful period to forge consensus for GST, draw up the Constitutional Amendment Bill and introduce it in the Parliament and lay the IT enabled network for the implementation of GST.[145]

However, just as the Standing Committee submitted a report (August 2013) to the Parliament suggesting improvements, the Lok Sabha was dissolved ahead of the general election. Thus, the Bill lapsed.

The (122nd) Constitution Amendment Bill on GST was passed in the Lok Sabha in May 2015 and then in the Rajya Sabha in August 2016. I was informed of the passage of the GST Bill by Prime Minister Modi the very next day. He called me early in the morning to congratulate me and graciously insisted that my efforts had paid rich dividends. However, we must not forget the constitutional challenge that awaits this game-changing reform. The legislation, in its present form, can be questioned by the Supreme Court as it affects the basic structure for tax imposition as envisaged in the Constitution.

---

[145] Budget 2013–2014, Speech of P. Chidambaram, Minister of Finance, 28 February 2013, http://indiabudget.nic.in/ub2013-14/bs/bs.pdf

PUBLIC DEBT MANAGEMENT

The management of the Central government's public debt is mandated to the RBI through the Reserve Bank of India Act, 1934. Given the possible conflict of interest in any central bank discharging this role, many have expounded on the value of an independent Public Debt Management Agency (PDMA). In recent times, many committees on financial reform, too, have made a case for it—Percy Mistry Committee on Making Mumbai an International Financial Centre (2007), Raghuram Rajan Committee on Financial Sector Reforms (2008), Jahangir Aziz Internal Working Group on Debt Management (2008) and Financial Sector Legislative Reforms Commission (2011).

Keeping that in mind, in the budget for 2007–08, we announced the setting up of a Middle Office of PDMA, which began to acquire skills in public debt management. In the 2011–12 budget, I announced that we would introduce the PDMA Bill in the next financial year. This announcement generated a certain amount of resistance, which was overcome through regular engagement with all stakeholders.

WAR AGAINST BLACK MONEY

We were seized of the fact that the generation and circulation of black money was an area of serious concern. To deal with this problem effectively, the government, as announced in the budget of 2011–12, operationalized a five-fold strategy.[146]

- Joining the global crusade against 'black money'
- Creating an appropriate legislative framework

---

[146] Budget 2011–2012, Speech of Pranab Mukherjee, Minister of Finance, 28 February 2011, http://indiabudget.nic.in/budget2011-2012/ub2011-12/bs/bs.doc

- Setting up institutions for dealing with illicit funds
- Developing systems for implementation
- Imparting skills to the manpower for effective action

We constituted a committee, headed by the CBDT chairman to examine ways to strengthen laws to curb the generation of black money in India, its illegal transfer abroad and its recovery. Its report, submitted on 28 March 2012, noted that while there was no dearth of laws to deal with the menace of black money, some new laws, such as to regulate the cash economy, and some changes to the existing legal provisions needed consideration. The multiple administrative agencies dealing with the problem needed to be strengthened in terms of manpower and other resources, and better coordination amongst these agencies was required.

Figures relating to the quantum of illegal funds stashed abroad in tax havens range from $500 billion to $1,500 billion. But these figures were based on unverified assumptions. Therefore, the government commissioned a study on unaccounted income and wealth held within and outside India. This study, which was conducted jointly by the National Institute of Public Finance and Policy (NIPFP), the National Institute of Financial Management (NIFM) and the National Council of Applied Economic Research (NCAER), was mandated to understand the nature of activities that encourage money laundering, examine causes and conditions that result in generation of unaccounted money and suggest ways and means for its detection and prevention. The report emanating from this study, 'The White Paper on Black Money', was tabled in the Parliament in May 2012. The White Paper set out several broad strategies for curbing the generation of black money including reducing disincentives against voluntary compliance, reforms in the vulnerable sectors of the economy, creating effective credible deterrence, strategies for repatriation of black money stashed abroad and issues related to confidentiality of information and other supportive measures.[147]

Further, the government took several steps to implement this five-pronged strategy. These included finalizing 82 Double Taxation Avoidance Agreements (DTAA) and 17 Tax Information Exchange Agreements (TIEA), dedicated exchange of information cell for speedy exchange of tax information with treaty countries and establishment of Directorate of Income Tax Criminal Investigation in the CBDT. Further, India became the 33rd signatory of the Multilateral Convention on Mutual Administrative Assistance in Tax Matters.[148]

Our sustained efforts, both domestically as well as internationally, helped in creating an environment where a regular flow of banking information had started. The revised tax treaty with Switzerland was particularly beneficial in this regard. The Double Tax Avoidance Agreement (DTAA) with France allowed us to obtain information from the European nation in specific cases from April 2011.

The investigation wing of the income tax (IT) department unearthed concealed income of ₹3,014 crore in the last five months of 2011. This was after sleuths carried out focused searches on the basis of information from abroad. The total black money unearthed by the wing from 2009–11 was ₹18,750 crore.

The NDA government's drive against black money and the subsequent demonetization exercise to deal with this festering

---

[147]Black Money; White Paper, Ministry Of Finance, Department Of Revenue, Central Board of Direct Taxes, New Delhi, May 2012, http://mof.gov.in/reports/WhitePaper_BackMoney2012.pdf
[148]Budget 2012–2013; Speech of Pranab Mukherjee, Minister of Finance, 16 March 2012, http://finmin.nic.in/sites/default/files/bs1.pdf?download=1

issue will have limited impact. These endeavours launched with great fanfare, just like L.K. Advani's 'Jan Chetna Yatra' in 2011, will not be able to get to the root of the malaise. I have always believed that we must work with individual countries to recover the unaccounted wealth stashed away in their banks. Tax treaties with foreign countries must be amended to enable Indian authorities to get their hands on the details of black money. Searches, seizures and raids, which I advocated in 1975–76, earning me the sobriquet of 'operator of raid raj', must be employed with care to deal with this issue.

UID MISSION

The setting up of the Unique Identification Authority of India (UIDAI) was a major step in improving governance in terms of the delivery of public services.

There had been a long-felt need in the country for a system of unique identification of every individual for a variety of reasons: better targeting of government's development schemes, regulatory purposes (including taxation and licensing), security purposes, banking and financial sector activities, etc. In the absence of such a nationwide system, each sector of the economy or department agency of the government had been adopting its own system of identification such as PAN card, ration card and electoral photo identity card. Such specific-purpose identities often had inherent limitations. Moreover, the multiplicity of such systems rendered it impossible to correlate information across sectors and even across institutions within the same sector. Similarly, different agencies of government were unable to correlate their data relating to any particular individual.

In addition, a major worry for the government was the sharp increase in the subsidies in the central budget. In the absence of a reliable identification system, leakages in the payment of subsidies were enormous. Apart from the loss to the exchequer, the intended beneficiaries were being denied their due.

Though the government's first effort to provide an identity to residents was in 1993, with the issue of photo identity cards by the Election Commission, the genesis of a Unique Identification (UID) scheme can be traced back to my discussion with Deputy Prime Minister L.K. Advani during the NDA rule, in which I proposed the idea of a unique identity number for every Indian citizen. I explained the need for this initiative with an example from my village, which witnessed the influx of daily-wage workers from Bangladesh. These workers would use their daily earnings to buy sugar, salt and kerosene. I insisted that this practice could only be curbed by giving a unique number to every citizen within 25 km inside Indian territory.

The concept received a fillip in 2006 when the scheme, 'Unique ID for BPL families', received administrative approval by the Department of Information Technology. It was conceived as an initiative that would provide identification for each resident across the country, to be used primarily as the basis for efficient delivery of welfare services. Since the Registrar General of India was engaged in the creation of the National Population Register (NPR) and issue of Multi-purpose National Identity Cards to citizens of India, the Prime Minister constituted an Empowered Group of Ministers (EGoM) in December 2006 to collate the two schemes—the NPR under the Citizenship Act, 1955, and the UID scheme. I was the External Affairs Minister then, and headed this Empowered Group; its members were Union Home Minister and ministers for IT and Communications, Law and Panchayati Raj, while the Deputy Chairman of Planning Commission was a standing invitee. Since UPA was a coalition government, a concerted effort was made to evolve a consensus. Through patient deliberations, we ironed out differences and increased the areas of convergence. Hence, once the decision was taken, there was quick progress in the implementation.

On 4 November 2008, the Empowered Group, approved the establishment of a Unique Identity Authority for all residents of the country. The authority was to be anchored in the Planning Commission for which a notification was issued in January 2009. A provision of ₹100 crore was made in the Annual Plan 2009–10 for this.[149] In the budget for the year 2010–11, I allocated ₹1,900 crore to the authority, since it had entered the operational phase.[150]

By the next financial year, the UID Mission had generated 20 lakh Aadhaar numbers. From 1 October 2011, 10 lakh identity numbers were generated per day, thus setting the stage for realizing the potential of Aadhaar to improve service delivery, accountability and transparency in governance of various schemes. In the subsequent year, the enrolments into the Aadhaar system crossed 20 crore. I allocated adequate funds to complete another 40 crore enrolments starting from 1 April 2012. The Aadhaar platform was now ready to support the payments of MGNREGA; old age, widow and disability pensions; and scholarships directly to the beneficiary accounts in selected areas.[151]

However, my colleague P. Chidambaram, the then Home Minister, had strong reservations about this project. He was opposed to the idea of the UIDAI headed by Nandan Nilekani to be the sole in-charge of the Aadhaar enrolment. He wanted the Registrar General of India to be made responsible for this exercise.

---

[149]Budget 2009–2010, Speech of Pranab Mukherjee, Minister of Finance, 6 July 2009, http://indiabudget.nic.in/ub2009-10/bs/speecha.htm
[150]Budget 2010–2011, Speech of Pranab Mukherjee, Minister of Finance, 26 February 2010, http://indiabudget.nic.in/ub2010-11/bs/speecha.htm
[151]Budget 2012–2013, Speech of Pranab Mukherjee, Minister of Finance, 16 March 2012, http://finmin.nic.in/sites/default/files/bs1.pdf?download=1

Despite these challenges, the project was very close to my heart and we made good progress. This also marked the beginning of an era of private sector talent engaging with the public sector on vital national priorities.

Manmohan Singh chose Nandan Nilekani to lead this project, once again proving that he had good judgement about people, just like Kaushik Basu and Arvind Virmani. Singh was clear that Nandan was the right man for the job. Though I was uncertain about Nilekani agreeing to lead this ambitious project, Singh was sure that he would get Nilekani on board. I shared excellent relations with Nilekani. Despite the bureaucratic delays and the turf war over biometrics with the Home Ministry, he always remained focused, motivated and delivered results on time.

RETROSPECTIVE TAX

This decision of mine, born out of my conviction that India's Direct Tax Policy should not discriminate between domestic and foreign entities, was a subject of much debate and remains so to date. The controversy began when I announced in my 2012–13 budget speech that I proposed to amend the Income Tax Act, 1961, with retrospective effect to undo the Supreme Court judgement in the Vodafone tax case.

THE BACKGROUND

Hutchison Telecommunications International Limited, through its various subsidiaries located in tax havens such as Cayman Islands, British Virgin Islands and Mauritius, had made investments in the Indian telecom sector since 1992. In December 2006, it held 66.98 per cent shares in Hutchison Essar Limited which had seven 100 per cent subsidiaries. These eight companies together held telecom licenses in 23 telecom circles in India. Hutchison Telecommunications decided to exit India in December 2006 and sold its stake to Vodafone International Holdings BV, incorporated in the Netherlands, a 100 per cent subsidiary of Vodafone Group Plc, UK. The two companies entered into a sale purchase agreement on 11 February 2007, for the sale of 'entire issued share capital' (which incidentally was only one share) of CGP Investments (Holdings) Limited, a company incorporated in the Cayman Islands for a total consideration of $11,076,000,000-plus at Libor from the date of agreement to the date of completion. In the recital to the sale purchase agreement, it was mentioned that CGP owned, directly or indirectly, companies which controlled the 'company interests.' This was defined to mean the aggregate interests in 66.98 per cent of the issued share capital of Hutchison Essar.

After the sale purchase agreement, Essar Group raised an objection to the transaction in view of the Right of First Refusal granted to it by Hutchison Telecommunications. A settlement agreement was reached between them on 15 March 2007. Hutchison Telecommunications agreed to pay $415 million to Essar Group. Through a deed of retention entered between Vodafone International and Hutchison Telecommunications on 8 May 2007, Vodafone retained an amount of $351.8 million from the sale consideration by way of Hutchison Telecommunications' contribution towards acquisition cost of options. After deducting this retention amount, Vodafone paid $10,854,229,859.05 to Hutchison Telecommunications on 8 May 2007. In the Hutchison Telecommunications annual accounts, this was shown as 'profit from discontinued operations' and was computed at HK$69,343 million. Out of this profit, Hutchison Telecommunications paid a special cash dividend of HK$ 6.75 per share (HK$ 32,234 million in aggregate).

Since Hutchison's source of profit was entirely from the

capital appreciation through its Indian operations (the subsidiaries in Cayman Islands, British Virgin Islands and Mauritius did not earn any profit), the tax department in September 2007 issued a show-cause notice to Vodafone. The department contended that the transaction of transfer of shares in CGP had the effect of indirect transfer of assets situated in India.

This notice was challenged in the Bombay High Court which gave its decision in favour of the revenue department on 3 December 2008. This verdict laid down the legal position, following which, several other multinational corporations paid taxes leading to an increase in tax revenue.

The Special Leave Petition (SLP) filed against this decision was dismissed on 23 January 2009 and the Supreme Court directed the assessing officer to consider the preliminary issue of jurisdiction. Vodafone International was directed to submit all the relevant documents. A jurisdiction order was passed by the assessing officer on 31 May 2010, which was again challenged before the Bombay High Court which passed an order on 8 September 2010 again in favour of the revenue department. When the SLP was filed against this decision, the Supreme Court directed the assessing officer to determine the tax liability, which came to ₹11,218 crore.

While the Supreme Court, in an interim order on 15 November 2011, had directed Vodafone International to pay ₹2,500 crore and provide a bank guarantee of ₹8,500 crore, its decision of 20 January 2012 directed the tax department to refund ₹2,500 crore with interest of 4 per cent within two months and asked its registry to return the bank guarantee within four weeks. With the Supreme Court setting aside the judgement of the High Court, it created an unusual situation where the tax department would have to return several thousands of crores to several companies.

One of the major concerns of the Supreme Court while delivering its judgement was the potential effect on FDI. I maintain that these concerns, which might have persuaded them to give a decision against the revenue department, were unfounded. First, this was not a case of FDI. Rather, money was paid by one foreign company to another for purchasing the former's assets in India. Second, the nature of the FDI policy is entirely the prerogative of the Executive.

THE RATIONALE

It is pertinent to note that FDI investments are not dependent upon tax; rather, crucial deciding factors include the size of the domestic market, low costs of operations and labour and skilled manpower. Competition from relatively low-tax countries without these advantages is unlikely for the location choice of FDI. Since India offers a huge domestic market, low costs of operations and a cheap and skilled workforce, a direct tax policy that does not discriminate between domestic and foreign entities has very little role to play in attracting FDI.

As a matter of policy, the source country should protect its tax base by ensuring that those foreign investors who have earned through their investments in the source country should also pay taxes like any other domestic investor or resident taxpayer. Just because some foreign investors choose to structure their investments through tax havens, they should not, as a matter of policy, get away without paying any taxes.

What foreign investors need is certainty in tax laws and not a tax-free environment, which no emerging economy can afford. I was convinced that this certainty of payment of taxes needed to be embedded in our tax policy.

The budgetary proposal to amend the Income Tax Act with

retrospective effect from 1962 to assert the government's right to levy tax on merger and acquisition (M&A) deals involving overseas companies with business assets in India was an enabling provision to protect the fiscal interests of the country and avert the chances of a crisis. This retrospective arrangement was not merely to check the erosion of revenues in present cases, but also to prevent the outgo of revenues in old cases. As the Finance Minister, I was convinced of my duty to protect the interest of the country from the revenue point of view.

THE REACTION

The budget proposal to undo the Supreme Court judgement evoked sharp reactions, not only domestically but also internationally. Some said that the Indian Government was 'going back to its old socialist ways.'

> [Harish] Salve was deeply critical of the United Progressive Alliance's budget on the whole. We should show that we have institutions in this country which work. I think the country will pay a dear price for this. I think we are on course for elections this year. It's a government which is politically rattled. They don't want to take tough decisions and introduce reformist measures. This is waging war on foreign investment. If a client asked me 'should I invest in India today? I would say "no",' he said.[152]

Manmohan Singh was convinced that the proposed amendment in the IT Act would impact FDI inflows into the country. I

---

[152] Nikhi Kanekal and Kian Ganz, 'Vodafone-Hutch deal | Retrospective change to I-T Act,' *Livemint*, 17 March 2012, http://www.livemint.com/Politics/n4zC41fejoQ7ObfL4Bue6N/VodafoneHutch-deal--Retrospective-change-to-IT-Act.html

explained to him that India was not a 'no-tax' or 'low-tax' country. Here all taxpayers, whether resident or non-resident, are treated equally. I insisted that as per our country's tax laws, if you pay tax in one country, you need not pay tax in the other country of your business operation which is covered by the Double Tax Avoidance Agreement (DTAA). But it cannot be a case that you pay no tax at all. I clarified that some entities had done their tax planning in such a way that they didn't have to pay tax at all. My intention was clear: where assets are created in one country, it will have to be taxed by that country unless it is covered by the DTAA.

Later, Sonia Gandhi, Kapil Sibal and P. Chidambaram also expressed the apprehension that the retrospective amendments would create a negative sentiment for FDI. I explained to them that FDI comes when there is profitability and not on account of zero tax. Clarificatory amendments were proposed to make the intent of the legislature clear. This would bring tax certainty and would clarify that India had the right to tax similar transactions. Two more Cabinet colleagues separately advised me to take a middle path, and to reconsider the decision. But I remained resolute.

Days ahead of introducing the Finance Bill in Parliament 2012, several colleagues, including one along with a high-ranking Vodafone official, approached me seeking reconsideration of the move to retrospectively amend laws.

Despite the angst that my proposal generated at that time, and even now, both from within my party and outside, I wonder why every succeeding finance minister in the past five years has maintained the same stance.

GROUP OF MINISTERS

This was the period when I headed the maximum number of Group of Ministers (GoMs). While the practice of instituting a GoM had been followed by earlier prime ministers, during Dr Singh's tenure this system was firmly institutionalized. In fact, some people joked that this was a government of GoMs and EGoMs. Manmohan Singh found it an extremely effective instrument to run the coalition government.

In the early days of UPA-I, Manmohan Singh expressed his displeasure at the delayed decision-making at Cabinet meetings despite detailed discussions and multiple interactions. He sought my views to find a solution. I agreed with him, and knew that the situation was a function of the fact that UPA-I and UPA-II were coalitions of diverse political parties. At every Cabinet meeting, leaders of all participating parties would express their views on each agenda item. Thus, the allocated time for the meeting would be routinely exhausted in endless discussions, mostly minus decisions.

As an immediate response, I suggested that Singh give me the floor at the beginning of the next Cabinet meeting. So at that meeting, I made a request to the Prime Minister, 'I would like to share some of my ideas with my Cabinet colleagues and may I suggest to you, Mr Prime Minister, to request the officials to leave the Cabinet room.'

Singh agreed and it was done. Then, very candidly, I made some observations, 'I am asking myself, after attending the previous Cabinet meetings, what are we doing here? Do not mind if I say that I have the longest experience as a minister in the Union Cabinet than any one of you around this table. I have never seen such Cabinet meetings. The Cabinet is not a talking shop. It is the highest decision-making body in the Union, which presides over the fate of such a vast multitude of people living in the Indian subcontinent.'

Naturally, my comment generated strong reactions from all those present. 'What are you suggesting?' one asked, 'we do not belong to your party. We have our views and we would like to express them.' I replied, 'Endless discussion can never lead to a decision and simply because we are running a coalition government does not dilute the functions and responsibilities of the Cabinet as prescribed in the Constitution. Therefore, I suggest that we may express our views if we feel strongly on any agenda item keeping in mind the time constraints. After listening to the observations, the Prime Minister would announce the decision of the Cabinet and we should agree and move on to the next agenda.'

There was much consternation with someone saying, 'In that case, the UPA government would collapse. We cannot accept your dictatorship.' I was equally strong in my response. 'I have a responsibility with 147 members in the Lok Sabha. I do not find it acceptable that a party with just a dozen members harasses the largest party in the coalition. We must deliver and fulfil our commitments. Otherwise what is the purpose of running a government?'

At this point, Sharad Pawar came forward to manage the situation and requested me to calm down. He suggested that the Prime Minister resume the meeting and take up the agenda items. Surprisingly, things moved faster this time as most of them were old agenda items and the ministers had expressed their views on two or three earlier occasions.

My show of temper did not make me popular with my colleagues, but I felt that it was necessary in the long-term interests of governance.

Subsequently, in order to make decision-making more

efficient and governance more effective, we resorted to referring all crucial or contentious issues to GoMs. I was the chairman of more than 95 GoMs and EGoMs. Several of my ministerial colleagues marvelled at my ability to juggle engagements to conduct these meetings that looked at complex issues requiring detailed study.

The institutions of GoMs and EGoMs had very positive outcomes in the decision-making process in the Cabinet. All contentious issues were discussed threadbare, taking note of views of all concerned parties and ministers. After some time, the Cabinet also developed the practice of not discussing the agenda further when it was pointed out that the matter was considered by the GoM's and their recommendations were submitted for its consideration. The Cabinet usually agreed to the proposals. All stakeholder parties were well represented in specific GoMs and were given the space to present their points of view. Thereafter, the Chair reported comprehensively to the Cabinet. As it turned out, Dr Singh was very happy with this arrangement.

LOKPAL

When the UPA government first came to power in 2004, its national common minimum programme had envisaged legislation of the Lokpal. The Cabinet had earlier referred it to a GoM set-up in January 2005 under my chairmanship. I was the defence minister then.

The need for a legislation to set up the institution of Lokpal at the Centre to inquire into allegations of corruption against designated public functionaries had been a long-felt one. The recommendation for establishing such an institution was made in 1966 by the Administrative Reforms Commission in its Interim

Report on the 'Problems of Redressal of Citizens' Grievances.[153] To implement this recommendation, eight bills on Lokpal were introduced in the Lok Sabha at various points in time. Seven of those had lapsed upon the dissolution of the respective Lok Sabhas. The 1985 bill was withdrawn after its introduction.

Detailed discussions on the bill took place at two meetings of the GoM, held on 21 April and 30 November 2005. At the first meeting, it was felt that the bill would require a thorough examination to remove any deficiencies, and an objective assessment followed. At its second meeting, the GoM made its recommendations on the Bill. It felt that since three organizations pertaining to grievance redressal already existed, there was no need for the Lokpal to deal with the redressal of grievances. The group recommended the inclusion of MPs within the purview of the Lokpal. It however observed that while complaints against MPs could be inquired into by the Lokpal, prosecution may be taken up only under the Prevention of Corruption Act, subject to the permission of the sanctioning authority, that is, Speaker of the Lok Sabha or the Chairman of the Rajya Sabha, as the case may be. The GoM felt that there was no requirement of the Judiciary to be included within the purview of the Lokpal as a law to prescribe an authority to look into allegations against the Judiciary was under consideration then. The GoM recommended that all other statutory bodies, except the Election Commission of India and other constitutional bodies should be brought within the purview of the Lokpal. As regards the inclusion of the Prime Minister, it recommended that the Cabinet may take a final view in the matter. In the Lokpal Bill under consideration, a time limit of ten years was prescribed for inquiring into complaints.

---

[153]Interim Report of the Administrative Reforms Commission on the Problems of Redressal of Citizens' Grievances, 20 October 1966, http://mohallalive.com/wp-content/uploads/2011/09/Morarjee-Interim-Report.pdf

The GoM felt this time period was rather long and suggested to reduce it to five years.

Based on these recommendations, the Lokpal Bill 2008 was submitted to the Cabinet, which considered it on 22 May and directed that all legal aspects should be examined in consultation with the Law Ministry. Subsequently, a revised Lokpal Bill 2010 was drafted.

Meanwhile, several representations and suggestions were being received on the proposed bill. On 7 March 2011, activist Anna Hazare and some of his associates of the India Against Corruption movement met Manmohan Singh and handed over a memorandum with a request for drafting a new Lokpal Bill urgently. Dr Singh requested me to include this as an agenda within my GoM on tackling corruption. He assured the delegation that the GoM would meet them immediately after the conclusion of the ongoing budget session of the Parliament.

At the GoM's meeting of 16 March, a sub-group under Defence Minister A.K. Antony was formed to look into the suggestions on the Lokpal Bill, particularly the one proposed by India Against Corruption. The sub-group invited Anna Hazare to attend a meeting on 28 March. Hazare refused to interact, and instead declared a fast onto death from 5 April.

Hazare's rigid stand, to my mind, was prejudiced. He insisted that the existing draft of the Bill would patronize rather than check corruption. The anti-corruption movement was able to turn public perception against the government, indicating the government was not keen to have a strong legislation. This was far from true. A strong and sound legislation also needs to be balanced. While the need to have a robust law is beyond any argument, we also need to factor in constitutional proprieties and exigencies associated with constitutional positions.

Anna Hazare demanded a joint committee to discuss the

draft bill. Though I had my reservations—law-making, which is a sacred duty of the legislators, reflects the collective will of the people; this role cannot be usurped, even partially, by a group of persons who claim, rightly or otherwise, to work in public interest. Yet, we paid heed to the public sentiment and constituted a Joint Drafting Committee (JDC) on 8 April. I was the chairman of this committee, which comprised Home Minister P. Chidambaram, Law Minister Dr M. Veerappa Moily, HRD and Communication and IT Minister Kapil Sibal and Water Resources and Minority Affairs Minister Salman Khurshid, and five non-official, civil society representatives Anna Hazare, Justice N. Santosh Hegde, Prashant Bhushan, Arvind Kejriwal and Shanti Bhushan (co-chairman). I was unwilling to be a part of any committee on Lokpal because I did not view it as a solution to the festering issue of corruption. However, Ms Gandhi was of the opinion that only I could control the proceedings of the committee with my temper. The JDC held nine meetings in a span of just two months.

At the first meeting, held on 16 April, I mentioned that the joint drafting of the Lokpal Bill was a unique experiment without precedent. It was the first instance of a section of society being made part of the drafting process. While pointing out that the parliamentary and government committees had their own laid-down procedures, the JDC was to evolve its own procedure for carrying out the drafting exercise.

It was decided to record the deliberations of each meeting. Since the JDC would be closely watched, we also decided that its functioning and progress should be made public on a periodic basis to share major decisions. To project a unified approach to the drafting of the Bill, I suggested that the press may be briefed after the JDC meetings by Anna Hazare or Prashant Bhushan or Kapil Sibal. The civil society members wanted video recordings of the

JDC proceedings instead of the audio recordings. It was pointed out to them that audio recordings without the visual impact were less susceptible to possible misinterpretation by the media.

Civil society representatives wanted continuous involvement of citizens in the drafting process by making the day-to-day proceedings and deliberations public. I suggested that once the basic principles were agreed upon, it would then be appropriate to involve the public by initiating the exercise of inviting comments through wider consultations. The government was not averse to sharing information. In fact, a dedicated website had already been created, which contained the background and other material, and a provision for feedback.

With a focus on the smooth functioning of the committee, we then set a deadline of 30 June for finalizing the draft legislation to enable it to be introduced in the ensuing monsoon session of the Parliament.

The discussions in the JDC meetings were based on the 40 basic principles (with 31 points supplementing the principles added later) and the statement of objects and reasons circulated by the civil society members. Basically, the scope and vision of the proposed bill was discussed. Despite agreement on many issues (like independence of the Lokpal from the point of view of financial resources, having independent investigation and prosecution wings, and autonomy in its functioning and manpower), there were six areas where the views of the minister-members of the JDC and civil society members differed. These were the exact powers of the Lokpal: provision of one single Act for both the Lokpal in the Centre and Lokayuktas in the state, inclusion of the PM and judges of the Supreme Court and High Court within the purview of the Lokpal, including conduct of MPs inside the Parliament (speaking or voting in the House) within the purview of the Lokpal, and subjecting members of a civil service of the Union to enquiry and disciplinary action including dismissal/removal by the Lokpal/Lokayuktas.

At the JDC meeting on 30 May, I pointed out that the prime minister was a keystone of our parliamentary structure and should be kept outside the purview of the Lokpal. My contention was that any complaint against the prime minister would render the incumbent dysfunctional and would lead to institutional instability. I went on to highlight that the prime minister was otherwise answerable to the Parliament.

As regards the Judiciary, I informed the committee that a Judicial Standards and Accountability Bill was already under the consideration by the parliamentary standing committee and that suggestions being proposed with regard to the Judiciary may be used for strengthening that Bill. The Judiciary has to remain independent for its effective functioning. It is self-regulated and should not be subject to the Lokpal.

The civil society representatives proposed covering all functionaries from village level to the highest executive. I opined that it would overburden the Lokpal, which should cover only senior functionaries—officers of joint secretary level and above and ministers—who were in a position to influence government policy and decision. The focus of the Lokpal should be to tackle corruption at high places and it was also necessary to address corruption at higher levels first.

As regards members of the Parliament, I reported that articles 105(2) and 105(3) allowed freedom of speech to the members and every speech or vote of a member in the Parliament, even with an allegation attached, were part of the privileges. The conduct of an MP inside the House cannot come within the domain of the Lokpal. However, conduct outside the Parliament ought to be within the ambit of the Lokpal.

The civil society members wanted the Lokpal to be

comprehensive, anti-corruption setup taking up the work of the entire existing anti-corruption machinery, that is, CBI, CVC and police. I explained to them that this arrangement would leave the government devoid of any powers to check corruption. The Constitution placed a responsibility on the government to discharge its responsibility in such areas. Addressing and tackling corruption was part of governance. Hence, it was not acceptable to dispense with the existing anti-corruption infrastructure available with the government.

Some of the issues on which the two sides did not agree upon also concerned the states. Consultations across the broad political firmament were also necessary given the import of the proposed legislation. I wrote to the chief ministers and leaders of political parties on 31 May and sought their views on the six major issues. This became a problem, and the civil society members did not attend the next JDC meeting on 6 June and instead sent a letter signed by Shanti Bhushan. He expressed a view that my letter was drafted in the form of a questionnaire and was therefore inappropriate. I clarified that the questionnaire was added to the letter only for ease of response. It did not prevent the CMs and political leaders to offer their opinion in detail, which was the aim behind the letter.

The JDC received responses from six political parties including BJP, BSP, SP and CPI, and from 25 chief ministers. An all-party meeting was held on 3 July, the representatives from various political parties emphasized that the supremacy of the constitution had to be maintained, and institutions of democracy could not be undermined. They also emphasized that laws had to be made by the parliamentarians who are elected representatives of the country, and that few nominated members of the drafting committee cannot have precedence over elected members of the Parliament. It was agreed through a resolution that the government would bring a strong and effective Lokpal Bill before the next session of Parliament following the established procedures.

In the JDC forum, it was decided that wherever there was convergence of views between the government members and the civil society members, it would be put in legal language. For those there was disagreement, views of the civil society would be put alongside the views of the government. The report would then be sent to the ministry concerned for follow-up action. The JDC completed its work with its final meeting held on 21 June.

Hazare often resorted to agitation. Realizing that public sympathy was on his side, he exerted pressure for passage of the version of the Lokpal Bill his movement was championing. Even when the JDC was active, a major protest at the Ramlila Grounds took place on 4 June.

The passage of a bill in the Parliament is a well-laid-out process. It can be fast-tracked to an extent possible but the procedures cannot be discarded. In short, the Parliament would have to follow parliamentary practices and procedures to enact a bill and no political exigency can cause a deviation. In pursuance of the directions of the all-party meeting held on 3 July, the government worked on the draft Lokpal Bill prepared by the JDC, and after following the formal process of inter-ministerial consultations and Cabinet approval, the Bill was introduced in the Parliament on 4 August. This entire process required patience. Tempers ran high on all sides. I had to become a listening post and get all parties to talk across the table. Nevertheless, Hazare went on a fast on 16 August. At another all-party meeting held on 24 August, a unanimous resolution was passed:

> This meeting of all political parties in Parliament requests Shri Anna Hazare to end his fast. The meeting was also of the view that due consideration should be given to the

Jan Lokpal Bill so that the Final Draft of the Lokpal bill provides for a strong and effective Lokpal which is supported by a broad national consensus.[154]

The government not only incorporated the suggestions coming from various sections, including the suggestions made by the civil society representatives in the JDC, but also the recommendations of the standing committee, and formulated the Bill.

While initiating the debate on the Lokpal Bill in the Lok Sabha, I said,

> 'We have taken oath to abide by the Constitution. So whatever we do has to be within the Constitution. We are at a crossroads. It is a rare occasion that proceedings of this House are attracting the attention of entire nation and outside world. I would request the Members to have a dispassionate and objective discussion to find out the solution of the problem without compromising parliamentary Democracy... I am sure that members of this House will seize this moment and demonstrate the commitment of the House in dealing with corruption which is gnawing at the vitals of our polity.[155]

The Lok Sabha passed the Lokpal and Lokayukta Bill on 27 December 2011. It was later passed by the Rajya Sabha on 17 December 2013. Amendments made by the Rajya Sabha were agreed to by the Lok Sabha on 18 December 2013. The Bill was notified in the gazette on 1 January 2014.

As the largest functional democracy having multiple parties

---

[154]'Anna Should End Fast, Govt Should Withdraw Bill: Opp', Outlook, 24 August 2011, New Delhi, https://www.outlookindia.com/newswire/story/anna-should-end-fast-govt-should-withdraw-bill-opp/732376

[155]With this speech, Pranab launched Lokpal debate, NDTV, 27 August 2011, http://www.ndtv.com/india-news/with-this-speech-pranab-launched-lokpal-debate-465688

and a population of 120 crore-plus people, I believe the Lokpal issue should have been addressed within the democratic structure and constitutional norms. But, at the same time, popular sentiment, as reflected in a peaceful agitation, should be addressed adequately. We have rules, norms, systems and procedural aspects that must be determined within the framework of the Constitution.

My stint as finance minister for the second time was a lot more challenging, not only for the difficult times we faced but also for the people (or coalition partners) one had to manage. There were several interactions with Mamata where I had to broker a middle-path or to deal with her emotional outbursts at Cabinet meetings.

I am happy that I was able to take action or set in motion a proactive and reformist programme aimed at growth and efficiency, some of which included the FSLRC, Aadhaar, GST, DTC, oil pricing and government debt management.

CHAPTER 10

TO RASHTRAPATI BHAVAN

The latter half of the budget session of 2007 witnessed much speculation in political circles about the choice of the presidential candidate. The incumbent A.P.J. Abdul Kalam was due to retire in July that year.

Around May–June, Sonia Gandhi and Manmohan Singh began discussions with our coalition partners about the prospective presidential candidate. I am told that my name was proposed by the Left parties first and then seconded by others. However, the final decision was left to the Congress party. Sonia Gandhi called me and said, 'Your name is being suggested by some political parties as the presidential candidate, but it would be difficult for us to spare you as you are a strong pillar of the party in the government and in the Parliament.' I told her that the decision was for her to take, and I would abide by it.

Sometime later, Prakash Karat came to my residence and informed me of his discussion with Sonia Gandhi on the issue of the presidential candidate. He mentioned that she had ruled out my name citing a number of reasons, including the fact that she did not have a substitute for me as the leader in the Lok Sabha, and could not spare me from the ministry. Further, my experience and knowledge about party matters was crucial for her as the Congress president.

I understood, and reconciled myself to the situation. But Sonia Gandhi, perhaps to assuage me, sent R.K. Dhawan to explain her rationale to me. I repeated to Dhawan what I had said to Sonia, and that is where the matter finally rested.

Pratibha Devisingh Patil was chosen as the UPA-I candidate for the presidential election. She won by a huge majority defeating Vice President Bhairon Singh Shekhawat.

2012: CHOOSING THE UPA NOMINEE

The question of presidential elections came up once again when President Patil was set to retire on 25 July 2012.

Towards the end of March that year, Sonia Gandhi asked me about the numerical strength of various political parties in the presidential electoral college and the value of their voting power. I informed her that the total value of the electoral college for the 13th presidential election was about 10,95,000 votes and the successful candidate would require a minimum of 551,000 'first preference' votes to get elected. Hence, broadly speaking, the UPA nominee could win if we could manage 100,000 additional votes. UPA, including TMC, had 461,000 votes.

It was around this time that my name started doing the rounds once again in the media and within political circles. I read that Sushma Swaraj, leader of the Opposition in the Lok Sabha and a leader of the NDA, had announced that the NDA would not support either Mohammad Hamid Ansari or myself as the presidential candidate.[156] This announcement caused some

---

[156] Sunetra Choudhury Sunil Prabhu, 'BJP will not support Pranab Mukherjee for President: Sushma Swaraj', 30 April 2012, http://www.ndtv.com/india-news/bjp-will-not-support-pranab-mukherjee-for-president-sushma-swaraj-479554

flutter among political parties, particularly within the NDA.

Nitish Kumar, Chief Minister of Bihar and leader of the second-largest party in the NDA, expressed his displeasure at Sushma Swaraj's comment and said that his party—the JD (U)—considered both Mohammad Hamid Ansari and myself to be suitable candidates for the presidential office. He insisted that the opinion expressed by Sushma Swaraj might be the views of her party, but certainly not that of the NDA. Some other political parties similarly expressed their disagreement with Swaraj.

P.A. Sangma was another strong contender with impeccable credentials. He had been chief minister and a Cabinet minister with a long tenure as Lok Sabha MP (since 1977). He had rendered distinguished service as Speaker of the Lok Sabha between 1996 and 1998. Young, educated and articulate, he checked all boxes, some said, and would be a good choice as India's first 'tribal' president. But they seemed to have forgotten that he had soured his relationship with Sonia Gandhi when he raised the issue of her foreign origin.

There had been reports of Sangma meeting various political leaders, and he informed the media that he was likely to get support of the Biju Janata Dal (BJD) and AIADMK.[157] However, he had even not been sponsored by his own party—NCP—which was a constituent of the UPA. To muddy waters further, his daughter Agatha Sangma had been appointed an MoS on the recommendation of Sharad Pawar.

In the meantime, from May onwards, Sonia Gandhi had initiated the process of consultation with leaders of other political parties—both UPA-II partners and others who were likely to support a Congress-led UPA nominee—to get a sense of their views.

---

[157]Rohit, 'Presidential elections: The race heats up!', the PRS blog, 14 June 2012, http://www.prsindia.org/theprsblog/?p=1690

On 27 May, M.J. Akbar came to meet me. Once a fierce critic, he had later become a good friend and had been working hard to further the cause of my presidential nomination. He apprised me of his informal discussions earlier that day with L.K. Advani and Jaswant Singh about my candidature, and insisted that both of them were supportive. They had told him that if the Congress officially nominated me, they would extend support, thus making me the unanimous choice. However, the conversation between M.J. Akbar and the BJP leaders was not made public, and I thought it imprudent to do so as the Congress was yet to take a decision in this regard.

On 29 May, Ahmed Patel informed me that Sonia Gandhi had perhaps finalized my name as the presidential nominee of the UPA. He went on to say that she was also exploring the possibility of adequate support for Hamid Ansari. The bone of contention about my nomination remained the same as that in 2007.

I sought time for a meeting with Sonia Gandhi on 1 June to discuss matters of the government and the party. I met her on the evening of 2 June. It was a frank discussion about a variety of issues: the functioning of the government and the PMO, ways to improve UPA's image, the apparent distance between the party and the government and the lack of proactiveness within the UPA. We reviewed party positions on the presidential election, and discussed probable candidates and the possibility of garnering the required support for those candidates. During the course of this discussion, she told me frankly, 'Pranabji, you are most eminently suited for the office, but you should not forget the crucial role you are playing in the functioning of the government. Could you suggest a substitute?'

'Madam,' I said, 'I am a party-man. Throughout my life, I have acted as per the advice of the leadership. Therefore, whatever be the responsibility given to me, I will discharge it with all the sincerity at my command.' She appreciated my stance.

The meeting ended, and I returned with a vague impression that she might wish to consider Manmohan Singh as the UPA presidential nominee. I thought that if she selected Singh for the presidential office, she may choose me as the prime minister. I had heard a rumour that she had given this formulation serious thought while on a holiday in the Kaushambi Hills.

However, there is no doubt that Sonia Gandhi saw me as an organizational man. This is best illustrated by an important incident. The parliament was debating an issue with great fervour, with Sushma Swaraj leading the charge and demanding answers. Soon there was commotion as all MPs began to outshout one another. When the Parliament adjourned for lunch, I told Sushma Swaraj that she should allow the Legislature's work to be completed, and assured her that she would get a response to the issue she had raised. Despite my assurances, the commotion continued, and Pawan Bansal called my office for me. I went to the Parliament and got extremely agitated on seeing the chaos. In anger, I told the members that they seemed to have forgotten that they were leaders; and that they were behaving like petulant children. I reiterated, as I had done earlier in the day to Sushma Swaraj that I would take up the matter. However, nobody had the right to hold the House to a standstill.

Sensing my indignation, Murli Manohar Joshi said, 'Dada is very angry. Someone please give him some water,' and Sonia Gandhi passed it to me. Subsequently, Sushma Swaraj came across and apologized, saying that she had been unable to communicate my message to her colleagues. The matter was thus sorted out, but not before Sonia Gandhi commented, 'This is why you can't be President.'

Nothing exemplifies my temper more than the episode that

involved the arrest of Jayendra Saraswati, the Shankaracharya of Kanchi, on 12 November 2004. It was a time when the entire country was celebrating Diwali. During the Cabinet meeting, I was extremely critical of the timing of the arrest and questioned if the basic tenets of secularism of the Indian state were confined to only Hindu monks and seers? Would the state machinery dare to arrest a Muslim cleric during Eid festivities? M.K. Narayanan, then Special Adviser to Prime Minister, also agreed with me. I immediately issued instructions for the Shankaracharya to be released on bail.

On 13 June, Mamata Banerjee met Sonia Gandhi. Later, Sonia Gandhi told me that Mamata had flagged off to her the names of two potential UPA nominees for the presidential election: Hamid Ansari and myself. Mamata said she was in discussions with Mulayam Singh Yadav on this issue, and would speak to him and revert. However, she did not inform Sonia Gandhi about her decision.

I am not aware of the discussions at Mulayam Singh Yadav's residence. But at a press conference that they jointly held that evening, they declared that their presidential nominees were A.P.J. Abdul Kalam, Manmohan Singh and Somnath Chatterjee, in that order. Mamata also mentioned her meeting with Sonia Gandhi and insisted that Sonia had suggested two names—Hamid Ansari and Pranab Mukherjee—both of which were unacceptable to them.[158]

I heard of this development, but chose not to comment. A certain sadness and disappointment spread amongst my family and friends. My daughter Sharmistha, who was in Ranikhet at that time, sent a message consoling me, and quoted a few lines

---

[158]Smita Gupta & Gargi Parsai, 'Dramatic twist to Presidential race', *The Hindu*, 13 June 2012, http://www.thehindu.com/news/national/dramatic-twist-to-presidential-race/article3523934.ece

from one of Tagore's famous songs (which I myself frequently consoled people with):

'Dukhero raatey nikhilo dhora jedin korey bonchonatomarey jeno na kori shongshoy.'

(So that on the darkest of nights when the world turns away I may not doubt your benevolent presence.)

Later that night, I received a call from Sonia Gandhi. She requested me to meet her the following morning. We did not discuss anything further on the phone.

Mamata and Mulayam Singh Yadav's press conference made front page news the next morning, with Mamata subsequently reiterating that under no circumstances would they support me.

On 14 June, I went to meet Sonia Gandhi at 11 a.m. and had a long discussion with her. I found her to be in a decisive mood. She told me about her meeting with Mamata Banerjee. She was dismayed that Mamata had not informed us about her decision after the meeting with Mulayam Singh Yadav and, instead, had disclosed information to the media.

She suggested that the issue be discussed further at the Core Group meeting, which was already scheduled at 7 Race Course Road, and was to be attended by her, A.K. Antony, P. Chidambaram, Ahmed Patel and myself, along with the PM. I recommended to Sonia Gandhi that she discuss the implications of my nomination with both the party and the government.

There were a slew of scheduled meetings of the Cabinet and some Cabinet committees that evening, after which Dr Singh informed me of his discussion with Sonia Gandhi and their joint decision to nominate me. However, the formal decision would be taken in the next day's Coordination Committee meeting. Both of them were seized of the fact that we could not afford to lose the presidential election.

Thereafter, Singh asked me if I would have to resign from the Cabinet immediately on being nominated. I told him that to the best of my knowledge, two incumbent Cabinet ministers had previously become president—Fakhruddin Ali Ahmed in 1974 and Giani Zail Singh in 1982. Also R. Venkataraman, who was the incumbent defence minister, was nominated for vice president's office. All three of them resigned from their respective ministerial offices before filing the nomination papers. In addition, Pratibha Devisingh Patil resigned from the office of the Governor of Rajasthan when she filed her nomination in 2007. However, I added, that in the 2007 presidential election, Bhairon Singh Shekhawat, who was then the vice president, did not resign from that office till his term came to an end in August 2007.

Keeping all this in mind, I proposed to resign from the Cabinet and the Working Committee around 24–25 June, before filing the nomination papers.

On the day of the announcement of my candidature, I found an unusually large crowd in front of the gate when I returned from the Coordination Committee meeting to my office in North Block. As soon as I got off my car, I was surrounded by them. There was a volley of questions about Mamata's opposition to my candidature and whether I would request Mamata for her support. I told reporters that Mamata Banerjee was like my younger sister and that I would talk to her if there was a need for the same. In fact, this was my standard reply whenever I was confronted with this question during my campaign period.

Within an hour of the announcement, Mayawati and Mulayam Singh Yadav expressed their parties' support—Mayawati at a press conference in Delhi and Mulayam Singh Yadav in Lucknow. In the meantime, L.K. Advani tried to persuade Jayalalithaa not to support P.A. Sangma, but to support Kalam instead, in which case the chances of winning the election would be higher.

However, this strategy came to nought as Kalam, at a press conference on 18 June, declared that he was not in the race.[159] But Mamata Banerjee persevered, and tried to persuade him. In fact, she organized a rally of her party workers and legislators in Kolkata to mobilize public sentiment in favour of Kalam. In this way she hoped to urge on Kalam to reconsider his decision and put pressure on the political spectrum to consider Kalam as a candidate of the people. Her emotional and irrational antipathy towards me seemed to have overpowered her. She had forgotten that the common man does not elect the president; rather, the president is elected by an electoral college consisting of members of the Parliament and State Legislative Assemblies. Perhaps all this was the result of her expectations not being met by me as the finance minister.

Mamata Banerjee had been unhappy with me for quite some time. She seemed to be under the misconception that I was deliberately not meeting her demand for a waiver of the outstanding loan to the government of West Bengal, which had accumulated during the Left Front rule. She had also been demanding a moratorium of five years for the current debts. She expected me to fulfil these demands as the finance minister.

On several occasions, I had explained to her that total debt moratorium was not possible, for every state has a debt burden. I assured her that the 13th Finance Commission had made some recommendations for providing relief to debt-burdened states. While most states accepted and implemented the recommendations, West Bengal had not—and as a result, the state could not get full relief. I also reminded her that I had helped West

---

[159]'Presidential poll: Kalam rebuffs Mamata, Advani says will not contest against Mukherjee', *The Indian Express*, 18 June 2012, http://archive.indianexpress.com/news/presidential-poll-kalam-rebuffs-mamata-adv/963452/

Bengal during her chief ministership by substantially enhancing the quantum of funds of the Backward Area Development Grant and through certain other relief measures. I had explained the details of the financial package to her Finance Minister, Amit Mitra. I do not know what he conveyed to her but she remained dejected, frustrated and angry with me.

On 22 June, two chief ministers—Kiran Kumar Reddy of Andhra Pradesh and Vijay Bahuguna of Uttarakhand—met me in North Block. Kiran Reddy confirmed that he was talking to Chandrababu Naidu to ensure his support of my presidential candidature.

That night I left for Kolkata, en route to my village home in Kirnahar to meet the eldest member of my family—my eldest sister—and my elder brother, who was visiting Kirnahar from Shantiniketan. On 23 June, I left for Kolkata early in the morning and reached Kirnahar at 2.30 p.m. There I met a large number of media persons and faced numerous questions. I explained the nature of the Indian presidential election to them. I informed the gathering that members of the electoral college are limited to elected MLAs of State Assemblies and Members of both the Houses of the Parliament. Therefore, the election should be looked at from that angle, and it was expected that voting would take place as per the party lines. Party sponsored candidates were expected to obtain votes of their respective sponsor parties. I told them that up until then, apart from UPA's partners, party leaders of the BSP, SP and JD(S) had expressed their support for my candidature. The aggregate votes of these parties in the Parliament and State Legislatures and the value of that aggregate could ensure my victory. I added that after filing the nomination, I would start visiting states and meeting leaders of those political parties and their legislators who had extended their support to me. These meetings, I reiterated, were not meant for canvassing since they had already expressed their support, but simply to convey my gratitude to my supporters. I explained to them that after the completion of the presidential election, there would be only two days before the declaration of results and the swearing-in, and that time would not be enough for me to visit all the states.

I stayed a day in Kolkata on my way back from the village. There was much speculation in the media that I might meet Mamata Banerjee (who had incidentally boycotted the UPA Coordination Committee meeting). There was no effort either from her side or from mine to establish any contact. I returned to Delhi without having met her in Kolkata.

On 25 June, the CWC met at 7 Race Course Road with Congress President Sonia Gandhi in the Chair. All members of the Committee—including the Prime Minister, office bearers and the Congress chief ministers, who were normally invitees in CWC—were present. After briefing the meeting on the presidential elections, Sonia Gandhi bid me an emotional farewell. In her speech she said:

> I believe, like me, all of you will miss Pranabji in the meetings of the Congress Working Committee (CWC) and other Congress forums where his visible presence was so impressive and effective that we cannot imagine to have a meeting of CWC without Pranabji.

Thereafter, with a mischievous smile she looked at me and said: 'Along with that, of course, I will miss some of his tantrums.'

In my response, I said:

> I was born in a Congress family. My father was a lifelong Congress worker. He joined the party at the clarion call of Gandhiji in the days of non-cooperation in 1920 and

26 January 2009: External Affairs Minister Pranab Mukherjee and President Pratibha Patil welcome Kazakhstan President Nursultan Nazarbayev at the ceremonial reception at the Rashtrapati Bhavan.

27. *May 2009: (From left to right) Jaipal Reddy; Ghulam Nabi Azad; Mamata Banerjee, A.K. Antony; Pranab Mukherjee, Sonia Gandhi and Dr Manmohan Singh at the swearing-in ceremony at the Rashtrapati Bhavan.*

28 January 2010: Finance Minister Pranab Mukherjee with Bangladeshi Prime Minister Sheikh Hasina in New Delhi.

29. February 2010: Finance Minister Pranab Mukherjee speaks to the media after his budget speech in New Delhi.

30. April 2011: Finance Minister and Chairman of Lokpal Bill Drafting Committee Pranab Mukherjee with Ministers P. Chidambaram, M. Veerappa Moily, Kapil Sibal and Salman Khurshid at the first meeting of the panel at North Block in New Delhi.

31. February 2012: Finance Minister Pranab Mukherjee, Nandan Nilekani, Sharad Pawar and Jairam Ramesh with the final report of the Task force on an Aadhar-enabled Unified Payment Infrastructure in New Delhi.

32. March 2012: Prime Minister Dr Manmohan Singh chairs the all party meeting on the Lokpal Bill in New Delhi.

33. June 2012: Pranab Mukherjee filing the nomination papers for the Presidential Election in the presence of Prime Minister Dr Manmohan Singh, Chairperson National Advisory Council, Sonia Gandhi and other dignitaries in the Parliament.

34. July 2012: The Chief Justice of India Justice S.H. Kapadia, President-elect Pranab Mukherjee, President Pratibha Patil, Vice President Mohammad Hamid Ansari and Lok Sabha Speaker Meira Kumar proceeding for the swearing-in ceremony in the central hall of the Parliament.

35. July 2012: Pranab Mukherjee signs the oath as the new President of India at the swearing-in ceremony in the central hall of the Parliament.
The Chief Justice of India, Justice S.H. Kapadia looks on.

36. July 2012: President Pranab Mukherjee arrives to inspect the guard of honour in the forecourt of the Rashtrapati Bhavan.

37. July 2012: President Pranab Mukherjee takes salute during the guard of honour ceremony in the Rashtrapati Bhavan.

served as a humble worker of this great organization till 1964 when he retired from active politics. As a child, I nurtured the ambition to be a member of the CWC one day, after reading biographical sketches of CWC members in my Rapid Reader textbook in school in 1945. I am grateful to this national organization in which I could serve as a member of the CWC from 1978–86 and again from 1991 till date... I will never forget the support I received from all Congress Presidents starting from Smt. Indira Gandhi to Smt. Sonia Gandhi, and my colleagues in the CWC who tolerated my temperament and short-tempered behaviour. I sincerely apologize for that.

It was an emotional send-off.

On 26 June, I resigned from the Cabinet. I handed over my resignation letter at 4.45 p.m. to the Prime Minister. After receiving my resignation and recommending to the President that it be accepted, Singh wrote to me:

> Our Government owes a deep debt of gratitude to you for your invaluable contribution to this Government over the last 8 years. It is a testimony of your extraordinary abilities and your stature in public life. You have carried an enormous range of responsibilities with ease and accomplishment. Our colleagues in the Cabinet and myself have benefitted from your wise counsel on innumerable occasions and we will deeply miss your presence amongst us.[160]

Earlier, on 27 June, the CPI-M politburo decided to support me but at the Left Front Meeting, the CPI and RSP expressed their

---

[160]'PM writes to Shri Pranab Mukherjee', Prime Minister's Office, Press Information Bureau, Government Of India, 26 June 2012, http://pib.nic.in/newsite/mbErel.aspx?relid=85026

desire to oppose. Ultimately, however, they remained neutral and did not participate in the presidential elections.[161]

On 28 June, I filed my nomination papers with the Secretary General, Rajya Sabha, who was the ex-officio Returning Officer of the presidential election. At 10.15 a.m., Pawan Bansal got the nomination papers signed by me and left. I accompanied V. Narayanasamy in his car and proceeded to the Parliament House. (I had given up my official car since I ceased to be a minister). At the Parliament House, I went to the chamber of the Prime Minister and joined the waiting team—Mulayam Singh Yadav (SP), Ajit Singh (RLD), Ram Vilas Paswan (LJP), Satish Mishra and Dara Singh Chauhan (BSP), D.P. Tripathi (NCP) and Ram Gopal Yadav (SP). From there, we proceeded to the Returning Officer's room. A large number of ministers from the Centre and the States, chief ministers, MPs and MLAs lined up on both sides of the corridor. The first set of nomination papers was handed over to the Returning Officer by Sonia Gandhi and all of us touched it—a mandatory photo op! The first set of nomination papers was deposited at 11.00 a.m. Motilal Vora and leaders of other political parties submitted the second set. I then took the Oath of Allegiance to the Constitution, which was read out by the Returning Officer. Thereafter, we returned to the Prime Minister's room and had a cup of tea.

In the evening, I gave a lengthy interview at my residence to Arnab Goswami, then the editor-in-chief of *Times Now*, during which, as expected, I was grilled, not only on the presidential elections, but also on the flurry of criticism on my economic policies that had built up as soon as I resigned from Government. It seemed akin to a systematic campaign against my economic

---

[161]'Prasenjit Bose's Letter of Resignation from CPM', 4 July 2012, *Mainstream*, Vol. L, No. 28, 30 June 2012, https://www.mainstreamweekly.net/article3534.html

policies, especially my retrospective tax proposal. This was expected, but not to such an extent.

The scrutiny of nomination papers of the presidential candidates was conducted on 2 July. Sangma and his lawyer, Satya Pal Jain, argued that my nomination papers should be declared invalid as I had, according to them, violated the provisions of Clause 2 of Article 58 of the Constitution of India, which states that the President shall not hold any office of profit. Their contention was that I was the President of the Council of the Indian Statistical Institute (ISI), which is a central organization and a deemed university.

My election agent Pawan Bansal, assisted by P. Chidambaram and P.H. Parekh, stated that the office of the President of the Council of ISI was not an office of profit as that neither carried any salary or financial benefit, nor was I the executive head of the institute. They also pointed out that according to their recollection and knowledge, I had resigned from all organizations I had been associated with. To confirm this, they requested that the hearing be deferred for a day so that they could provide the necessary documents supporting this claim.

Pawan Bansal, Chidambaram and Parekh then came to my residence to explain the situation. I told them that I recalled having resigned from the ISI, and that a copy of the acceptance letter of my resignation might be available with my Adviser, Omita Paul. She brought out a copy of my handwritten resignation letter as President of the ISI Council. The President of the Institute, M.G.K. Menon, had made a handwritten notation—'accepted with immediate effect', on that letter on 20 June.

Chidambaram, Bansal and Parekh then assured me that there was nothing to be worried about. They were fully satisfied and convinced that they had a cast-iron case.

I did not realize then that this was part of a larger conspiracy to get me disqualified. I am told that some people, including Subramanian Swamy, Ram Jethmalani and Satya Pal Jain, briefed the media that each organization I was associated with was an office of profit—Asiatic Society, ISI, Rabindra Bharati Society, Nikhil Bharat Banga Sahitya Sammelan, and a host of other literary and academic organizations. However, what they did not know was that after my candidature was announced, I had resigned from all of them. It is possible that the organization websites and sundry documents had not yet been corrected, which would have prompted these people to raise a hue and cry.

I began my visit to the states on 30 June and completed this exercise on 16 July. I had been to all state headquarters except Shimla (Himachal Pradesh), Aizawl (Mizoram), Itanagar (Arunachal Pradesh) and Shillong (Meghalaya). MLAs of these states had come to meet me at Chandigarh and Guwahati respectively. I met the MLAs and MPs of all supporting parties and UPA partners. I could not address the MLAs and MPs of TMC as I did not have that party's support. Mamata Banerjee's decision to support me came much later. At all my stops, I was received very warmly, and met not only with Congress people but all supporting parties. They all reiterated their support for my candidature.

A few interactions stand out in my memory.

On my visit to his state, I recall the Meghalaya Chief Minister Mukul Sangma, telling me, 'Dada, you will see he (P.A. Sangma) will not even get half the votes he expects in his own state Meghalaya, and you will be well-ahead of him.'

My visit to West Bengal, not surprisingly, received a lot of attention. The media was present in large numbers both at the airport and at my residence. They were keen to know about the possibility of meeting or a discussion with Mamata Banerjee regarding my candidature. I gave them my stock reply, 'I shall certainly speak should the need arise.'

I recall Nitish Kumar, who had already promised me his support even though he was an NDA partner, asking me not to visit Bihar. He said it would be embarrassing for him if he received me at the airport and organized meetings with his MLAs since his alliance partner—the BJP—would not take it kindly. He told me that since he had openly declared his support for my candidature, and Sharad Yadav had, on behalf of his party, signed my nomination papers, there was no need of my visiting Patna.

My visit to Maharashtra on 13 July was significant. Though Shiv Sena was a part of the NDA, Bal Thackeray, had, without being asked, extended his support to my candidature. This was completely unexpected.

I had asked both Sonia Gandhi and Sharad Pawar—who was instrumental, I think, in influencing Thackeray towards me—whether I should meet Thackeray during my visit to Mumbai. I had received several messages from him for an interaction at his residence. Sonia Gandhi was not enthusiastic about my meeting Bal Thackeray and advised me to avoid it if possible. Sonia Gandhi's reservations about Thackeray were based on her own perception of his policies.

Expectedly, Sharad Pawar's advice was completely different. Pawar insisted that I meet Thackeray since he and his followers were waiting to receive me at his residence and had made elaborate arrangements for my visit. Pawar added that Thackeray would consider it a personal insult if I did not meet him during my visit to Mumbai. I took a decision to meet Thackeray despite Sonia Gandhi's disapproval because I felt that the man who had broken away from his traditional coalition partner to support my candidature, should not feel humiliated. I requested Sharad Pawar to take me to Thackeray's residence from the airport, and he readily agreed to do so.

There was a large gathering of the media and curious onlookers at Thackeray's residence. I had a brief chat with him, his son and daughter-in-law. The meeting was very cordial. He jokingly told me that it was but natural for the Maratha Tiger to support the Royal Bengal Tiger. We discussed some issues of internal security and he shared with me his very clear perceptions on the same.

I had known Thackeray as a politician with a sectarian approach, but at the same time, I could not ignore the fact that the man had gone out of the way to support my candidature. His decision to support the Congress nominee Pratibha Devisingh Patil in 2007 could still be explained—he himself had said that Patil was Maharashtra's 'bahu' and he had to support his 'daughter-in-law' for the highest office, irrespective of the party she contested from. In my case, it was his deliberate decision to support me—he even told me that he found me distinctly different from other Congress politicians. Whatever be the reason, I thought it was my duty to thank him personally for his support.

I returned to Delhi, and the following morning Girija Vyas called on me. She informed me that Sonia Gandhi and Ahmed Patel were upset about my meeting with Thackeray. I understood the cause of their unhappiness but, as I have explained, I did what I believed was right. I had to keep in mind the sensitivity of the advice of Sharad Pawar—an important ally of UPA-II. Already, Mamata Banerjee-led TMC had opted out of the UPA and presidential elections. If Sharad Pawar became similarly disenchanted, it wouldn't augur well for the UPA. The UPA had two more years in office as the ruling coalition; without the effective intervention and support of its partners it would not be possible for it to complete the term. It was already known that Sharad Pawar was unhappy on various issues and the relationship amongst coalition partners was under stress. I did not want to give him further cause for unhappiness. However, I decided not to raise this issue either with Sonia Gandhi or Ahmed Patel, and left the matter at that stage.

It was on my trip to Chandigarh on 16 July, that there was seemingly positive news from West Bengal.[162] Before my departure for the airport, Pradyut Guha took me aside and told me that he had just received a message from Mamata Banerjee. He read it out: 'Tell Dada not to worry about me.'

I had always had a feeling that Mamata would come around, which is why I had maintained a stoic silence all along and ignored all comments, including abuses, from her cronies.

I met Sonia Gandhi on the evening of 16 July to update her on my travels. It was a cordial but emotional meeting that lasted for an hour. I assured her that as per my assessment, of the total voting share of the presidential electoral college, I would receive about 70 per cent. At the end of the meeting, I told her, 'Madam, this would perhaps be my last meeting with you at your residence, since after 25 July, it would not be possible for me to come and meet you. I have visited your residence since Rajiv shifted to this house in 1990. In the last two decades, we have met countless times, shared views and argued on numerous occasions.'

She was also visibly moved and told me almost in a choked voice, 'Pranabji, I will miss you.'

'This will remain a cherished memory for me.' I said. Thereafter, I left.

Around that time, Somen Mitra and Subhendu Adhikari informed me that though it was very difficult for them to read Mamata's mind, there was little doubt that if she decided to vote

---

[162]Khushboo Sandhu, 'Pranab winds up Prez poll campaign in city', *The Indian Express*, 16 July 2012, http://indianexpress.com/article/cities/pranab-winds-up-prez-poll-campaign-in-city/

against me by supporting Sangma, it would lead to cross voting. About 10 MPs and 50 MLAs would defy the party decision and cast their votes in my favour. However, it would be very difficult for all of them to vote if she decided to boycott the presidential election and issue the Whip to abstain. In that case, about seven to eight MPs would openly defy her and cast their votes. But the MLAs would not have the courage to go against Mamata's decision.

I informed them that the process of voting by the Members of Legislature does not come within the purview of the Whip and party discipline because it is neither a Legislative action nor a proposal of Vote of Confidence or No Confidence. The member has the right, as per the Constitution, to elect a person. Therefore, here the job of a legislator was simply that of a voter—to cast his or her vote, and not to participate in any Legislation or Resolution of the House.

On 17 July, Mamata Banerjee announced at a press conference that she would support my candidature and directed the MLAs and MPs to vote in my favour.[163] I became aware of this development when I was awakened by some commotion outside my room that afternoon. I noticed a large number of media persons at the gate. Even as I tried to comprehend the reason behind this excessive media presence, I got a call from Anil Singh of *Aaj Tak*. He informed me of Mamata Banerjee's announcement, and wanted my reaction to the same. I told him that I had only heard about this decision from him, and would need to confirm first from Mamata before offering any reaction.

At the camp office, Pradyut assured me of the authenticity of the information, which he had confirmed from the Kolkata

---

[163]'Pranab gets Mamata's backing in Presidential bid', *The Hindu Business Line*, 17 July, 2012, http://www.thehindubusinessline.com/news/national/pranab-gets-mamatas-backing-in-presidential-bid/article3649539.ece

press. This also matched the text message Mamata had sent for me a few days earlier. I asked Pradyut to contact Mamata Banerjee on the phone. She was enthusiastic and told me that all MLAs and MPs would vote in my favour and she would ensure that not a single vote was wasted. She assured me that on the day of voting, she would personally monitor the casting of votes by each and every voting MLA and MP. Thereafter, she requested me to visit Kolkata first after my election. I thanked her and concluded our telephonic conversation. I was absolutely certain of the fact that she would ensure complete implementation of her decision.

Mamata Banerjee is a true politician. It was not that she did everything casually or as per her whims and fancies. On most occasions, she was carried off by emotions. But even behind her emotional outburst, she had a cool, calculated and well worked-out strategy. All her actions are backed by very strong reasons.

Her decision was to support me with a 'heavy heart'—the term she expressed before the media.[164] Major successes in two consecutive elections—Lok Sabha in 2009 and West Bengal Assembly in 2011, along with her massive victory in local body elections in West Bengal and a general appreciation of her performance had created an aura of her being a major player in national politics.

Throughout the entire campaign, she had provoked me and urged her supporters to use un-parliamentary language against me. She possibly wanted to goad me to comment, thus giving her an excuse to abstain from voting. She made every possible attempt to exert pressure on me and ensure that my nomination gets invalidated. However, I refused to retaliate against her personal

---

[164]'Pranab gets Mamata's backing in Presidential bid', *The Hindu Business Line*, 17 July 2012, http://www.thehindubusinessline.com/news/national/pranab-gets-mamatas-backing-in-presidential-bid/article3649539.ece

attacks on me. In the end, my strategy of waiting patiently and abstaining from offending her by any statement or even responding to abusive statements by some TMC leaders, paid off. I got her total support.

VOTING COMMENCES

On 19 July, voting for the presidential election began at the Parliament House and at the State Legislature buildings at respective state headquarters. I had appointed Election Observers at all places to represent me at the polling booth and to monitor the progress.

I cast my vote in the Parliament House, along with Manmohan Singh and Sonia Gandhi. At the polling hall, I came across Satya Pal Jain, Sangma's lawyer who had tried to stir trouble for me. He came up to me and said apologetically, 'Dada, please forgive me. Whatever I did, I had to do at the insistence of my party.' I just smiled at him. This was a historic election for me at a personal level. In this election, both my son and I cast our votes—I as an MP and my son as a member of West Bengal Legislative Assembly. It was indeed a unique moment.

In the evening, Pawan Bansal and V. Narayanasamy came to my residence. We checked the list and found that some of our voters were marked absent. Mulayam Singh's vote was invalidated by the Returning Officer as he had displayed the ballot paper before the media to show that he had voted for me.

On 20 and 21 July, I asked my staff and daughter to check the arrangements at Rashtrapati Bhavan. I had no knowledge of the life at the Presidential House, as I had been there only for official purposes. I also instructed Pradeep Gupta and some other officers to sort out and pack my papers and files. Pradeep did a good job by working out a detailed inventory of papers and mementos that I had collected over the years.

I had spent almost 17 years at 13 Talkatora Road, the longest I had ever stayed in a government accommodation in Delhi. I had changed ministerial bungalows in 1973, 1974, 1980, 1985, 1995 and 1996. In 2004, Sonia Gandhi insisted that I shift my residence to a house near 10 Janpath. However, my wife strongly resisted this idea. She had said, 'I am tired of changing residences according to the change in your political fortunes. Now I will only shift when you become either the prime minister or the president.' And so, she had to move house one more time when I became the President of India. It is my lasting regret that she didn't stay with me till my last day in Rashtrapati Bhavan.

Counting started at 10 a.m. on 22 July. News from the states started pouring in by noon and the results were on predicted lines. I got a clear majority in Mizoram, Meghalaya, Sikkim, Arunachal Pradesh, Nagaland, Tripura, Assam, Manipur, West Bengal, Bihar, Uttar Pradesh, Himachal Pradesh, Uttarakhand, Jammu & Kashmir, Haryana, Delhi, Rajasthan, Maharashtra, Goa, Kerala, Andhra Pradesh, Puducherry and Jharkhand. But, as expected, I had lost in Odisha, Tamil Nadu, Chhattisgarh, Madhya Pradesh and Karnataka. In the Parliament, I got an overwhelming majority. The final results were based on the total value of votes polled in the elections i.e. 10,28,872, out of the total voting value of 10,98,882. More than 70,000 vote values were not polled. Some political parties like CPI, RSP, TDP and TRS had declared that they would not cast their votes. Some MPs and MLAs also made mistakes while casting their votes.

Be that as it may, I won by a huge margin. The value of votes polled in my favour was 7,13,763 against my opponent P. Sangma, who secured 3,15,987. I won by a margin of almost 4 lakh votes. In terms of percentage, it was a little less than 70 per cent.[165]

Interestingly, Sangma did not get a single vote in the three tribal-dominated states of Nagaland, Mizoram and Tripura, and in Sikkim and Kerala. However, he got three votes from MLAs in West Bengal.

The results were followed by congratulatory calls, first from Manmohan Singh, followed by Sonia Gandhi, Hamid Ansari and Meira Kumar. Sonia Gandhi said, 'I am congratulating you over telephone and I will come personally to greet you after the results are formally declared by the Returning Officer.'

Around 8 p.m., Returning Officer Dr V.K. Agnihotri came to my residence and handed over the certificate of my election to the office of the President of India. After the official announcement, I received calls well past midnight both from India and abroad.

On the morning of 23 July, I was inundated with visitors and the media. At 11.30 a.m. Sharad Pawar, along with all senior leaders of the NCP, came to congratulate me. My departure from the Cabinet had created a rift between the Congress and the NCP since Sharad Pawar had expected to be elevated as he was the most senior member of the Cabinet. But after my resignation, the PM and Sonia Gandhi decided that A.K. Antony would occupy this position.

That same evening, Sharad Pawar and Praful Patel were conspicuous by their absence at the PM's customary farewell dinner for President Pratibha Patil. My wife and I were invited. Manmohan Singh informed me of Pawar's meeting with Sonia Gandhi the following day and the expectations of a resolution at that meeting.

But matters only got worse. Pawar and Patel, once again, skipped the customary dinner hosted by the outgoing president on

---

[165] Appendix 7: Presidential Election, 2012.

24 July for the Council of Ministers, to which I was also invited.[166] That evening, P. Chidambaram along with Home Secretary and a couple of other senior officers of the ministry explained the procedures to be followed the next day, including the swearing-in. This was followed by a briefing from the presidential side by the Military Secretary to the President, Lieutenant General A.K. Bakshi.

JOURNEY TO RAISINA HILL

On the morning of 25 July, dressed in a black sherwani and white kurta-pyjama, I left 13 Talkatora Road, my home of 17 years, not to return again. I proceeded to Rajghat followed by Shanti Van, Shakti Sthal, Vir Bhumi and finally, Vijay Ghat.

I arrived at Rashtrapati Bhavan and was received by President Pratibha Patil and her husband, Devisingh Shekhawat. Thereafter, I left for the Parliament House, accompanied by President Patil. She was saluted by the President's Bodyguard before boarding the car. She sat on the right side of the car and I sat on the left. We were led and followed by the President's Bodyguard convoy. Officers and jawans of the Army, Navy and Air Force stood on both sides of the road from the main gate of Rashtrapati Bhavan to gate no. 5 of the Parliament House to bid farewell to the outgoing President.

At the Parliament House, we were received by the Vice President, the Prime Minister, the Speaker of Lok Sabha and the Chief Justice of India. Here too, the President's Bodyguard offered Rashtriya Salute to the President, and Pratibha Patil took the salute. Thereafter, we proceeded to the Central Hall. We reached the podium and the Vice President, the President, the

---

[166]'President's Engagements', President's Secretariat, Rashtrapati Bhavan, New Delhi, 24 July 2012.

President-elect, the Speaker, the Prime Minister and the Chief Justice of India stood before their seats and the National Anthem was played by the Rashtrapati Bhavan band. Two decorated high chairs were kept on the podium—one for the President and the other for the President-elect. After the National Anthem, the Home Secretary came forward and sought permission of the President to commence the proceedings. He then read out the notification of the election commission declaring the election of the 13th President of India. The Home Secretary then called upon the Chief Justice of India to administer the oath of office to the President-elect.

The then Chief Justice of India, Justice S.H. Kapadia, read out the oath and I repeated it after him.

> I, Pranab Mukherjee, do swear in the name of God that I will faithfully execute the office of President of India and will to the best of my ability preserve, protect and defend the Constitution and the law and that I will devote myself to the service and well-being of the people of India.

Having completed the oath, the outgoing President and I symbolically exchanged chairs. I occupied the chair of the President while Ms Patil, the outgoing President, occupied the chair where I was seated earlier.

Thereafter, I delivered my brief but important acceptance speech. I emphasized that I would strictly adhere to the oath by which I had just committed to protect, preserve and defend the Constitution—in letter and spirit. I also mentioned that the rise of a village boy from flickering oil lamps in an obscure village, to the blazing chandeliers of the high dome at Raisina Hill, symbolizes the strength of Indian democracy and its pervasiveness. After the acceptance speech, the Home Secretary came forward again and sought my permission, now as the President, to conclude the ceremony.

We left Central Hall in a procession as before, and reached gate no. 5. This time it was I who took the Rashtriya Salute of the President's Bodyguard and then boarded the car. I sat on the right and the outgoing President Pratibha Patil, sat on the left. I was seen off by the Vice President, the Speaker, the Prime Minister and the Chief Justice of India. In the return procession, I greeted Sonia Gandhi and other leaders, governors, chief ministers and other guests.

Thereafter, the outgoing President was given a farewell salute by the President's Bodyguard. Both of us boarded the car, which took her to her new residence in New Delhi. Subsequently, I returned to the Rashtrapati Bhavan and went upstairs to the Dwarka Suite adjacent to Nalanda Suite—the first one for me and the second one for Mrs Mukherjee—and started my first day in Rashtrapati Bhavan. My entry into Rashtrapati Bhavan on the afternoon of 25 July 2012 marked the end of my 46-year-old political career which began in February 1966. It had indeed been a long and arduous journey.

EPILOGUE[167]

Our founding fathers, with the adoption of the Constitution, set in motion powerful forces that liberated us from the stranglehold of inequity in gender, caste and community along with other fetters that had tied us for too long. It inspired a social and cultural evolution which put Indian society on the track to modernity.

Our national mission must continue to be what it was when the generation of Mahatma Gandhi, Jawaharlal Nehru, Sardar Patel, Rajendra Prasad, Ambedkar and Maulana Azad offered us a tryst with destiny: to eliminate the curse of poverty, and create such opportunities for the young that they can take India forward by quantum leaps. For development to be real, the poorest of the land must feel that they are a part of the nation's narrative. Trickle-down theories do not address the legitimate aspirations of the poor. We must lift those at the bottom so that poverty is erased from the dictionary of modern India. For us, creation of an inclusive society has to be an article of faith. Gandhiji saw India as an inclusive nation where every section of our population lived in equality and enjoyed equal opportunity. He wanted our people to move forward unitedly in ever-widening thought and action. Financial inclusion is at the core of an

---

[167]Address by the former President of India, Shri Pranab Mukherjee, at the Farewell Function, http://pranabmukherjee.nic.in/

equitable society. We must ensure that the fruits of our policies reach the last person in the line.

A modern nation is built on some essential fundamentals—democracy or equal rights for every citizen, secularism or equal freedom to every faith, equality of every region, and economic equity. The soul of India resides in pluralism and tolerance. Plurality of our society has come about through assimilation of ideas over centuries. The multiplicity in culture, faith and language makes India special. We derive our strength from tolerance. It has been part of our collective consciousness for centuries. There are divergent strands in public discourse. We may argue, agree, or disagree, but we cannot deny the essential prevalence of multiplicity of opinion. Otherwise, a fundamental character of our thought process will wither away. Our social harmony is the sublime coexistence of temple, mosque, church, gurudwara and synagogue; they are symbols of our unity in diversity.

The capacity for compassion and empathy is the true foundation of our civilization. But every day, we see increased violence around us. At the heart of this violence are darkness, fear and mistrust. We must free our public discourse from all forms of violence, physical and verbal. Only a non-violent society can ensure the participation of all sections of the people, especially the marginalized and the dispossessed in the democratic process. Power of non-violence has to be resurrected to build a compassionate and caring society.

Peace is the most important ingredient of prosperity. History has often been written in the red of blood; but development and progress are the luminous rewards of a peace dividend, not a war trophy. Gandhiji taught by example, and gave us the supreme strength of non-violence. India's philosophy is not an abstract for textbooks. It flourishes in the day-to-day life of our people, who value the humane above all else. Violence is external to our nature; when, as human beings, we do err, we exorcise our sins with penitence and accountability.

But the visible rewards of peace have also obscured the fact that the age of war is not over. We are in the midst of a fourth world war—the war against terrorism. It is a world war because it can raise its evil head anywhere in the world. India has been on the frontlines of this war long before many other recognized its vicious depth or poisonous consequences. I am proud of the valour and conviction and steely determination of our Armed Forces as they have fought against this menace; of our brave police forces as they have met the enemy within; and of our people, who have defeated the terrorist trap by remaining calm in the face of extraordinary provocation. The people of India have been a beacon of maturity through the trauma of whiplash wounds. Those who instigate violence and perpetuate hatred need to understand one truth: few minutes of peace will achieve far more than years of war. India is content with itself, and driven by the will to sit on the high table of prosperity. It will not be deflected in its mission by noxious practitioners of terror.

In my view, education is the alchemy that can bring India its next golden age. Our oldest scriptures laid the framework of society around the pillars of knowledge; our challenge is to convert knowledge into a democratic force by taking it into every corner of our country. Our motto is unambiguous: All for knowledge, and knowledge for all.

The weight of office sometimes becomes a burden on dreams. The news is not always cheerful. Corruption is an evil that can depress the nation's mood and sap its progress. We cannot allow our progress to be hijacked by the greed of a few.

We have achieved much in the field of agriculture, industry and social infrastructure; but that is nothing compared to what India, led by the coming generations, will create in the decades ahead. What has brought us thus far, will take us further ahead. India's true story is the partnership of its people. Our wealth has been created by farmers and workers, industrialists and service-providers, soldiers and civilians.

Our citizens have the basic right to lead healthy, happy and productive lives. Happiness is fundamental to the human experience of life. Happiness is equally the outcome of economic and non-economic parameters. The quest for happiness is closely tied to the quest for sustainable development, which is the combination of human well-being, social inclusion and environmental stability. Eradication of poverty would provide a strong boost to happiness. A sustainable environment would prevent damage to the planetary resources. Social inclusion would ensure access to the fruits of progress to all. Good governance would provide the ability to people to shape their own lives through transparent, accountable and participatory political institutions.

I envisage an India where unity of purpose propels the common good; where the Centre and State are driven by the single vision of good governance; where every revolution is green; where democracy is not merely the right to vote once in five years but to speak always in the citizen's interest; where knowledge becomes wisdom; where the young pour their phenomenal energy and talent into the collective cause. As tyranny dwindles across the world, as democracy gets fresh life in regions once considered inhospitable...India becomes the model of modernity.

As Swami Vivekananda said in his soaring metaphor, 'India will be raised, not with the power of flesh but with the power of the spirit, not with the flag of destruction, but with the flag of peace and love. Bring all the forces of good together. Do not care what be your colour—green, blue, or red, but mix all the colours up and produce that intense glow of white, the colour of love. Ours is to work, the results will take care of themselves.'

Appendix 1

ELECTION OF SMT. SONIA GANDHI AS CONGRESS PRESIDENT

The Congress Working Committee adopted the following resolution:

Resolution

'This meeting of the Congress Working Committee takes note of the special situation arising out of the public announcement of Shri Sitaram Kesri to resign from the office of Congress President in favour of Smt. Sonia Gandhi at a press conference held on 9.3.98 at the AICC headquarters.

'After considering the special situation since this announcement the Congress Working Committee feels that the organizational work has come to stand still and that a hiatus has been created in the smooth functioning of the Party. To remove the confusion and state of uncertainty, leading to the irreparable and immense harm to the party, the Congress Working Committee elects Smt. Sonia Gandhi as President of the Indian National Congress in exercise of the power conferred in clause "J" of Article XIX of the Congress Constitution with immediate effect.'

The resolution was put to vote. It was adopted unanimously.

The meeting concluded with a vote of thanks to the Chair.

Appendix 2

THE PACHMARHI DECLARATION
6th SEPTEMBER, 1998

THANKING the Madhya Pradesh Congress Committee, its workers and leaders, and the Chief Minister of Madhya Pradesh for the excellent arrangements made for the Vichar Manthan Shivir (Brainstorming Session) at Pachmarhi.

RECALLING the noble heritage of the Party as bequeathed to it by leaders of the stature of Mahatma Gandhi, Pandit Jawaharlal Nehru, Sardar Patel, Maulana Azad, Subhas Chandra Bose, Rajaji, Acharya Kripalani, Perunthalaivar Kamaraj, Shri Lal Bahadur Shastri, Shrimati Indira Gandhi and Shri Rajiv Gandhi, among others too numerous to name individually.

RE-DEDICATING itself to the ideological sentinels of the Party:

- *Democracy,* including the strengthening of the Parliamentary system and the promotion of the third tier of governance through the Panchayats and Nagarpalikas, as enshrined in the Constitution;
- *Secularism,* that is the bedrock of our nationhood, draws its essence from catholicity, humanism and respect for every faith and religious denomination in the world, is consecrated in our Constitution, is the immutable commitment on which our democratic polity rests, and is enshrined in the Congress concept of secularism as

defined in the past, the present and will continue into the future;
- *Socialism*, directed to the task of promoting equity and social justice, based on sustained, balanced and high economic growth, through a mixed economy allied to democratic institutions of governance; and
- *Non-alignment*, as relevant as even in the post-Cold War era to the conservation of our sovereignty, and our relentless struggle to end what Shri Rajiv Gandhi called the 'quest for dominance' which regrettably continues to characterise international relations;

HAVING SECURED the approval of the Congress Working Committee,

PROCLAIMS the following Plan of Action and calls upon its workers everywhere in the country and abroad to work tirelessly towards the realisation of these goals and objectives:

A. POLITICAL

1. Scheduled Castes/Scheduled Tribes/Other Backward Classes/Weaker sections of society/Minorities

Notes with dismay the erosion of the affirmative action taken in favour of these sections of society in accordance with the letter and spirit of the Constitution, and

Pledges itself to vigilance and determined steps to:

(a) foretall and oppose any move to dilute reservations, the filling of vacancies, promotions and preference in government employment for these sections, as established by law;

(b) prevent any discrimination against them, ensure their safety and security and insist on stern action in regard to atrocities inflicted on them, especially their womenfolk;

(c) remove distortions and discrepancies that have crept into the implementation of policies in respect of education, subsidies and assistance in economic and poverty alleviation programmes;

(d) ensure full representation for these sections at all echelons of the Party;

(e) vigoriously pursue the 15 point programme for the Minorities as enunciated by Shrimati Indira Gandhi and reformulated by Shri Rajiv Gandhi;
(f) resolve the Babri Masjid issue expeditiously according to the law and ensure the rigorous observance of the Places of Worship Act which guarantees the status of all places of worship as they stood on Independence Day 1947.
(g) unflinchingly meet the challenge of the communal forces as represented by the BJP and its associates in the Sangh Parivar, such as the RSS, the VHP, and the Bajrang Dal, and those outside, such as the Shiv Sena, with no compromise or dilution of the well-established principles and practice of secularism, defined and evolved by the Party as crucial to our nationhood.

2. Women

Regrets the failure of the Government to introduce the Constitution (84th Amendment) Bill, as prepared by Parliament's Joint Select Committee, and seeks its passage at the next session of Parliament on the basis of a broad based consensus among all political parties;

Commits itself to the substantial enhanced representation of women at all echelons of the Party organisation and in the distribution of tickets for elections to the State Assemblies and Parliament.

3. Youth

Notes that 60 percent of the electorate is below the age of 30.

Recognises the crucial importance of the empowerment of youth as we move into the next millennium:

Underlines the necessity of

- being sensitive to their concerns and relevant to their aspirations,
- involving them in the work of the Party,
- ensuring adequate representation for them in the Party organisation and effective positions,

- and thus rejuvenating itself at the springs of youth, as it has repeatedly done over the last 113 years.

4. Population Control

Notes with concern the inadequacy of attention to the question of voluntary population control;

Decides to make this a key element of the Party programme;

Decides accordingly that any party member who becomes the parent of more than two children after the 1st January, 2000 would be ineligible for selection or election to any Party office or for selection as a Party candidate for any election.

5. Proposed Review to the Constitution

Notes the proposal to establish a Commission to review the Constitution;

Expresses it apprehensions regarding the ulterior motives of those piloting this wholly unnecessary proposal at present;

Stresses that the basic structure of the Constitution, including its essential secularism and the Parliamentary system, cannot be altered; and *Calls* upon the Government to hold prior consultations with all political parties before taking any decisions on this issue.

6. Electoral Reforms

Decides to appoint a committee to examine electoral reforms with special reference to curbing the use of money and muscle power in elections.

7. Coalitions

Affirms that the Party considers the present difficulties in forming one-party governments a transient phase in the evolution of our polity;

Pledges to restore the Party to its primacy in national affairs;

Decides that coalitions will be considered only when absolutely necessary and that too on the basis of agreed programmes which will not weaken the Party or compromise its basic ideology.

8. National Water Policy

Considers continuing and unresolved disputes over the sharing of river waters a matter of serious concern which impinges upon the progress of the country and even its unity;

Recalls the contribution of Shri Rajiv Gandhi to the elaboration of a National Water Policy;

Decides to accord high priority to the evolution of a policy which will treat river waters as a national asset to be used and developed as a national grid for the welfare of all its people.

9. North-East

Notes with anguish the growing alienation of a section of the people of the North-East from the national mainstream owing to inadequate development;

Resolves to restore priority to the North-East in Party matters and the governance of the nation as it was when the Congress was in office at the centre.

10. Jammu & Kashmir

Views with deep concern the developing situation in the State of Jammu & Kashmir;

Expresses its deep sympathy with the innocent families who have been the tragic victims of militant activites and cross border terrorism; and

Resolves to ensure that there is no erosion in the secular traditions of the State as secularism has always been the binding and motivating force in the State to which the Congress has consistently contributed since Independence.

11. Uttar Pradesh, Bihar and Tamil Nadu

Notes with concern the weakening of the Party in the. States of Uttar Pradesh, Bihar and Tamil Nadu; and

Decides to accord the highest priority to the revival and renewal of the Party in these States.

12. Jain Commission of Inquiry follow up

Expresses its profound concern at the failure of the agencies concerned to investigate the remaining leads identified by the Jain Commision, which have been pointedly brought to the attention of the Government by the Party and which the Government have committed themselves to fully investigating through the proposed Multi Disciplinary Monitoring Agency (MDMA)

Resolves not to rest till the truth, the whole truth and nothing but the truth about the dastardly assassination of its beloved leader, Shri Rajiv Gandhi, and the conspiracy, if any, behind. It, is fully and completely revealed, and the guilty parties, whoever they are, punished under the law of the land.

B. FOREIGN POLICY

Decides, to establish, as recommended, two Working Groups within the AICC's Department of Foreign Affairs to deal respectively with.

a. monitoring and preparing policy options on matters related to our neighbourhood, especially with a view to maintaining a sustained dialogue with our neighbours and servicing the Party-to-party relations which the Party intends to promote with political parties in neighbouring countries;

b. updating and rendering into treaty language the Action Plan for a Nuclear-Weapons-free and Non-violent World Order presented by Prime Minister Rajiv Gandhi to the Third Special Session of the UN General Assembly on Disarmament in 1988, to serve as a basis for discussions between the Party and its interlocutors on global nuclear Issues;

Directs the chairman of the Foreign Affairs Department to take ste⋯ towards sending high-powered Party delegations to China and ⋯ Africa, as recommended by the Group;

Cautions the Government against taking any precipitate decisions and accending to the CTBT, keeping in mind that no final decisions are called for over the next 12 months and that, in any case, the decision will have to be taken in consultation with all political parties;

Calls for the restoration of the national consensus on foreign policy, disrupted by the BJP-led Government.

C. ECONOMIC AFFAIRS

Reassert its commitment to socialism and the socialistic pattern of society as spelled out at Avadi in subsequent resolutions of the Party; 1955 and in subsequent resolutions of the Party;

Appreciates the remarkable recovery and impressive economic achievements secured through the reforms of the period 1991-96;

Deplores the squandering of that legacy by successive governments since the Congress demitted office in May 1996;

Reaffirms that the removal of poverty and the empowerment of the poor as effective partners in the growth process is the essence of the Party's economic policy;

Stresses the importance of redefining the role of Government at all levels to make it a more effective instrument of economic change and social transformation.

Commits itself to programmes aimed at the realisation of growth rates of 7%-8% per annum on average through the mixed economy model, adjusted pragmatically to meet the ends of growth with social justice;

Underlines the inescapable importance of conserving the environment to ensure sustainable development;

Demands the control of inflation and the dampening of inflationary expectations;

Urges the revival of investment and employment opportunities through policies that promote savings, productive investment, physical and social infrastructure, productivity and competitiveness, protection to industry against unfair external competition through an effective anti-dumping regime, and effective social security safety nets;

Commits itself to the direct transfer of funds to the Panchayats and Nagarpalikas for anti-poverty programmes in rural and urban areas;

Commits itself also to the reform of the educational system, in particular vocational education, to deal with the priority problem of educated unemployment among youth;

Assures the better targeting of subsidies for the poor, the needy and the disadvantaged, which will be continued and strengthened;

Agrees with the need to persist with a significant role for the public sector but equally with the need to make these viable and genuinely autonomous; and

Draws attention to the challenges posed by growing urbanization and calls for special programmes to improve the quality of life in town and cities;

Emphasises the importance of financial sector reforms, strengthening the small scale sector, energy supplies in all forms, and the centrality of agriculture and rural development in economic policy.

D. AGRICULTURE, RURAL DEVELOPMENT AND PANCHAYATI RAJ

Adopts the 35-point Programmmes of Action for Agriculture, supplemented by six additional points, as recommended by the Group, dealing, *inter alia*, with larger outlays for agriculture and agriculture-related activities by the public, private and cooperative sectors; the status of industry to agriculture; water management, including watershed management and a National Water Policy and National Grid for river waters; prevention of fragmentation and sub-division of land holdings combined with the vigorous implementation of land reforms and the maintenance of records of rights of proprietors, tenants and sharecroppers; assured supply of fertilizer, appropriate pesticides and quality seeds; cooperative credit and reasonable rates of interest within the capacity of farmers to pay; bank pass books and credit cards for access to credit;

the targeting of agricultural subsidies to farmers not industrial suppliers; comprehensive crop insurance; horticulture and aquaculture; dryland and and areas technology missions, including urgent attention to nascent problems in the cultivation of oil-seeds; agribusiness; exports of agricultural produce; the urgent passage of the Sui Generis Bill; the end of all harassment to farmers; and the elaboration and adoption of a National Agriculture Policy, etc.

Further adopts the 14-point Programmes of Action for Panchayat Raj, supplemented by one additional point, as recommended by the Group, dealing, *inter alia*, with the finances of the Panchayats in the light of recommendations by the State Finance Commissions and the terms of reference of the Eleventh Finance Commission with regard to the sound finances of the panchayats; the imperative need to elect and establish District Planning Committees, as provided for in the 74th Amendment, to serve as the foundation for the elaboration of the Ninth Five-Year Plan; the effective devolution of the functions delegated to the pachayats in pursuance of the Eleventh Schedule to the Constitution and subsequent State Legislation, including the need to establish a nexus between the functions devolved upon elected local authorities and the funds, as well as administrative and technical personnel, made available to them to carry out these functions; effective and active Gram Sabhas to ensure that Power to the Panchayats becomes Power to People, attempted by the Congress Government of Madhya Pradesh through its Panchayat Raj System and its Rajiv Gandhi Missions; free and fair elections, etc.

Pledges the Congress to taking all necessary action to ensure strict adherence to the letter and spirit of Part IX of the Constitution, conceived by Shri Rajiv Gandhi and brought to realisation by the Congress.

E. ORGANISATIONAL MATTERS

Approves the proposal to establish a Congress Election Authority, composed of eminent, impartial and respected senior Congress leaders to ensure fair elections at all levels of the Party;

Approves also the short-term and long-term Programmes of Action proposed by the Group immediate implementation by the Party at all levels within the prescribed time-frames; and

Transmits to the Congress Constitution Review Committee the suggestions made by the Group for strengthening the Party organisation and its frontal organisations, including relations with INTUC.

F. CONCLUSION

Under the leadership of Shrimati Sonia Gandhi,

Commits itself to becoming again the Party of the brightest and the best, a Party of principles and ideology, a Party of ethics in politics; and thereby

Entitled to primacy in the country's polity as the Party which mirrors the hopes and aspirations of the millions of downtrodden and dispossessed of this country.

Appendix 3

SHIMLA SANKALP JULY 9TH, 2003

Taking stock and reviewing the current political, social and economic situation in the country,

Being concerned with the state of the nation brought about by the comprehensive and glaring failures of the BJP-led NDA government and its divisive policies,

Responding to the public sentiment against the sharp fall in the rate of economic growth, mounting unemployment, stagnant investment, dire distress of *kisans* and *khet mazdoors,* increasing neglect of rural India and youth, grievous damage to social harmony and amity, growing jeopardy to defence preparedness and national security, rampant corruption and scams and the erosion of the independence of the country's foreign policy,

Conscious of the uniqueness of the Indian National Congress arising from several basic features of Congress's history, its character, its ideology and the legacy of its leadership,

Continuing to be inspired by the life and the message of Mahatma Gandhi and recalling at this critical moment the yeoman contribution to nation building and social reform of a galaxy of remarkable Congressmen and women like Jawaharlal Nehru, Sardar Patel, Rajendra Prasad, Maulana Azad, Subhas Chandra Bose, Rajaji, Acharya Kripalani, Kamaraj, Lal Bahadur Shastri, Indiraji, Rajivji and many other stalwarts,

Appreciating the successful stewardship of the country under successive Congress governments at the centre and in states that have resulted in economic growth and social transformation,

Acknowledging the support, goodwill and affection of all sections of our society, particularly the weaker sections like *dalits, adivasis,* OBCs, minorities and women,

Taking inspiration from Smt. Sonia Gandhi's inaugural speech at this *Vichar Manthan Shivir* in which she had spelt out a comprehensive vision, strategy and action programme for our party, from her relentless efforts to give voice, respect and position to the *karyakartas* across the country,

Proclaims the following Shimla Sankalp

POLITICAL CHALLENGES

1. The Indian National Congress announces that it stands fully prepared and ready to face the national elections at any time. No sacrifice should be too great for each and every Congressman and woman to ensure defeat of the BJP and its allies in the forthcoming elections. Throughout its annals, the dedication and sacrifices of lakhs of its workers across the length and breadth of this vast country that has sustained the Congress, in and out of power. It will be the dynamism of this committed cadre along with the support of the people that will ensure the victory of the Congress under the leadership of Smt. Sonia Gandhi.
2. The Indian National Congress will launch and sustain a *Jan Jagran Abhiyan* across the country to expose the BJP-led NDA government's comprehensive and glaring failures on security, defence, communal harmony, economic growth, social welfare, good governance, foreign policy and probity and transparency in public life.
3. The Indian National Congress re-emphasises its unwavering commitment to fight religious fundamentalism of all kinds. It also reiterates its resolve to combat in as determined a manner

as possible the evil and cynical attempts being made by the BJP, the RSS, the VHP and the Bajrang Dal to distort and destroy the liberal and tolerant essence of the Hinduism. It will also ensure that the essence of all great religions and faiths that have flourished for millennia on the soil of our country are protected and respected.

4. The Indian National Congress rededicates itself to strengthening the forces of nationalism that celebrate India's multiple diversities and nurture its many unities. The Indian National Congress expresses its commitment to the people that the communalisation of education will not go unchallenged and that the values of our Freedom Movement, of our Constitution and of our culture will resonate in schools and educational institutions through the *Bapu Sadbhavna and Shiksha Trust*. It calls upon all like-minded, progressive people to participate in this historic endeavour.

5. The Indian National Congress applauds the courage of the people of Jammu and Kashmir who have reinforced their commitment to secular democracy. It was the sagacity and concern for the welfare of the people of Jammu and Kashmir and the concern for the national interest that led Smt. Sonia Gandhi to agree to the formation of a PDP-led coalition government in J&K. The Indian National Congress accords the highest priority to the success of this coalition and to the formulation and execution of an effective strategy to deal with cross-border terrorism by the Centre. At the same time, the Indian National Congress will forcefully resist all attempts at using the issue of cross border terrorism to polarise our society on religious and communal lines.

6. The Indian National Congress is committed to the rapid and equitable development of all regions of our vast country. The special challenges and concerns of the people of the northeast will receive our undivided attention. The dangerous and nefarious political game being played by the BJP-led NDA government in collaboration with various insurgent groups will be exposed and resisted determinedly in the larger interests of our country.

7. The Indian National Congress promises the people of the country

an accelerated, time-bound programme for the modernisation of defence and a programme for providing full educational and housing facilities to the families of our armed forces and for the welfare of ex-servicemen and their families as well.

8. The Indian National Congress is firm in its commitment to Jawaharlal Nehru's vision of foreign policy. That framework has in-built flexibility to respond to the dynamics of a changing world keeping our national interests paramount. For the Congress, non-alignment has essentially meant independence in foreign policy. Recalling Rajiv Gandhi's historic efforts for the establishment of the nuclear weapons free world, the Indian National Congress reiterates its commitment to universal nuclear disarmament. As part of this process, the Congress Party believes in the need for initiating a dialogue with our nuclear neighbours for confidence building measures and for managing the consequences of nuclearisation.

People-Oriented Governance, Rural Transformation and Social Empowerment

9. The Indian National Congress identifies the following as the core priorities in its agenda of governance in keeping with its beacon *Congress Ka Haath, Garib Ke Saath*:

    - The assurance of reliable power, cheaper credit, better seeds, assured irrigation and remunerative prices to *kisans* across the country.
    - The devolution of funds, functions and functionaries so as to fully empower *panchayats and nagarpalikas* and make them vibrant institutions of local self government.
    - The enactment of a national rural employment guarantee by law and making employment growth for educated youth the overriding objective of all economic policies.
    - The establishment of food and nutrition security for all at more affordable prices and more particularly for the destitute and vulnerable sections of our society and for those living in the poorer and backward regions of the country.
    - The introduction of social insurance and other schemes for

the protection and welfare of all workers but particularly for those in the unorganised sector who constitute over 93% of our labour force.

- The acceleration of the implementation of land reforms and the initiation of reforms in land laws and record of rights to enable the conversion from the present system of presumptive titles to conclusive titles guaranteed by the State.
- The launching of major programmes for the economic advancement, social empowerment, political representation and legal equality of *dalits, adivasis, OBCs* and minorities.
- The time-bound implementation of the Mahila Sashaktikaran Sankalp adopted by the AICC on October 1, 2002.
- The start of a purposeful dialogue with private industry on how best India's social diversity could be reflected in the private sector in different ways like reservations and fiscal incentives, how privatisation where inevitable can protect the welfare of the weaker sections of society and how government procurement can promote entrepreneurship among *dalits and adivasis*.
- The introduction of liberal loan and scholarship schemes to ensure that no boy or girl belonging to the weaker sections of society is denied the benefit of school and college education.
- The deepening of fiscal and other economic reforms to make Indian agriculture, industry and services productive and competitive and to increase public investment particularly in irrigation, power, education and health.
- The functioning of government in a completely transparent, responsive and accountable manner with special focus on major administrative, police and judicial reforms.

10. The Indian National Congress recalls with pride that it was Rajiv Gandhi who brought India into the IT, computer and telecom age. The Indian National Congress also recalls with pride that it was a Congress government that launched economic reforms in the early 1990s to consolidate and expand on the gains made in

earlier decades. Social mobility and the expansion of the middle class in India is a direct consequence of the Congress's economic policies followed after Independence. The dynamic entrepreneurial base in India is a direct result of the Congress's vision and policies. The Indian National Congress is the only party that integrates pro-poor policies, programmes and perspectives with the concerns and aspirations of the middle classes and entrepreneurial communities.
11. The Indian National Congress fully recognises that the youth are our country's most precious and productive assets. They will get the Congress's maximum political, social and economic support to realise their aspiration in education, employment and entrepreneurship.

ORGANISATIONAL REFORMS

12. The Indian National Congress rededicates itself to a renaissance of the country's political culture along the lines identified in the Congress President's opening speech at this *Vichar Manthan Shivir*. It renews its commitment to major electoral reforms, among other things, to make party funding more transparent and to combat criminalisation of politics.
13. The Indian National Congress decides to establish a national training institute. Every Congressman and woman will go through an annual orientation course on contemporary political, economic and social issues and constructive work.
14. In keeping with the sentiments expressed by the Congress President in her opening speech at Shimla, the Indian National Congress reiterates its firm commitment to giving grassroots workers across the country a respected place in the party organisation.

CONCLUSION

The Indian National Congress fought for Independence and secured it for our people. We must now fight to preserve it and its time-tested values in their truest form. Our unshakeable commitment is to the politics of principles, to democracy, secularism, economic growth and social empowerment. We now seek the support of the people to bring India back on the path of Progress with Congress under the leadership of Smt. Sonia Gandhi. We invite all progressive thinking men and women, institutions and political movements who share our understanding of India's past, our concerns with India's present and our vision of India's future to join us in this historic endeavour.

Appendix 4

SUO MOTU STATEMENT BY MINISTER OF EXTERNAL AFFAIRS MR PRANAB MUKHERJEE IN LOK SABHA ON FOREIGN POLICY-RELATED DEVELOPMENTS (AN EXTRACT)

New Delhi
March 3, 2008

Sir,

India is closely monitoring developments in Sri Lanka and is concerned about the recent upsurge in the violence and conflict in that country. As Hon'ble Members are aware, our policy towards Sri Lanka is based on the conviction that there is no military solution to the conflict. The way forward lies in a peacefully negotiated political settlement within the framework of a united Sri Lanka acceptable to all communities, including the Tamils. The interests of the Tamil community in Sri Lanka are a matter of particular significance to us in our dealings with Sri Lanka. With this in mind, we have welcomed as a first step the declared intention of the Sri Lankan government to fully implement the 13th Amendment. We are also fully conscious of the need to provide for the safety of our fishermen. While it is important for our fishermen to respect the International Maritime Boundary Line (IMBL), especially keeping in mind the on-going operations in Sri Lanka, we have impressed on the Sri Lankan Navy to act with restraint and for our fishermen to be treated in a humane manner.

Appendix 5

TEXT OF HOME MINISTER P. CHIDAMBARAM'S SPEECH IN THE LOK SABHA ON THE MUMBAI TERROR ATTACKS

I wish to make a statement on the terrorist attacks that took place in Mumbai between November 26, 2008 and November 29, 2008. With deep regret, I have to report to this House that 164 persons (civilians and security personnel) lost their lives and 308 persons were injured. Among the civilians killed were 26 foreigners belonging to many nationalities. Besides, nine terrorists were killed in the operations by the security forces. One terrorist was overpowered and captured.

At the outset, I wish to pay homage to the innocent civilians who were killed and the brave security personnel who laid down their lives in order to save the lives of many others. I offer my heartfelt condolences to the bereaved families. The Government of India and the Government of Maharashtra have announced a set of measures as compensation for the terrible loss suffered by the families. Monetary compensation and free treatment have been offered to the injured. While words of sympathy and money can never adequately recompense the loss, I sincerely hope that our gesture will bring some comfort to the affected families.

The broad facts of the horrific tragedy are, by now, known

to the Honourable Members and the people of India. According to information gathered during the course of the investigations, it appears that 10 Pakistani nationals belonging to the Lashkar-e-Toiba, a proscribed terrorist outfit, had left Karachi on November 23, 2008; boarded a launch by the name of Al Hussaini; accosted and hijacked an Indian fishing vessel, MV Kuber, off the coast of Gujarat; killed its occupants; and a few miles short of the coast of Mumbai abandoned the fishing vessel, got into an inflatable rubber dinghy, and landed near Budhwar Park, Colaba, Mumbai between 8.00 p.m. and 8.30 p.m. on Nov 26, 2008.

The terrorists split into four groups and the main targets of the four groups were (i) Chatrapati Shivaji Terminus (CST); (ii) the Leopold Café and Taj Hotel; (iii) the Oberoi-Trident Hotel and; (iv) the Nariman House. These attacks involved indiscriminate firing, throwing of grenades and bomb blasts at 13 locations. Considering the extensive publicity that the whole episode has already received in the media and through official statements, it may not be necessary for me to go into the details of what happened at each of these locations.

I shall now give you a brief account of the response of the authorities to the terrorist attack. At the CST, security personnel belonging to the Mumbai police and the RPF confronted two heavily armed terrorists. After causing mayhem at CST, the two terrorists escaped via a lane opposite the station. Meanwhile, as soon as news of the firing at the CST and near Cama Hospital was received, police officers rushed to the sites.

There was an unexpected—and fortuitous—confrontation between the two terrorists and the police personnel in which three officers were killed. Subsequently, the two terrorists were challenged by a police party and, in an exchange of fire, one terrorist was killed and one was captured alive. The name of the apprehended terrorist is Mohammed Ajmal Amir. Interrogation and investigation have revealed that he belongs to Village Faridkot, in District Ukada, in the province of Punjab in Pakistan.

As information about the terrorist attacks poured in from the

Nariman House, Taj Hotel and the Oberoi-Trident Hotel, police parties were rushed to the places.

Shortly before 11 p.m. on November 26, 2008, information was received by the Central Government that there were incidents of firing in several places in Mumbai. Immediately, the Central Government authorities got in touch with the authorities of the Government of Maharashtra.

At the request of the Government of Maharashtra, the local Army and Navy authorities were asked to provide assistance. Accordingly, the Army deployed five columns to cordon off the affected areas and the Navy deployed their commandos to deal with the terrorists. Meanwhile, at about 11.30 p.m., the Government of Maharashtra asked for the National Security Guards.

The Central Government immediately alerted the NSG and mobilized their counter terrorist units, based at Manesar in Haryana. A group of around 200 men (which was reinforced the next day) was airlifted to Mumbai late that night. They were deployed at the various sites of the operation in the early hours of November 27, 2008.

The operations were conducted under very difficult circumstances: the terrorists were heavily armed, there was a hostage situation, and the terrorists had the advantage of shield and height afforded by the tall buildings that they had entered. Nevertheless, through their patience, skill and bravery, the security forces were able to neutralise the terrorists and rescued hundreds of persons who had been trapped in the buildings. The operations came to an end at about 8.20 a.m. on Nov 29, 2008.

Cases have been registered and the investigations have been entrusted to the Crime Branch of the Mumbai Police. The authorities of the Maharashtra Police and the Central agencies have extended their full support to the Mumbai Police in the conduct of the investigations. Honourable Members will appreciate that it would not be appropriate to disclose any details of the investigations except to draw attention to the official briefings given by the Mumbai Police. Nor would I be able to comment on the many reports that have appeared in the media from time to time. I would respectfully urge patience until the investigations are completed and the reports are filed before the court of law.

I am, however, able to say that the finger of suspicion unmistakably points to the territory of our neighbour, Pakistan. The interrogation of the captured terrorist has yielded valuable material evidence. The origins of the ten terrorists who entered India have been established conclusively. There is also abundant evidence gathered from the inflatable rubber dinghy, the fishing vessel and the bodies of the terrorists that has enabled the investigators to reconstruct the sequence of events from the origin to the targets.

I know that Honourable Members—as well as the people of the country—would wish to ask a number of questions concerning the nature and extent of the terrorist threat to India, the intelligence gathering machinery, the preparedness of our security forces, the effectiveness of the operations, and on the path forward. There are genuine concerns on each of these matters. I share these concerns. In the last ten days, even while familiarizing myself with the security situation and the working of the Ministry of Home Affairs, the intelligence agencies, the Central Paramilitary Forces and the State Police forces. I have initiated a number of steps that will, I believe, enhance security and restore the confidence of the people.

Honourable Members, in my assessment, South Asia is in the eye of the storm of terror. Several terrorist organisations operating from territories beyond India's borders have been identified as the source of the terrorist attacks in India that have occurred over the last several years.

India told the United Nations Security Council yesterday, 'India will act to safeguard and protect its people from such heinous attacks; however long and difficult that task may be. We have acted with restraint in the face of terrorist attacks. We must do our duty by our people and take all actions as we deem fit to defend and protect them.' That is our policy. My colleague, Shri Pranab Mukherjee, Minister for External Affairs will intervene in the discussion and deal with the external and diplomatic aspects of the situation arising out of the terrorist attacks in Mumbai.

We have a number of intelligence gathering agencies. Intelligence is shared, evaluated and acted upon. However, I have found that there is a tendency to treat some intelligence inputs that are not specific or precise as not actionable intelligence. Further, the responsibility for acting upon intelligence inputs is quite diffused. In the case of the Mumbai attacks, intelligence regarding a suspected LeT vessel attempting to infiltrate through the sea route was shared with the Director General, Coast Guard and the Principal Director, Naval Intelligence.

The Coast Guard made a serious effort, including deploying vessels and aircraft, to locate the suspect vessel, but was not successful. The Navy found that the coordinates of the vessel, as reported, placed it well within the territorial waters of Pakistan. Nevertheless, the Navy had committed several surface units and aircraft in the zone during the period on November 19–20, 2008. In the absence of further inputs or information from the agencies concerned, the Navy concluded that no further action could be taken on the basis of the available information.

I wish to inform Honourable Members that all aspects concerning intelligence are under my examination. While the basic structure seems sound, there is a need to make intelligence gathering and intelligence sharing more effective and result oriented. Some changes have already been made and more are underway.

The NSG is our best trained and best equipped force to counter a terrorist attack. On many occasions in the past—and in Mumbai too—they have displayed exceptional courage and skill. They are hampered by the distance between their headquarters and the airport; the absence of a dedicated aircraft; and the poor logistics in the theatre of operations.

Nevertheless, once deployed, the NSG is a very effective counter terrorist force. I have initiated a number of steps to remove the logistical weaknesses in mobilising and deploying the NSG. A decision has been taken to locate NSG units in a few regional hubs. A decision has also been taken to draw upon the commando units of the Armed Forces to create more regional hubs until a decision is taken to locate

NSG units in those hubs too. These decisions will be implemented as expeditiously as possible.

The Mumbai terrorist attacks have brought into sharp focus the vulnerability of our coastline that extends to 7,500 km and the imperative need to enhance maritime and coastal security. A coastal security scheme was approved in January 2005 for implementation over a period of five years with an outlay of Rs 400 crore for capital expenditure and Rs 151 crore for recurring expenditure during the first five years.

We have reviewed the scheme and we have concluded that there is a need to strengthen it and integrate it into a larger security system. A decision has been taken in-principle to create a Coastal Command for overall supervision and coordination of maritime and coastal security. The mandate of the Coastal Command will be to secure India's coastline.

I may also report to this House a number of other decisions that have been taken in order to enhance security:

Intelligence gathering requires human resources and technical resources. We have identified the gaps. Steps are being taken to fill the vacancies in the intelligence organisations expeditiously and to provide them with advanced technical equipment.

India Reserve Battalions are being raised in a number of states with financial assistance from the Central Government. Government have already authorized that two companies of each battalion may be raised as special commando units for which additional assistance will be provided for training, equipment, etc.

It has been decided to set up 20 counter-insurgency and anti-terrorism schools in different parts of the country for training the commando units of the State police forces.

A separate exercise is underway to strengthen the laws relating to terrorist acts. We are in the process of consulting different political parties and I hope to introduce in this session, with the leave of this House, a set of Bills to strengthen the legal provisions relating to the prevention, investigation, prosecution and punishment of terrorist acts. One of the Bills is for setting up a National Investigation Agency. I would urge this House to consider and pass these Bills in this session. I would also urge this House to pass the Amendment Bill to the Prevention of Money Laundering Act, 2002.

The Prime Minister, in his address to the Nation on November 27, 2008 declared the resolve of the Government to take the strongest possible measures to ensure the security of the Nation and the people. I promise, on behalf of the Government, that we will strain every nerve to carry this resolve into determined action. There is one thing that I wish to make clear: given the nature of the threat, we cannot go back to 'business as usual'. In the next few weeks and months, it will be my endeavour to take certain hard decisions and prepare the country and the people to face the challenge of terrorism.

I appeal to all sections of this Honourable House and to the people of India to stand united and brave in the face of the challenge of terrorism. I ask you to remember the extraordinary courage of Assistant Sub-Inspector Tukaram Ombale who grabbed the barrel of the gun and took all the bullets in his chest to enable his fellow policemen to overpower Mohammed Ajmal Amir.

I ask you to remember the supreme sacrifice made by Major Sandeep Unnikrishnan who ordered his men to stay back while he confronted the terrorists. Ordinary men and women like us cannot match their bravery, but we can stay united in our resolve and in our actions. Nothing should divide us—not religion, not language, not caste. In our fight against terror, there will be need for self-restraint, discipline and even some sacrifice. I seek your support; and I have no doubt that, with your support and the support of the people, we shall overcome and vanquish the forces of terror.

Appendix 6

INDIA–US JOINT STATEMENT (AN EXTRACT)

Washington, DC
July 18, 2005

Prime Minister Manmohan Singh and President Bush today declare their resolve to transform the relationship between their countries and establish a global partnership. As leaders of nations committed to the values of human freedom, democracy and rule of law, the new relationship between India and the United States will promote stability, democracy, prosperity and peace throughout the world. It will enhance our ability to work together to provide global leadership in areas of mutual concern and interest.

Recognizing the significance of civilian nuclear energy for meeting growing global energy demands in a cleaner and more efficient manner, the two leaders discussed India's plans to develop its civilian nuclear energy program.

President Bush conveyed his appreciation to the Prime Minister over India's strong commitment to preventing WMD proliferation and stated that as a responsible state with advanced nuclear technology, India should acquire the same benefits and advantages as other such states. The President told the Prime Minister that he will work to achieve full civil nuclear energy cooperation with India as it realizes its goals of promoting nuclear power and achieving energy security. The President would also seek agreement from Congress to adjust US laws and policies, and the United States will work with friends and allies to adjust international regimes to enable full civil nuclear energy cooperation and trade with India, including but not limited to expeditious consideration of fuel supplies for safeguarded nuclear reactors at Tarapur. In the meantime, the United States will encourage its partners to also consider this request expeditiously. India has expressed its interest in ITER and a willingness to contribute. The United States will consult with its partners considering India's participation. The United States will consult with the other participants in the Generation IV International Forum with a view toward India's inclusion.

The Prime Minister conveyed that for his part, India would reciprocally agree that it would be ready to assume the same responsibilities and practices and acquire the same benefits and advantages as other leading countries with advanced nuclear technology, such as the United States. These responsibilities and practices consist of identifying and separating civilian and military nuclear facilities and programs in a phased manner and filing a declaration regarding its civilians facilities with the International Atomic Energy Agency (IAEA); taking a decision to place voluntarily its civilian nuclear facilities under IAEA safeguards; signing and adhering to an Additional Protocol with respect to civilian nuclear facilities; continuing India's unilateral moratorium on nuclear testing; working with the United States for the conclusion of a multilateral Fissile Material Cut Off Treaty; refraining from transfer of enrichment and reprocessing technologies to states that do not have them and supporting international efforts to limit their spread; and ensuring that the necessary steps have been taken to secure nuclear materials and technology through comprehensive export control legislation and through harmonization and adherence to Missile Technology Control Regime (MTCR) and Nuclear Suppliers Group (NSG) guidelines.

The President welcomed the Prime Minister's assurance. The two leaders agreed to establish a working group to undertake on a phased basis in the months ahead the necessary actions mentioned above to fulfill these commitments. The President and Prime Minister also agreed that they would review this progress when the President visits India in 2006.

The two leaders also reiterated their commitment that their countries would play a leading role in international efforts to prevent the proliferation of weapons of mass destruction, including nuclear, chemical, biological and radiological weapons.

In light of this closer relationship, and the recognition of India's growing role in enhancing regional and global security, the Prime Minister and the President agree that international institutions must fully reflect changes in the global scenario that have taken place since 1945. The President reiterated his view that international institutions are going to have to adapt to reflect India's central and growing role. The two leaders state their expectations that India and the United States will strengthen their cooperation in global forums.

Prime Minister Manmohan Singh thanks President Bush for the warmth of his reception and the generosity of his hospitality. He extends an invitation to President Bush to visit India at his convenience and the President accepts that invitation.

Appendix 7

PRESIDENTIAL ELECTION, 2012

STATEMENT OF VALUE OF VOTES OF ELECTED MEMBERS OF THE STATE LEGISLATIVE ASSEMBLIES AND BOTH HOUSES OF PARLIAMENT AS PER PROVISIONS OF ARTICLE 55(2) OF THE CONSTITUTION OF INDIA

Sl. No.	Name of State	Number of Assembly Seats (Elective)	Population (1971 Census)	Value of Vote of Each M.L.A.	Total Value of Votes for the State
1	2	3	4	5	6
1.	Andhra Pradesh	294	43502708	148	148 × 294 = 43512
2.	Arunachal Pradesh	60	467511	8	008 × 060 = 480
3.	Assam	126	14625152	116	116 × 126 = 14616
4.	Bihar	243	42126236	173	173 × 243 = 42039
5.	Chhattisgarh	90	11637494	129	129 × 090 = 11610
6.	Goa	40	795120	20	020 × 040 = 800
7.	Gujarat	182	26697475	147	147 × 182 = 26754
8.	Haryana	90	10036808	112	112 × 090 = 10080
9.	Himachal Pradesh	68	3460434	51	051 × 068 = 3468
10.	Jammu & Kashmir*	87	6300000	72	072 × 087 = 6264
11.	Jharkhand	81	14227133	176	176 × 081 = 14256

12.	Karnataka	224	29299014	131	131 × 224 = 29344
13.	Kerala	140	21347375	152	152 × 140 = 21280
14.	Madhya Pradesh	230	30016625	131	131 × 230 = 30130
15.	Maharashtra	288	50412235	175	175 × 288 = 50400
16.	Manipur	60	1072753	18	018 × 060 = 1080
17.	Meghalaya	60	1011699	17	017 × 060 = 1020
18.	Mizoram	40	332390	8	008 × 040 = 320
19.	Nagaland	60	516449	9	009 × 060 = 540
20.	Odisha	147	21944615	149	149 × 147 = 21903
21.	Punjab	117	13551060	116	116 × 117 = 13572
22.	Rajasthan	200	25765806	129	129 × 200 = 25800
23.	Sikkim	32	209843	7	007 × 032 = 224
24.	Tamil Nadu	234	41199168	176	176 × 234 = 41184
25.	Tripura	60	1556342	26	026 × 060 = 1560
26.	Uttarakhand	70	4491239	64	064 × 070 = × 4480
27.	Uttar Pradesh	403	83849905	208	208 × 403 = 83824
28.	West Bengal	294	44312011	151	151 × 294 = 44394
29.	NCT of Delhi	70	4065698	58	058 × 070 = 4060
30.	Puducherry	30	471707	16	016 × 030 = 480
	Total	4120	549302005		= 549474

*Constitution (Application to the Jammu & Kashmir) Order

(A) Value of each vote of members of parliament total members
Lok Sabha (543) + Rajya Sabha (233) = 776

$$\text{Value of Each Vote} = \frac{549474}{776} = 708$$

(B) Total value of votes of
776 members of parliament = 708 × 776 = 549408
(C) Total electors for the
Presidential election = MLAs (4120) + MPs (776) = 4896
(D) Total value of 4896 electors for
The presidential election 2012 = 549474 + 549408 = 1098882

ACKNOWLEDGEMENTS

I gratefully acknowledge the contribution of several of my friends and well-wishers who have encouraged me to write this book. The list is long and I may not be able to mention all of them, but this book would not have been possible without their encouragement.

I would like to express my sincere gratitude to all the coalition partners of the UPA government, who enriched me with their knowledge and experience. My team at Rashtrapati Bhavan, for providing valuable assistance with research and structuring this book. Omita Paul, an associate of several years, for reading the manuscript and offering suggestions for improvement.

I am grateful to Kapish Mehra, Managing Director, Rupa Publications and his team, comprising Elina Majumdar, Yamini Chowdhury, Tanima Saha and Nishtha Kapil, for meticulously editing each draft and their complete dedication. Boundless thanks to them for their unflagging interest in bringing out this volume.

I conclude with a general expression of gratitude to all who have contributed to the writing and publication of this book.

INDEX

123 Agreement, 132–134, 136, 147, 152–154
   negotiations of the, 131

Accelerated Irrigation Benefit Programme, 168
Accidental prime minister, *See* Singh, Manmohan, 76
Accredited Social Health Activists (ASHAs), 168
Adhikari, Subendu, 221
Administrative Reforms Commission, 194
Advani, L.K., 57, 60, 143–144, 177–178, 183–184, 207, 211
Aggressive unilateralism, 143
Agreement on Mutual Legal Assistance in Criminal Matters, 104
Ahamed, E., 100
Ahluwalia, Montek Singh, 73
Ahmed, Fakhruddin, 113–114, 211
Ahmed, Iajuddin, 113
AICC, 18–19, 22, 25, 31, 34, 36, 39, 41–42, 49
Aiyar, Mani Shankar, 42
Akali Dal, 44
Akbar, M.J., 207
Akshardham Temple terror attack (2002), 57
Al-Qaeda, 119, 124
Alva, Joachim, 1
Anna Dravida Munnetra Kazhagam (AIADMK), 6, 14, 44, 48, 206
Annan, Kofi, 47
Ansari, Hamid, 205–206, 207, 209, 226
Anti-BJP sentiment, 30
Anti-corruption movement, 196
Anti-terror mechanism, 116
Antony, A.K., 26, 99, 196, 210, 226
Antulay, A.R., 26, 75
Anwar, Tariq, 19, 21, 26, 40, 53–54
Asiatic Society, 218
Asom Gana Parishad, 44
Automation of Central Excise & Service Tax (ACES), 178
Awami League, 115
Azad, Ghulam Nabi, 40, 69, 178

Baalu, T.R., 72
Bahujan Samaj Party (BSP), 141, 143, 200, 213, 216
Bakshi, A.K., 227
Balakrishnan, K., 141
Balayogi, G.M.C., 49
Banerjee, Mamata, 24–25, 32–37, 209–212, 214, 218, 220–223

support's president candidature, 221
   emergence of, 25
Bangla Congress, 1
Bangladesh, 113–116
   connection of ethnicity and kinship, 113
   crisis, 83
   Line of Credit Agreement, 115
   politics in, 115
Bansal, Pawan, 208, 216–217, 224
Bardhan, A.B., 76, 135
Basu, Jyoti, 71, 76, 140–141
Basu, Kaushik, 166, 186
Bengal Provincial National Trade Union Congress, 33
Bhai Mahavir, 1
Bharat Nirman programme, 168
Bhardwaj, H.R., 97
Bhattacharya, Malini, 33
Bhushan, Prashant, 197
Bhushan, Shanti, 197, 200
Biju Janata Dal (BJD), 206
Bilateral relationships, 106–116
   Bangladesh, 113–116
   Bhutan, 106–108
   Nepal, 108–111
   Pakistan, 116
   Sri Lanka, 111–113
Biswas, Debabrata, 135
BJP,
   13 days government, 15
   13 months government, 46–48
   1996 general elections, 12
   alliance with state-based parties, 44
   alliances with regional parties in UP, 6
   anti-BJP sentiments, 30
   campaign against Sonia's foreign origin, 54
   'India Shining' campaing, 63, 68
   rise of, 44
Bofors, 20–21

Bose, Subhas Chandra, 26–27
Bringing the Green Revolution to Eastern India (BGREI), 169
Brown, Ron, 92
Budget-related issues, 50
Bush, George W., 115

Carnegie Endowment for International Peace, 93
Caste-based parties, 4
Chagla, M.C., 1
Chandrachoodan, 135
Chandrika Kumaratunga, 30
Chatterjee, Somnath, 32, 76, 209
Chauhan, Dara Singh, 216
Chavan, Prithviraj, 145
Chavan, Y.V., 74
Chhatra Parishad, 33
Chidambaram, P., 14, 16–18, 73, 83, 121–122, 135, 160, 176, 179, 185, 191, 197, 210, 217, 227
Chowdhury, Adhir, 64
Citizenship Act, 1955, 184
Civil nuclear initiative, 149, 153, 156
Coalition consultations, 70–74
Coffin scam, 97
Cold War, aftermath of, 91
Common Minimum Programme, 76
Commonwealth of Independent States (CIS), 91
Communist Party of India (CPI), 1, 6, 16, 33, 43, 45, 64–66, 76, 135, 142–143, 200, 215, 225
Comprehensive Nuclear Test Ban Treaty (CTBT), 155
Compulsions of politicians in Tamil Nadu, 30
Congratulatory calls, 67, 226
Congress,
   Constitution, intricacies of the, 40
   presidency, 26–28
   1996 electoral loss, 13

Constitution's silence, 39
Congress Legislature Party (CLP), 33, 41, 68
Congress Parliamentary Party (CPP), 1, 68
Constitutional amendments, 4, 6, 177
Consumer Price Index (CPI), 168
Customary farewell dinner for President Pratibha Patil, 226

Dasgupta, Gurudas, 143
Dasmunsi, P.R., 33, 56
Daulatram, Jairamdas, 1
Decriminalization of politics, 63
Defence
    budgetary allocations, 82–85
    coffin scam, 97
    defence framework agreement, 93–95
    Defence Offset Facilitation Agency (DOFA), 88
    Defence Procurement Procedure (DPP), 86–89
    equipment shortages of armed forces, 79
    funding acquisitions, 81–82
    Indo–US defence relations, 92
    mandatory integrity pact, 87
    maritime security, 102
    modernization of forces, 80–81
    morale of the armed forces, 85–86
    naval war room case, 89–91
    NFU policy, 97
    'no-first use' policy (NFU), 96
    P-75 submarine-building project, 84
    'Sagarika' project, 96
    scams, 97–98
    scandals, 73
    services long term perspective plans, 87
    war-fighting capability shortcomings, 81
    zero defect system to ensure secrecy, 91
Demonetization, 182
Dhawan, R.K., 26, 205
Dhebar, U.N., 27
Direct Tax Policy, 186
Direct Taxes Code (DTC), 174–175, 178, 203
Domestic savings, 163
Double Tax Avoidance Agreement (DTAA), 182, 191
Drive against black money, 182

Emergency, 3, 23, 59, 113
EXIM Bank, 115
Exports, growth rate of, 163
External Environment, 100
    neighbourhood, 103–106
    vision for India's foreign policy, 101

Father of reforms, See Singh, Manmohan
FDI, 57, 189–191
Fernandes, George, 59, 73, 97
Financial inclusion, 231
Financial Sector Reforms Commission, 173–174
Financial sector reforms, 171, 173
Financial Stability and Development Council (FSDC), 171–172
Fiscal deficit, 163
Fiscal package, 164
Fiscal Responsibility and Budget Management Act (FRBMA), 174
Fiscal stimulus, 164
Fissile Material Cut-off Treaty, 150
Five-Year Plan, 8, 81, 167
    First, 8
    Tenth (2002–07), 81
    Eleventh (2007–12), 167
Flying coffin, See MIG-21, frequent crashes

Food Security Bill, 170–171
Foreign policy, ultimate objective of, 159
Fractured mandate, 53

G-8 summit, 140
Gamang, Giridhar, 48, 52
Gandhi, Indira, 2–3, 10, 16, 19, 23, 29, 32, 78, 215
Gandhi, Rajiv, 24, 28, 36, 74, 149
   assassination, 28, See also Jain Commission
Gandhi, Sanjay, 23
Gandhi, Sonia, 20, 24–25, 31, 36, 38–43, 47, 50, 53–56, 58, 62–63, 66, 68–72, 75, 121, 136, 160, 165, 167, 170, 191, 204–210, 214–216, 219–221, 224–226, 229
   1999 elections, 55–56
   advisers, 41
   brainstorming session of senior Congressmen, 41
   campaign during elections, 39
   elected leader of CPP, 68–70
   foreign origin, 53–55
   Pachmarhi conclave, 41–43
   pan-India approach, 43
   primary member of Congress, 24, 31
   stakes claim to form government, 50–51
   willingness to accept the Congress presidency, 40
GDP growth rate, 130, 157, 166
General Anti Avoidance Rule (GAAR), 175
General election
   1996 election, 12
   1999 election, 55–56
   2004 election, 61–62
Global economic slowdown, negative fallout, 164

Godhra riots (2002), 58
Goods and Services Tax (GST), 8, 176–179, 203
   Constitution Amendment Bill, 179
Goswami, Arnab, 216
Gowda, H.D. Deve, 16, 20–21, 23, 30
Growth of income, 166
Guha, Pradyut, 221
Gujral, I.K., 16, 20, 23–24, 29, 31
   disagreements with Sanjay Gandhi, 23
   foreign policy, 23
   short tenure as PM, 23
Gupta, Bhupesh, 1–2
Gupta, Indrajit, 16
Gupta, Shekhar, 73
Gyanendra, King, 109

Hasina, Sheikh, 113–115
Hazare, Anna, 196–197, 201, See also Lokpal
Hegde, N. Santosh, 197
Hyde Act, 133–136

IAEA, 129, 132, 139–140, 142, 145–147, 150–151, 155–156
Illegal Migrants (Determination by Tribunals) Act, 60
Inclusive development, agenda, 166
Income Tax Act, 186, 189
India Against Corruption, 196
India Shining campaign, 63, 68
India Today-ORG-MARG opinion poll, 67
Indian Airlines flight hijacking (1999), 57
Indian Financial Code, 174
Indian National Congress (INC), 1
Indian Statistical Institute (ISI), 217
India–Nepal Treaty of Peace and Friendship, 108–109
India-specific safeguards agreement,

132, 140, 147, 150, 156
Indira Awaas Yojna, 168
Indo–Bhutan relationship, 106
Indo–Bhutan Treaty, 106
Indo–Pak equation, 93
Indo–Soviet Friendship Treaty, 144
Indo–US Civil Nuclear Agreement, 127–128, 145
   123 agreement, 132–133
   acceptance of safeguards, 134
   background, 128–132
   civil nuclear cooperation, 131
   costly source of power, 137–138
   Hyde Act, 133
   India–US Joint Statement, 131
   no first use (NFU) policy, 129
   nuclear isolation, 130
   Nuclear Suppliers Group (NSG), 129
   opposition, 146
   sovereign right to test, 136–137
Indo–US strategic relations, 95
Indra Dhanush programme, 60
Insurance Act, 173
Interim budget, 162, 164, 166
International Atomic Energy Agency (IAEA), 129
Investment-driven partnerships with the US, 100

Jahangir Aziz Internal Working Group, 180
Jain Commission, 24, 28, *See also* Gujaral, I.K.
Jain, Ajit Prasad, 1
Jain, Satya Pal, 217–218, 224
Jaitley, Arun, 177
Jamaat-ud-Dawa (JuD), 123
Jammu & Kashmir Assembly, bombing (2001), 57
Jan Chetna Yatra, 183
Jayalalithaa, 14, 48–50, 211
Jethmalani, Ram, 218
Jharkhand Mukti Morcha (JMM), 43
Joshi, Murli Manohar, 208
Judicial Standards and Accountability Bill, 199

Kalam, A.P.J. Abdul, 152, 204, 209
Kant, Krishan, 57
Karat, Prakash, 95, 135, 141–142, 204
Kargil conflict, 48, 79, 82–83, 85, 97
Karunakaran, K., 41, 51
Karunanidhi, M., 14, 72
Kejriwal, Arvind, 197
Kesri, Sitaram, 18–22, 24–27, 29, 38, 40, 54–55, 75
   as Congress president, 25–26, 32
   role in destabilizing the United Front, 20–23
Khan, Gohar Ayub, 80–81
Khurshid, Salman, 135, 197
Kidwai, Mohsina, 35
Kidwai, Rasheed, 53
Kisan Mazdoor Praja Party (KMPP), 27
Kissinger, Henry, 92
Kohler, Jeffrey, 95
Kolkata Plenary Session, 24–25
Kripalani, J.B., 27
Kumar, Meira, 76, 226
Kumar, Nitish, 206, 219
Kumari, Chandresh (Maharani), 178

Lahore Declaration, 48
Lashkar-e-Taiba (LeT), 123
Liberation Tigers of Tamil Eelam (LTTE), 28, 112
Lok Sabha election, 63–68
   Abul Hasnat Khan (opponent), 64
   election campaign, 64–65
Lokpal, 194–203
   focus of, 198
   inclusion of MPs, 195

recommendations, 195
representations and suggestions, 196
LTTE, 30, 32, 112

Mahajan, Pramod, 56–57
Mahatma Gandhi National Rural Employment Guarantee Act (MGNREGA), 167–170, 185
Mahila Congress, 33
Malhotra, Rashpal, 117
Maran, Dayanidhi, 72
Maran, Murasoli, 28
Maritime security, 102
Mayawati, 141, 211
  Taj Corridor case, 141
Media speculation, 70, 72
Menon, Shiv Shankar, 145
MIG-21, frequent crashes, 80
Mishra, Brajesh, 152
Mishra, Chaturanan, 16
Mishra, Satish, 216
Misra, Loknath, 1
Mitra, Somen, 33, 36, 67, 221
Modi, Narendra, 170
Moily, M. Veerappa, 135, 197
Moopanar, G.K., 14, 34–35
Mukherjee, Subroto, 33
Multiplicity in culture, 232
Multi-purpose National Identity Cards, See UIDAI
Mumbai serial blasts (1993)74
Mumbai terror attack (26/11), 117–121
  arrival of the terrorists through sea, 118
  media speculation about Indo–Pak relations, 118
  military intervention demand, 120
  Pakistan's 'non-state actors' excuse, 119
  parliament debate, 122–125
Musharraf, Pervez, 116

Narain, Raj, 1, 59
Narayanan, K.R., 45, 49, 52
Narayanan, M.K., 115, 145
Narayanasamy, V., 216
Nath, Kamal, 72
National Council of Applied Economic Research (NCAER), 181
National Institute for Smart Government, 125
National Institute of Financial Management (NIFM), 181
National Institute of Public Finance and Policy (NIPFP), 181
National Population Register (NPR), 184
National Rural Drinking Water Programme, 168
National Rural Employment Guarantee Act, 167
National Rural Health Mission (NRHM), 168, 170
Nazarbayev, Nursultan, 161
Nehru, Jawaharlal, 5, 27, 231
Nepal
  arms management, 110
  Comprehensive Peace Agreement, 110
  Indo–Nepal ties, 110
  multi-party democracy, 109
  Nepal-India relations, 109
  restoration of democracy, 110
Next Steps in Strategic Partnership (NSSP) initiative, 131
Nikhil Bharat Banga Sahitya Sammelan, 218
Nilekani, Nandan, 177, 185–186
No-confidence Motion, 78, 127, 146
No-first use policy (NFU), 96–97, 129, 155
Non-Congress Government, 56–58
Non-Proliferation Treaty (NPT), 47, 128–129, 155

Nuclear energy, peaceful uses of, 151
Nuclear isolation, 130
Nuclear Power Corporation of India, 152
Nuclear Suppliers Group (NSG), 129, 132, 134, 142, 145–148, 151–152, 155–156, 159
Nuclear Weapons Convention, 149

Pachmarhi Conclave, 41–43, 63
Panja, Ajit, 33
Parekh, P.H., 217
Parliament, 7–11
   3Ds—Debate, Dissent and Decision, 7
   absence of parliamentary debates, 8
   disruptions, 7
   effective use of time, 8
   evolutionary principle of effective functioning, 7
   ordinances, 9–11
Parliamentarian career, 3
Passport Seva project, 125
Paswan, Ram Vilas, 70–71, 216
Patel, Ahmed, 41, 66–67, 69–71, 207, 210, 220–221
Patel, Dahyabhai, 1
Patel, Maniben, 1
Patil, Pratibha Devisingh, 141–142, 161, 205, 211, 220, 226–227, 229
Patil, Shivraj, 73, 75, 117, 121–122
Patil, Vasantdada, 74
Patnaik, Janaki Ballabh, 48
Paul, Omita, 166, 217
Pawar, Sharad, 21–22, 25–26, 29, 39–40, 50–51, 53–54, 70–71, 73–75, 192, 206, 219–220, 226
   career with the Youth Congress, 74
   organizational capabilities, 74
   pragmatic policies, 75
   prime ministerial ambitions, 74
   role and position in Maharashtra politics, 74
   Sonia Gandhi foreign origin issue, 75
PDMA, 179
Percy Mistry Committee, 180
Phukan, S.N., 97
Pillai, Ramachandran, 141
Pilot, Rajesh, 25–26, 39
Planning Commission, 9, 33, 73, 169, 184–185
Pluralism, 232
Politics of the masses, 13
Portfolio, 67, 71–73, 98, 160, 173
Post-Congress polity, 43–44
Prabhakaran, V., 28, 30
Pradhan Mantri Gram Sadak Yojna, 168
Prakash, Arun (Admiral), 90
Prasada, Jitendra, 19, 21–22, 25–26, 29, 38–40, 178
Prevention of Corruption Act, 195
Preventive detention to maintain essential supplies, 2
Privy purses, abolished, 4
Public debt management, 180

Qureshi, Shah Mehmood, 117

Rabindra Bharati Society, 218
Raghuram Rajan Committee, 180
Raid raj, operator of, 183
Raja, A., 72
Rajapaksa, Mahinda, 112
Rajiv Gandhi Grameen Vidyutikaran Yojna, 168
Rajya Sabha
   composition of, 3
   history of creation, 5
   proposals for, 5
Ramachandran, K.T., 34
Rao, K. Chandrasekhar, 69–70
   ambition of separate Telangana, 71

Rao, P.V. Narasimha, 9, 12, 14, 17–20, 25, 33, 35, 55–56, 59, 76, 74, 77–78
   balance of payments crisis, 13
   economic reforms, 13
   inability to prevent the demolition of the Masjid, 14
Rashtriya Janata Dal (RJD), 43
Ray, Siddhartha Shankar, 34
RBI Act, 172
Reddy, Jaipal, 16
Reddy, Neelam Sanjiva, 52
Reddy, Sudhakar, 134
Reform process, 59
Religious extremism, 94
Retrospective tax, 185
Revolutionary Socialist Party (RSP), 16, 135, 143, 215, 225
Rice, Condoleezza, 119, 131, 153
Right to Education Act (RTE) Act, 168
Right to Food Bill, 170
Roy, Abani, 135
Rumsfeld, Donald, 92–93, 130

SAARC, 101, 103–106, 109, 112, 114, 116
   SAARC Bands Festival, 105
   SAARC Development Fund (SDF), 104
Sagarika, project, 96
Salim, Mohammad, 143
Salve, Harish, 190
Samajwadi Party (SP), 141, 144
Sangma, P.A., 41, 53, 206, 212, 217–218, 222, 224–226
Saran, Shyam, 145
Saraswati, Jayendra, 209
Sarkozy, Nicolas, 152
Scindia, Madhav Rao, 55
Secularism, 95, 113, 209, 232
Securities Contract Regulation Act, 173

Self-correction, 3
Sen, Ronen, 92
Shah Commission, 59
Shah, Amit, 177
Shank Ocean Engineering, 90
Shankaran, Ravi, 90
Sharma, Anand, 100, 145
Sharma, Naval Kishore, 42
Sharma, Shankar Dayal, 15, 45
Sharmistha, 209
Shekhar, Chandra, 52
Shekhawat, Bhairon Singh, 205, 211
Shiv Shankar, P., 54
Sibal, Kapil, 135, 145, 168, 191, 197
Simla Sankalp, 63
Singh, Ajit, 215
Singh, Arjun, 21–22, 29, 41
Singh, Charan, 52
Singh, Giani Zail, 211
Singh, J.J., 81
Singh, Jaswant, 47, 207
Singh, Joginder, 20
Singh, Madhvender (Admiral), 98
Singh, Manmohan, 50, 56–57, 63, 68–73, 76–78, 95, 108, 116–117, 131–132, 140, 142, 151–152, 159–161, 167, 170, 172, 177, 186, 190, 192, 196, 204, 208–209, 224, 226
   budget-related issues, 50
   leader of opposition in Rajya Sabha, 56
   views about Montek Singh, 73
   economic policymaker, 77
   diverse coalition, 78
   1991 economic reforms, 78
   Bhutan's visit as PM, 108
   meeting with Pervez Musharraf, 116
   congratulatory call, 226
   UPA presidential nominee, 208
   economic reforms (1991), 77–78
   G-8 summit, Japan, 140
   Vote of confidence, 142

US visit, 152
  Indo–US nuclear deal, 77
Singh, Natwar, 41–42, 69, 71, 73, 99, 107
  resignation, 99
Singh, Raghuvansh Prasad, 71
Singh, V.P., 16, 52
Sinha, Atish, 33
Sitaramayya, Pattabhi, 26
Sixth Central Pay Commission (CPC), 86
Social harmony, 232
Social inclusion, 234
Social Safety Net, 166–170
Soni, Ambika, 41
Soren, Shibu, 69–71
Speaker, 75–76
Sri Lanka
  civil war, 112
  peacekeeping force, 112
Sri Lankan Tamils, 30
Srikrishna, B.N., 174
Stock markets global crash, 163
Subbarao, D., 172
Surjeet, Harkishan Singh, 45, 69–70, 76
Surve, S.L., 89
Swamy, Subramanian, 218
Swaraj, Sushma, 177, 205–206, 208

Taj Corridor case, 141
Taliban, 119, 123
Tamil Maanila, 14, 16–17, 44, 73
Tandon, Purushottam Das, 27
Tax Information Exchange Agreements (TIEA), 182
Tax relief, 164
Tax-GDP ratio, 175
Telangana, 71
Telangana Rashtra Samithi (TRS), 43, 70, 76, 225
Telugu Desam Party, 44, 46
Thackeray, Bal, 219–220
Third Front, 50–51

Trickle-down theories, 231
Tripathi, D.P., 216
Tyagi, Mahavir, 1

UID Mission, 183–186
UNFCCC, 105
Unique Identification Authority of India (UIDAI), 183
United Front Government, 16–17
  talented ministers, 16
United Front II Falls, 28–32
United Nations Framework Convention on Climate Change (UNFCCC), 105
United Progressive Alliance (UPA), 37, 43, 68–69, 75–76, 126–127, 133, 135–136, 139–143, 145, 160, 162, 165, 167–168, 184, 192–194, 205–206, 209, 214, 218, 220
UPA–Left Committee, 135–136
UPA's President Nominee, 205–224

Vajpayee, Atal Bihari, 15, 21, 45, 49, 58–59, 67, 152
  13-month government, 46–48
  bus yatra to Lahore, 48
  economic reforms agenda, 56
  foreign policy, 57
  NDA coalition, 56
  Pokhran nuclear tests, 46–47
  signature in politics, 58
Varma, Abhishek, 89
Venkataraman, R., 15, 52, 211
Virmani, Arvind, 186
Vivekananda, Swami, 234
Vodafone tax case, 186–189
Vote of Confidence, 49, 51–52, 142–159, 222
Vyas, Girija, 220

Wangchuck, Jigme Khesar Namgyel, 106–108

War against Black Money, 180–183
War against terrorism, 233
Weapons of mass destruction (WMD), 94, 102
Weapons of Mass Destruction and their Delivery Systems Act, 150
West Bengal Pradesh Congress Committee (WBPCC), 25, 33–36
Wickramanayake, Ratnasiri, 112

Yadav, Lalu Prasad, 69–71
Yadav, Mulayam Singh, 209–211, 216, 224
Yadav, Ram Gopal, 216
Yechury, Sitaram, 76, 135
Yuva Congress, 33

Zardari, President, 120–121
Zia, Khaleda, 113, 115